1

Introduction

For the able-bodied and the physically handicapped alike, physical education is probably the most vigorous and physically demanding of all the compulsory elements of the school curriculum. Even in adulthood, it is surprising how vividly one can recall the feeling of anticipation which preceded the P.E. (or P.T.) lessons of one's schooldays. For those of us who in later years were to become physical educationists ourselves it was a feeling akin to adoration. For others it was closer to anathema or revulsion. Apparently it is just the same for children today. One way or the other very few of them are indifferent to the prospect of a P.E. lesson.

But what is physical education?

Although the main task of this book is to consider the appropriateness of physical education to the physically handicapped, it is perhaps as well to preface this by giving some thought to the nature of the subject itself.

During the past few years there has been a lot of soul searching by physical educationists, particularly those in tertiary education, in an attempt to justify not only *what* is done, but also *how* and *when* it should be done (e.g. Whiting 1969, Kane 1972, Munrow 1972). This, not surprisingly, has been reflected in the schools, with the result that even if over the years children's feelings towards physical education have remained constant, the underlying philosophy, the mode of administration and the content of the programmes themselves have changed almost beyond recognition.

At the beginning of this century the activity component of the school curriculum (it can scarcely be called P.E.) was advocated for purely physical reasons. Standards of health and nutrition were considered inadequate to the needs of growing children and, in an effort to compensate for this situation, all schools were obliged to provide daily exercise sessions. Although in the older public schools the loftier aspirations of the 'playing fields of Eton' were being fostered, in the majority of State schools the training given was far more rudimentary: as McIntosh (1968) described it 'haphazard games, and drill under an ex-army instructor'.

In 1909 a Syllabus of Physical Exercises was introduced by the Board of Education in an effort to draw teachers away from military drill 'along the road to therapeutic physical training'. Ten years later it was renamed a

An archery class: nowadays archery is practised worldwide by young and old alike with all manner of disabilities.

Syllabus of Physical Training for Schools; a change which according to McIntosh 'was significant of a broader content and a wider application'. It even incorporated a supplement 'Suggestions in regard to Games'. But even in 1933, which saw the introduction of a new syllabus, the emphasis, despite 'revised methods of teaching', was still upon 'exercises . . . introduced with a view to the special encouragement of posture and flexibility of muscles and joints'.

Gradually, however, the traditional English preoccupation with games and sports imposed itself upon the school curriculum and physical training receded. By the mid 1950s the designation 'physical training' had been almost universally superceded by 'physical education'. As this had never been a statutory requirement, it can only have reflected some apparent or intended shift in emphasis.

By this time children of school age were considerably stronger and healthier. In consequence the physical educationist was able to give consideration to aims and objectives other than those determined by medical expedience. Basically, these aims, equally valid today, are divisible into three main areas:

(i) Physical objectives – The importance of physical fitness and correct posture to the child's general health is still recognised, but, the general level of health being higher, more time can be devoted to the acquisition of skills and their incorporation into various forms of recreational activity.

(ii) Psychological benefits – Many physical educationists have come to realise that their subject, quite apart from its physical values, can also benefit a child's psychological development. The sense of physical well-being which can

2

result from their programmes is thought to instil confidence and poise, and to foster alertness and vitality. Additionally, the energies which are expended in strenuous physical activity seem to play a most useful role in offsetting the stresses and frustrations of everyday life.

(iii) Social factors – Activities which promote interaction and co-operation with others, the sharing of responsibilities and obligations, the exercise of qualities of leadership, etc., such as team games and outdoor pursuits, have all gained recognition as being valuable to the overall development of the child, both as an individual and as a member of society.

In 1972 a survey was carried out for the Schools Council (Kane 1974) in which teachers were asked what they believed to be the most valuable contributions made by physical education to the total development of the child. The findings provide an interesting and up-to-date validation of the areas of effect outlined above. The objectives given greatest importance were motor skills, self-realisation and leisure. These were followed (in descending order) by emotional stability, moral development, social competence, organic development, cognitive development and aesthetic appreciation.

Physical education in the comprehensive school

Within the last two decades concern has been felt that in the past there was too much emphasis on elitism (not only in physical education but in education generally) and too little attention paid to the needs of the majority, in particular the underachiever. This has contributed to the evolution of the comprehensive school. Because of the large numbers of children educated together in these schools (1500 is not uncommon), there has been a considerable growth both in the range of activities and the extent of the facilities available. Extensive physical education programmes are now commonplace at both Junior and Middle School levels (5–9 and 10–13 years of age respectively). But it is at the Senior level (14–18 years of age) that the changes have been most noticeable.

Fifteen years ago a secondary school might have had one, two or at best three physical education teachers. Depending on whether the school was mixed or single-sex, these might have offered between them one major winter game (rugby or soccer, netball or hockey), occasionally cross-country running or swimming, and cricket or tennis, with athletics in the summer. At the most, this meant that each child could expect tuition in five or six different activities. In the comprehensive system, there might be as many as eight or ten physical education specialists working in a single school and, according to Kane's survey, this has virtually doubled the number of activities that can be offered to any one child. As can be seen from Table 1, by the time they are in the Fifth or Sixth Form, children of either sex are able to select from a range of some ten or twelve different activities. In any one school these might include such diverse pursuits as basketball, climbing, judo, badminton, volleyball, fencing, karting, canoeing, golf and dance.

Table 1. Number of physical education activities for boys and girls in secondary schools: by year *(Kane 1974)*

Year	Boys' mean	Girls' mean
1	9.241	8.623
2	9.640	8.682
3	10.778	9.068
4	11.910	9.785
5	11.382	9.064
6	12.117	9.321
7	12.521	9.748

Physical education in the special school

Unfortunately there is óne sector of society in which, to a large extent, this rapid change in educational practice and opportunity has not kept pace. Ironically this is the field of 'special' education which, notwithstanding some slight international variation, commonly includes the educationally subnormal, the blind, the partially sighted, the deaf, the partially hearing, the speech defective, the maladjusted, the epileptic, the delicate and the physically handicapped. It is now widely held (though as yet less widely practised) that a well administered programme of physical education can contribute extensively to the overall education of children in *all* these categories. But as my own experience is not so widespread, it is with just two of these that this text is principally concerned: the delicate and the physically handicapped. It is my belief that it is for these children that physical education can probably do most.

To determine what is delicate and what is physically handicapped is not so much a question of kind as of degree. According to Jackson (1966) delicate children are defined as follows:

> pupils who by reason of impaired physical condition need a change of environment or cannot without risk to their health or educational development be educated under the normal regime of ordinary schools.

The presence of a physical handicap, on the other hand, implies an impairment of a more serious nature usually involving some degree of immobility, uncoordination or other motor dysfunction.

However, as it is nowadays common practice to educate both delicate and physically handicapped children in the same schools, for the purpose of this book the term 'physically handicapped' refers equally to both categories and this includes the whole spectrum of physical disability ranging from asthma

and haemophilia to muscular dystrophy and spina bifida. Blindness and deafness are *not* included as these are properly termed sensory and not physical handicaps, a distinction which has been concisely and clearly made by Taylor and Taylor (1960):

> English law defines physically handicapped pupils as those not suffering solely from a defect of sight or hearing who by reason of disease or crippling defect cannot be satisfactorily educated under the normal regime of ordinary schools.

But it should also be remembered that even in our 'normal' schools there is an estimated 6.7% (Brenner et al. 1967) who suffer from some minimal neurological dysfunction (our so-called 'clumsy' children and our 'slow-learners'); not to mention an increasing number of more severely handicapped children who are being placed in ordinary schools in the interests of integration.

For most of these children, both in the special school and in the normal school, there is, underlying even their intellectual and social handicaps, a disability of a physical nature. What could be more appropriate, therefore, than a truly physical education?

The benefits which can accrue from a physical education for able-bodied children have been outlined above. The fact that these other children have some kind of movement co-ordination problem does not lessen the appropriateness of this provision. On the contrary, it would seem to strengthen their claim to such programmes. This can probably best be demonstrated by reference to those same three areas of effect:

(i) PHYSICAL CONSIDERATIONS

Some physically handicapped children may have poor control over parts or all of their body, some may have no control at all over some body parts but quite normal control over the rest, whilst others with, say, a cardiac or respiratory deficiency, may have no motor impairment at all. But whichever is the case, they will all almost certainly have missed years of valuable movement experience through lengthy periods of hospitalisation or some other similarly protective environment. Whatever the specific nature of their condition the outcome will probably be that described by Morris and Whiting (1971):

> It is reasonable to suppose that a low standard of performance, coupled with the inability to perform certain simple tasks effectively, may result in a child having a limited vocabulary of motor skills and a correspondingly limited range of relevant experience upon which to base the development of abilities and the learning of further skills. This will inevitably lead to a slower rate of progress and a restriction in overall achievement and benefit. In extreme cases, there may be certain culturally desirable skills that some of these children never acquire.

Furthermore, the majority of these children need regular physiotherapy,

either remedially to assist in improving their condition, or prophylactically to prevent contractures, renal failure or some other complication. Although most of them appreciate the importance of these exercises, the physiotherapists recognise that they may find them repetitive and boring. The likelihood of a child continuing with such exercises after he has left school is therefore remote. If these exercises can be incorporated into some form of recreational activity, however, such as swimming or wheelchair basketball, there is a much higher probability that they will continue to be practised in adulthood.

(ii) PSYCHOLOGICAL EFFECTS

In the case of the handicapped child these can be particularly far-reaching. The frustrations with which a growing child with limited or uncontrolled movement must contend may be incomprehensible to the normal able-bodied observer. The effects of repeated failure, of the inability to perform even simple tasks and, perhaps more important, of realising that others too recognise one's inadequacies, may result in a rigidity or inflexibility of behaviour which prevents the child participating in any activities which are either novel or complex.

(iii) SOCIAL EFFECTS

If this relationship with the environment persists throughout childhood, the effects can be most damaging. Add to this the almost total reliance upon others which can permeate life in a residential establishment, and it is little wonder that some find it impossible to cope successfully with the outside world. Whilst some may avoid contact with other children, others may bear a grudge which they find difficult to control and which leads them to compensate by alternative forms of assertion or achievement which are socially unacceptable.

The physical education programme, properly implemented, may help in all these areas. What is more, it can do so not only through the medium of recreational activities (as in the conventional physical education programme), but also through assisting the child in his or her efforts to cope with life generally. Whether the problem be an athetoid's poor control of a pencil, a paraplegic's difficulty in getting in or out of the bath or up and down a kerb in his wheelchair, or simply a hemiplegic's inability to get up from the floor having fallen over, the physical education specialist, co-operating with the physiotherapist, may be in an ideal position to help in finding a solution.

But what sort of school is it that enables teacher and physiotherapist to co-operate so closely? And how did such a system come about? Before we look at the special school as it exists today, it is perhaps worth reflecting briefly on the background to our system of special education.

6

A fast-moving game, basketball is beneficial to cardiorespiratory and neuromuscular fitness.

An historical overview

As far back as 1893 the British Government passed an Elementary Education (Blind and Deaf Children) Act, which empowered school boards to provide education for blind and deaf children between the ages of seven and sixteen. A few years later in 1899 another Act was passed which required local authorities to ascertain the number of children in their area who were either epileptic or mentally defective, and to provide special instruction for them. Unfortunately it was a long time before similar provision was made for physically handicapped children.

Right up until the Second World War most physically handicapped children spent their lives either at home, in hospital units or in sanatoria. With the possible exception of a more fortunate but very small minority, the question of their educability was given scant consideration. In mitigation of this apparent neglect it should be remembered that at that time very few severely handicapped children were ever likely to outlive their childhood. Presumably the inadequacy of the provision reflected this fact. But whatever the reason, if congenitally physically handicapped children were sufficiently robust to survive beyond infancy, they were either confined to the home so as to avoid the possibility of familial stigma, or else, in the strictest sense of the words, 'institutionalised' or maintained 'in care'.

Since the war, however, and in many ways because of the war, a great deal has changed. Not only, as medical science and child management expertise have improved, have more and more severely disabled children achieved a

7

relative longevity, but also, as the social climate has improved and a better educated populus emerged, old fashioned stigmas and fears have been allayed. Gradually, through concerted efforts on the part of charitable organisations and the Ministries of Health and of Education (later the Departments of Health and Social Security and of Education and Science), the physically handicapped have repossessed their natural heritage: a right to an accepted place in society and to the same opportunities for education as are afforded to any other person.

It is interesting to note in this context that on December 9th 1975 the General Assembly of the United Nations resolved to adopt a Declaration on the Rights of Disabled Persons. Although it is too lengthy to reprint in full, one passage in particular merits quotation:

> Disabled persons, whatever the origin, nature and seriousness of their handicaps and disabilities, have the same fundamental rights as their fellow citizens of the same age, which implies first and foremost the right to enjoy a decent life, as normal and full as possible.

Admittedly, neither this country nor any other has yet achieved such a state of total social and educational integration; but in recent years certain noteworthy inroads have been made towards this end. The following have been of particular significance in England:

(i) The Chronically Sick and Disabled Persons Act (1970) This statute was aimed primarily at the local authorities and endeavoured to ensure that the needs of the disabled were not only recognised but catered for, both in the home and in the community at large. Two passages in particular stand out as being both typical of the spirit which underlies the whole of this act and of particular relevance to this text: Section Two requires that the authorities give help with adaptations not only to the home but to recreational and educational facilities as well; and Section Eight requires that special access, parking and toilet facilities be made available in all public buildings, including universities, colleges and schools.

(ii) The Education (Handicapped Children) Act (1970) This act, which became effective on April 1st 1971, required that *all* children, including those previously designated as unsuitable for education at school (and therefore the responsibility of the Department of Health), be brought under the jurisdiction of the Department of Education and Science. Probably the most significant line was the following:

> From the Appointed Day the procedure for determining a child as ineducable will cease to be used.

(iii) The Snowdon Report on Integration of the Disabled (1976) The working party which produced this report under the Chairmanship of Lord Snowdon was first convened in October 1974 by the National Fund for Research into

Crippling Diseases with the following terms of reference:

> To consider the areas in which disabled people are not fully integrated with the rest of society, to examine the reasons for this lack of integration and to consider ways in which, in the different areas, the situation can be rectified so that the disabled person may, so far as his personal disabilities permit, have equal opportunities and appropriate facilities as his non-disabled fellows.

To achieve the objects, the working party established seven sub-committees, each responsible for a different area, two of which were education and sport and leisure.

(iv) The Warnock Report on Special Educational Needs (1978) The Committee of Enquiry into the Education of Handicapped Children and Young People, chaired by Mrs Mary Warnock, first met in September 1974 and finally presented its report to the Department of Education and Science in March 1978. Its terms of reference were

> to review educational provision in England, Scotland and Wales for children and young people handicapped by disabilities of body or mind, taking account of the medical aspects of their needs, together with arrangements to prepare them for entry into employment; to consider the most effective use of resources for these purposes; and to make recommendations.

Like the Snowdon Report, its ideological commitment is on the side of an integrated system of education. However, it too is highly appreciative of the achievements of our special schools:

> It will be to no advantage to integrate unless the result is a real and worthwhile social and educational interaction between pupils and teachers in the tradition of the best special schools (T.E.S. 1977).

At the present time, according to the latest edition of the Department of Education and Science List 42 'Special Schools for Handicapped Pupils' (1974), there are in England and Wales some 175 schools serving the special needs of the delicate and physically handicapped. Some of these are run by charitable organisations, some cater for only one particular condition, some are residential, some are day schools, some are infant and junior, and some are secondary. But by far the most common is the school which is part of the local education authority provision, is at least partly residential, covers the whole age range (i.e. approximately 3–16 years of age) and cater for all types of physical handicap. (A complete list of various categories of handicap is given in Appendix One.)

It is with this provision and the contribution that physical education can make to it that this book is primarily concerned. That is not to say, however, that its contents are not applicable to other places where physically

handicapped children are educated, whether hospital school, charitable institution, unit attached to an ordinary school or fully integrated normal schools. Hopefully, it will be of value in all of these as well as to each of the many disciplines which provide their staff, whether teachers, physiotherapists, remedial gymnasts or therapeutic recreationists. It should also provide students in colleges and hospitals with an insight into a valuable specialist educational service which hitherto, in Britain at least, has been given scant coverage.

Timetabling in the special school

Let us suppose that a headteacher in a special school believes that a physical education programme might make a useful contribution to his curriculum. Where does he start? The task before him is by no means as straightforward as at first it might appear.

In an ordinary school with its much larger population, the introduction of a new subject does not appear to pose quite so many problems. Although the large numbers sometimes make for complications, the homogeneity of the groups or classes makes them easier to cater for and, as a result, timetables can be quite rigidly conceived. What is more, despite the problems that the size of a comprehensive school population might pose, it also has advantages. If a thousand children are to benefit (as opposed to the hundred or so of the special school) it is not nearly so extravagant either to employ numerous specialist teachers or to provide expensive equipment and extensive facilities. A further advantage in having a large population and a team of specialist teachers is that a wider range of activities can be offered, which in turn means that to some extent even minority interests can be accommodated.

In a smaller school, with perhaps only one specialist teacher, the number of activities or options available at any one time is limited. Even if the teacher is versatile enough to be able to introduce a wide range of activities, it is often only possible to do so if all children participate in all activities; a restriction which is only fully appreciated when one considers the provision of opportunities for competition. With the large numbers of pupils in normal secondary schools and with several such schools in any one area, it is possible to provide a wide range of activities, with different children involved in each, for participation both within the school and between schools. In the special school, with its population of 100–150 children spanning an age range of 12–13 years and an ability range of similar proportion and with the nearest comparable. school perhaps fifty miles away, the possibilities are not nearly so numerous.

But probably the biggest single advantage the headteacher in the normal school has is that his curriculum is exclusively educational. The administrator in the special school for physically handicapped, on the other hand, has to accommodate several disciplines in his timetable. Nurses, physiotherapists, speech therapists, occupational therapists, educational psychologists and

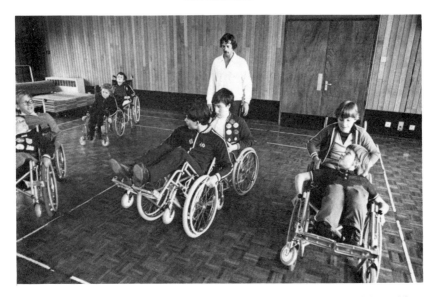

Tandem rides are more than just fun; they combine strenuous activity with unfamiliar attitudes, fostering strength and balance.

teachers all have a part to play and all make demands upon the children's time. Whilst these demands are more than justified, the result is that timetables are fragmented. Children are commonly required to attend sessions with each of these specialists, either alone or in small groups; for some this might be once a week, for others several times a day. For the class teacher, attempting to work to a timetable, this means that the class is rarely complete, and it is rarely the same children that are missing, and those who do remain are less alike in terms of maturation, mental age and physical ability or anything else than any similar group in a normal school.

Nonetheless, the fact that more and more headteachers in schools for physically handicapped children are now endeavouring to incorporate a physical education programme into their curriculum, despite these difficulties, is indicative of the growing awareness of the contribution that this subject can make to the overall development of such children.

But the successful negotiation of this first hurdle – the winning of a place for physical education on the special school timetable – still leaves us a long way from the finishing tape. The person responsible for administering this programme may have been trained as a teacher, a physiotherapist or a remedial gymnast; but whatever his or her professional background may be, certain decisions will have to be taken on a wide range of subjects, each requiring some knowledge of *all* these disciplines. Different ways of grouping children, different methods of instruction (for different situations), the selection of a varied yet complementary programme of activities, the length and frequency of lessons and so forth, each of these questions must be weighed against the

problems arising from the various handicaps of the children under instruction. It is with the solution of questions such as these that this book is principally concerned.

REFERENCES

Barnard, H. C. (1969) *A History of English Education from 1760* 2nd edition: University of London Press.

Brenner, M. W., Gillman, S., Zangwill, O. L. & Farrell, M. (1967) Visuo-motor ability in school children. *British Medical Journal*, 4, 259–262.

Department of Education and Science (1974) *Special Schools for Handicapped Pupils.* List 42. H.M.S.O.: London.

Her Majesty's Government (1970) *The Chronically Sick and Disabled Persons Act.* H.M.S.O.: London.

Her Majesty's Government (1970) *Education (Handicapped Children) Act.* H.M.S.O.: London.

Jackson, S. (1966) *Special Education in England and Wales.* Oslo University Press: Uppsala.

Kane, J. E. (Ed.) (1972) *Psychological Aspects of Physical Education and Sport.* Routledge and Kegan Paul: London.

Kane, J. E. (1974) *Physical Education in Secondary Schools.* Macmillan: London.

McIntosh, P. C. (1968) *Physical Education in England since 1800.* Bell: London.

Morris, P. R. & Whiting, H. T. A. (1971) *Motor Impairment and Compensatory Education.* Bell: London.

Munrow, A. D. (1972) *Physical Education: A Discussion of Principles.* Bell: London.

Snowdon Committee (1976) *Integration of the Disabled.* National Fund for Research into Crippling Diseases: Horsham.

Taylor, W. W. & Taylor, I. W. (1960) *Special Education of Physically Handicapped Children in Western Europe.* International Society for the Welfare of Cripples: New York.

Times Educational Supplement (1977) Leading article on the Warnock Report. T.E.S. No. 3217: 28 Jan. 77. Times Publishers: London.

United Nations General Assembly (1975) *The First Charter: A Declaration on the Rights of Disabled Persons.* International Rehabilitation Review: New York.

Warnock, H. M. (1978) *Special Educational Needs: Report of the Committee of Enquiry into the Education of Handicapped Children and Young People.* Her Majesty's Stationery Office: London.

Whiting, H. T. A. (1969) *Acquiring Ball Skill: A Psychological Interpretation.* Bell: London.

2

The present situation in special schools for physically handicapped children

The experience of a single individual is necessarily limited, and to ensure the widest possible basis for the information and advice in this book a survey was made of a wide range of schools for the physically handicapped. Information from the survey, coupled with personal experience in introducing and implementing a programme of physical education for handicapped children is the background to the text that forms the bulk of this book.

The survey

The main purpose of the survey was to identify common elements in the way in which special schools for physically handicapped children are organised, and the way in which (if at all) physical education is administered within them. More specifically the questionnaire sought information on the following areas: (i) the sort of children catered for in these special schools; (ii) the facilities available for use in these schools; (iii) the amount of time allocated to physical education; (iv) the ratio of staff to pupils considered appropriate to the various activities within the physical education programme; and (v) the actual activities constituting that programme.

The questionnaire was sent to all schools in England and Wales listed by the Department of Education and Science in 1974 as catering either exclusively for physically handicapped children or for physically handicapped and delicate together. It was not sent to schools taking only delicate children. Of the 160 questionnaires sent out, 90 were returned completed and 4 others were returned spoilt, making a total return of 58.75% and a useful return of 56.25%. The general character of these 90 schools and the extent to which their distribution is representative of the total number is shown in Table 2. All subsequent references in this chapter to situations in or pertaining to schools for the physically handicapped are derived principally from the data received from these 90 schools. The information is described, section by section, both graphically and literally. The implications for the institution of a physical education programme, coloured at times by the light of personal experience, are discussed as appropriate. As indicated above, the questionnaire (Appendix 2) comprised five parts, and the rest of this chapter details the findings in each area.

Table 2. Schools receiving the questionnaire. Figures in parenthesis indicate the number of schools which completed and returned the questionnaire

	All-age	Junior	Senior	Total
Mixed	123 (69)	24 (12)	4 (3)	151 (84)
Boys	1 (–)	– (–)	4 (3)	5 (3)
Girls	3 (2)	– (–)	1 (1)	4 (3)
Total	127 (71)	24 (12)	9 (7)	160 (90)

Part one: the children

The first question relates to the total population of each school. From Table 3 a difference is immediately apparent between the size of the normal school and that of the special school. (From here on unless indication is given to the contrary, the term 'special school' will refer to the special school for physically handicapped and delicate children.) Indeed, of the 90 schools which replied to this questionnaire, there were only 8 with more than 150 pupils; and in the majority of cases (60) there were less than 100 pupils.

Table 3. Total school populations

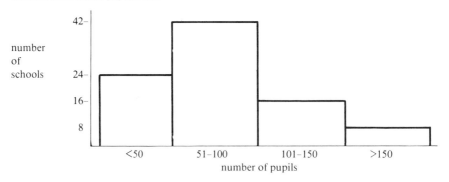

These figures are particularly significant when one considers the age range of these children. From Table 2 it can be seen that the majority (79%) of these schools cater for the whole age range, that is, approximately 3–16 years. With such small numbers spread over such a wide age range, the optimum size of groups for different activities must be either age-determined and therefore small in number, or a relatively large group of very diverse ages. Whilst small numbers might be advantageous for activities such as swimming and other individual pursuits, they obviously make team games rather difficult.

The third question concerns the incidence of different handicaps within the school population. Although a few schools evidently cater for one particular handicap, the majority accept children with all manner of physical disability. Unfortunately (from a statistical point of view), these conditions do not all

14

appear with the same frequency. Indeed, from the results of this enquiry it would appear that, whilst the overall range is very wide (Appendix One), approximately half the population of these schools suffer from just two conditions: spina bifida and cerebral palsy.

Whilst the data returned was not comprehensive enough to give statistically valid information in this respect, support for this estimate can be obtained by ranking the various handicaps according to the frequency of their occurrence in each school. From Table 4 it can be seen that, in the majority of schools, by far the most commonly occurring conditions are, indeed, cerebral palsy and spina bifida. The rest of the schools' population is made up of small numbers of children suffering from many different disabilities, the commonest being muscular dystrophy, haemophilia and asthma.

Table 4. Occurrence of handicaps (rank order)

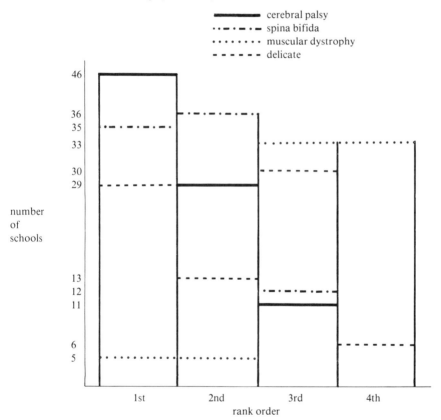

In summary, the wide range of ages, abilities and disabilities within a pupil population which is commonly less than a hundred greatly influences decisions about the size and composition of groups, whether in the classroom,

Table 5. Type of facilities available within the sample of special schools

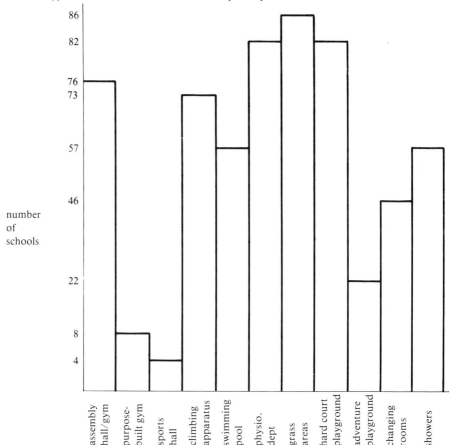

gymnasium or swimming pool. If these groupings are to be at all effective, a measure of flexibility in the timetable seems essential. As each group needs to be an appropriate reflection of both the objectives which are specific to the situation and the activity which constitutes that situation, it is not always possible to find such a group within a single class. This is not a situation which is peculiar to physical education however, and, in my experience, most teachers are willing to co-operate in trying to find a mutually satisfactory and workable system.

Part two: the facilities
From the replies to this section of the enquiry (Table 5) it would appear that, whilst there is still room for improvement, facilities in most schools are adequate for the introduction of a comprehensive programme of physical education.

The cycle ergometer is useful both for building strength and for establishing desirable movement patterns.

The major differences between the facilities available for use in the special school and those commonly found in ordinary schools would appear to be the following:

(i) There is an almost universal lack of purpose-built gymnasia and sports halls – only 8 schools out of 90 had a proper gymnasium. This seems to show the low priority still given to physical education in our special schools.

(ii) Without purpose-built gymnasia, it is perhaps not surprising that almost half of these schools have no changing rooms either.

Many of these schools, however, are at least partly residential and presumably have changing facilities in their dormitory wings. Many schools too have their own swimming pool, in which case it is sometimes possible for timetables to be so arranged that the pool changing area serves both swimmers and games players. At the very worst the classroom or activity hall itself can be used. The easy way out, not bothering at all, should be vigorously resisted; hygiene is at least as much a problem for handicapped children as it is for the able-bodied.

It is worth remembering, too, that handicapped children generally take a lot longer to dress and undress than do their able-bodied counterparts, and even if a houseparent or classroom assistant is available to help with dressing, it can be a time-consuming process. A thirty-five-minute lesson might be sufficient for normal children, but for the severely physically handicapped this is no time at all.

(iii) One area in which the special school is apparently better provided for than most ordinary schools is in the provision of a swimming pool; 57 of the 90 schools in the survey have their own pool and, even though most of these were installed with hydrotherapy in mind, and in consequence are often irregularly shaped, short in length, shallow and uncomfortably warm, they do make excellent teaching pools.

For more advanced swimming or sessions involving large numbers, it is of course necessary to seek more extensive facilities – something which no less than 35 of the schools had done.

(iv) There is also evidence to suggest that where certain schools have made a positive effort to provide their children with a wide range of physical experiences, the conventional equipment or apparatus has proved inadequate for their special needs. Adaptations or improvisations which have been specially made include low-level trolleys to provide an alternative to wheelchairs or crawling, and extensions to climbing frames provide opportunities for 'aerial travel' close to the ground.

Part three: time allocation

This part of the enquiry was designed to discover (i) whether or not there are physical education programmes in these schools, and (ii) if so, how much time is devoted to their three main constituents: P.E., games and swimming. (Although to differentiate between games and swimming on the one hand and 'P.E.' on the other is conceptually tautologous, this classification was adopted in the questionnaire because it is a distinction commonly made in schools; 'P.E.' representing the gymnastic/body awareness element in the programme.) In addition to these three areas of activity, it was expected that there would also be some provision in these schools for physiotherapy. For this reason information was also sought on the provision for individual activity sessions.

Table 6. Number of schools allocating time to physical education activities

	Number of Days per Week					
	0	1	2	3	4	5
P.E.	10	50+	15+	<5	<5	<5
Games	10	50+	15+	<5	<5	<5
Swimming	4	65+	10+	<5	<5	—
Individual Sessions	15+	variable				

Unfortunately the data obtained from this section of the questionnaire was rather imprecise, however at least the relative incidence of these activities can be seen (Table 6). In the majority of schools there is at least one session per week of between 30 and 60 minutes' duration allocated to each of 'P.E.', games and swimming. In some schools these activities feature on the timetable

two or three times a week, and in a few cases even every day – irrespective of handicap. The only exception to this is the provision for individual activity sessions. As most respondents equated these with physiotherapy, for which generalisations are quite impossible, there was no discernible pattern. Treatment will depend on the condition each child is suffering from, its degree, and the child's health at the time. The frequency of physiotherapy sessions can therefore vary from once a week or less to as much as three or four times a day.

However, quite apart from the individual sessions which children have with school therapists, there is much to commend the inclusion of similar sessions in the timetable for the physical education specialist. Despite the fact that its inclusion impinges even further on an already crowded timetable, even one session a week when the teacher is free to take 'clinics' for individuals, can form a most useful complement to the regular physical education programme (Price 1977).

In any conventional lesson, whether in the special school or elsewhere, a teacher has to communicate with and, hopefully, exert some influence on a whole group of children simultaneously, and no matter how gifted, it is sometimes difficult attending to the different needs of each individual within the group. In the special school these difficulties are greatly magnified. Even within matched groups the learning difficulties and behavioural problems of the child with motor impairment are so varied and so specific to each individual that some inevitably do not receive the attention and guidance they require. Whilst physical education is perhaps the most appropriate lesson in which to remedy these difficulties, such remedial work cannot always be incorporated into an ordinary lesson, and the physical education teacher must then provide the individual with a programme of compensatory education possible only on a one-to-one basis.

The position outlined above is encouraging. In most schools P.E., games and swimming have already won a regular place on the school timetable. But there are still some schools in which physical education plays no part at all. Although only four schools in this survey did not offer some kind of swimming instruction, there were ten which provided no physical education or games programme. And unfortunately, although 56 of the schools in this survey devote extra-curricular time to organised recreational activity (Table 7),

Table 7. Extra-curricular time devoted to organised physical activity

None	*0–5 hrs/wk*	*6–10 hrs/wk*	*More*
34	44	9	3

this only accounts in part (50%) for the lack of timetabled provision in these ten schools. Less surprisingly, of these 56 schools 29 are residential, representing 52% of all the residential schools in the survey, whereas the 27 day schools represent only 23% of all the day schools in the survey.

19

Exercising before a mirror enables a child to monitor his own performance and often encourages a child to maintain a higher standard of performance.

Wherever possible, equipment should be installed in such a way as to be equally accessible to ambulant and chairbound alike.

The advantages of a residential population are obvious: sports clubs, evening training sessions and general recreation periods can all be introduced on campus without regard for any of the factors which accompany such provision for day-school pupils, e.g., different domestic arrangements, transport problems, bad weather, etc. But in the school which is only partly residential the teacher responsible for these extra-curricular activities has to guard against the dangers of favouritism. Unless very real efforts are made to ensure that the activities provided for boarding children are also open to day pupils, the latter very quickly feel themselves to be second-class citizens.

The only other question included in this section deals more with the content of the programme than its size; namely, the extent to which a competitive element is allowed to pervade the programme. The figures in Table 8 need little amplification. Evidently even in special schools competition and physical education go hand in hand. After all, competition is a fact of life. From early childhood through into adulthood, we all strive to master new skills and, where possible, to perform old skills better. Strangely, one often hears argu-

ments against competition in physical education – there were even six schools in the questionnaire sample who claimed never to let competition feature in their programmes. But surely it is not competition itself that is undesirable, but only inappropriate competition. Given realistic objectives, an understanding of what is involved by all parties and the ability to participate purposefully (even if not to win), then competition, intergroup, interperson and even intraperson competition can be a most healthy, effective and enjoyable motivating force.

Table 8. The role of competition in physical education

Never	Occasionally	Usually	Always
6	59	22	—

Part four: staff-pupil involvement

The fourth part of the enquiry was an attempt to gather information on the following: (i) the criteria used for grouping children; (ii) the size of groups considered appropriate for different parts of the programme; and (iii) the background, qualification or training of the person(s) administering these programmes.

It appears that, wherever possible, most schools endeavour to group their children according to age, but where this is not appropriate it is heartening to see that selection is commonly made according to ability rather than disability. Only rarely and in special circumstances is selection determined by sex.

As can be seen from Table 9, apart from the almost universal tendency to group according to age, there is considerable variance amongst the other categories. In general, this can be assumed to reflect the extent to which group

Table 9. Criteria used for grouping children in physical education

	Never	Occasionally	Usually	Always
Age	3	18	53	7
Sex	23	45	7	4
Type of handicap	34	36	9	1
Ability	11	32	27	7
Mobility	19	37	14	4

structuring is specific to each situation. For example, the selection of a group for slalom competition (or any other wheelchair activity) is likely to be based not so much upon age, sex or handicap, as upon confinement to a wheelchair, whether that be a temporary or a permanent state. Similarly, as archery allows for equal participation by members of both sexes, whether wheelchair bound or ambulant, and of virtually any degree of disability, the selection of groups is probably best made according to peer equivalence.

But, however much variation there seems to be in the criteria for group selection, the size of the groups selected is subject to more general agreement. From Table 10 it is evident that in very few cases are groups composed of less than five children. (This is probably as much a reflection on timetabling difficulties and overall staff:pupil ratio as upon desirability.) More significantly, at the other extreme very few groups comprise more than fifteen children. This is markedly different from the usual pattern among normal schools and no doubt reflects a recognition of the difficulties of teaching children with so many diverse problems. These small numbers are particularly noticeable when children are placed in unnatural or unfamiliar surroundings; hence the smallness of swimming groups.

Table 10. Group sizes for physical education classes

	1–5	*6–10*	*11–15*	*More*
P.E.	5	33	32	5
Games	2	29	38	5
Swimming	20	37	18	6

Although the information obtained through this enquiry was not definitive, there is probably an additional relationship between the size of groups and the severity of handicap(s) of the children within them.

With regard to the training of the staff who administer these programmes, it would appear that the special school has taken as its model the conventional junior school. In both types of school 'P.E.' and games lessons are commonly taken by 'classroom teachers', although there is now a tendency to appoint a physical education specialist as well. Of the ninety schools which replied to the questionnaire twenty-eight are now employing a physical education specialist.

Table 11. The qualifications of staff who teach physical education

	P.E. Spec.	*Class Teacher*	*Physio.*	*Rem. Gym.*	*Other*
P.E.	28	53	39	5	9
Games	28	53	25	5	12
Swimming	28	53	47	3	30

The most noteworthy features to be inferred from Table 11, which sets out the different qualifications of the staff who teach physical education in these schools, are the following:

(i) in most schools the physiotherapist contributes extensively to the administration of the physical education programme, not only in swimming, but also in games and P.E.

(ii) In many schools more than one member of staff is assigned to an activity session. Particularly in swimming these assistants are often unqualified part-time volunteers; nonetheless, they do a most valuable job. It is often impossible for one person to cope with groups of children with gross motor problems as well as learning and/or behavioural difficulties. In an ordinary school if a child has an accident it is usually possible to send one of the other children for help. With a class of physically handicapped children this is not always possible. But if the teacher goes for help, who is to supervise the rest of the group? Whilst these emergencies do not happen every day, even in the special school, they inevitably occur more frequently than in other schools. Yet it is in the more routine matters that assistance is really welcome. Many motor impaired children have difficulty in dressing and undressing and many, even if they are willing, are simply unable to carry equipment or to move apparatus. If the teacher has to do all this himself, as well as remain alert for the possible mishap, his actual teaching time is likely to be greatly reduced.

Part five: activities
This section was included in the questionnaire to give a broad indication of the sort of activities currently being offered to children in special schools. Although one or two activities were added or subtracted the list is basically the same as that used by Kane (1974) in his survey of secondary schools. The more detailed and admittedly more valuable analysis of which activities are taught to which children would be a major survey in its own right and may well be done as a second phase at a later date. In its absence, some guidance as to which activities are suitable for which children is given later in the book (Chapters 6–9).

Despite this inadequacy, Table 12, which summarises the response to this question, at least focuses attention upon a number of interesting anomalies:

(i) Out of a total of forty different activities in only ten cases does the number of schools in which such activities are taught exceed the number in which they have never been taught. These activities are athletics, cricket, dance, handball, netball, riding, rounders, soccer, swimming, and table tennis.

(ii) Although, not surprisingly, swimming is the most commonly taught activity in the special school, the frequency with which the other activities are taught is perhaps not so predictable. In descending order these same ten activities are swimming, table tennis, cricket, soccer, rounders, athletics, riding, netball, handball and dance.

(iii) Alternatively, when ranked according to the regularity with which they feature in the timetable, swimming, soccer and riding head the list, followed by table tennis, cricket, rounders, educational gymnastics, athletics, archery and handball.

(iv) The activities which are taught least of all are lacrosse (no schools), skiing (one school), rowing (four schools), roller skating (four schools) and ice skating (six schools).

Table 12. Activities taught as part of the physical education programme

	Never	*Occasional*	*Regular*
Archery	42 (8)	21	19
Athletics	25 (8)	37	20
Badminton	38 (7)	33	12
Basketball	39 (9)	25	17
Bowling	63 (6)	15	6
Canoeing	60 (7)	14	9
Climbing	71 (10)	8	1
Cricket	15 (7)	34	34
Cross-country	68 (6)	13	3
Cycling	58 (8)	16	8
Dance (mod. educational)	40 (2)	32	16
Dance (folk, etc.)	38 (8)	34	10
Fencing	75 (5)	5	5
Golf	64 (9)	11	6
Gymnastics (educational)	35 (11)	21	23
Gymnastics (traditional)	57 (10)	21	2
Handball	32 (9)	30	19
Hockey	58 (11)	14	7
Judo	80 (8)	2	—
Keep Fit	56 (8)	22	4
Lacrosse	81 (9)	—	—

(v) At the end of this section space was provided for schools to name activities taught which were not included in the list. Although each such activity is played in only a minority of schools the list is impressive and demonstrates the extent to which the enthusiastic teacher is prepared to go to find activities suitable to the needs of children with many different disabilities. In alphabetical order, the activities mentioned in this section were angling, billiards, chess, croquet, darts, draughts, indoor rugby, modern dance (disco), orienteering, skittleball, skittles, snooker, squash, stoolball, table football, touchball, tricycling, wheelchair dance.

Table 12 continued

	Never	Occasional	Regular
Netball	34 (6)	36	14
Orienteering	71 (9)	10	—
Riding	26 (8)	13	43
Rounders	19 (8)	34	29
Rowing	79 (7)	3	1
Sailing	64 (8)	12	6
Shooting	74 (9)	7	—
Shinty	55 (7)	22	6
Slalom	49 (7)	16	18
Skating (ice)	76 (8)	6	—
Skating (roller)	79 (7)	3	1
Skiing	80 (9)	1	—
Soccer	17 (8)	15	50
Swimming	4 (9)	4	73
Table Tennis	11 (9)	33	37
Tennis	54 (8)	25	3
Trampolining	64 (8)	8	10
Volleyball	41 (8)	30	11
Weight Training	66 (8)	12	4

N.B. The figures in parenthesis denote the number of schools which left these sections blank. This has been interpreted as an indication that these activities are *not* taught.

Summary

The information collected from this questionnaire has been used in an attempt to describe the sort of school in which physically handicapped children are educated, and to suggest some of the implications and constraints which this might impose upon an administrator who is wanting to introduce a programme of physical education to such a school. Although there was considerable variation in the response to this questionnaire, it was at least possible to develop some notion of the typical special school.

Close formation drills of this kind demand precision of movement and timing; an ideal lead-up activity to wheelchair dance.

For the more competitive individual the slalom course is invaluable as an aid to improved chair control.

This school has approximately one hundred pupils, both boys and girls, of ages ranging from three to sixteen years, and with a wide range of physical handicaps. Two of these handicaps, spina bifida and cerebral palsy, account for almost half of the pupil population; and the remainder comprises a wide range of less frequently occurring conditions, such as muscular dystrophy, haemophilia, asthma, cystic fibrosis and various cardiac disorders. Although the school does not have a purpose-built gymnasium, it has a hall, a swimming pool and ample grass and playground areas. Other items of equipment, bats and balls, benches, climbing apparatus and the like, are also available. Games, swimming and 'P.E.' are all timetabled so that each group has at least one session of each per week. In addition to this, each child has a certain number of individual sessions according to his or her particular needs.

The person responsible for the physical education programme may be a classroom teacher, physiotherapist, remedial gymnast or physical education specialist. But the type of training would appear to be rather less important than the need for the teacher to be able to weigh a whole host of different variables: the selection of activities, the criteria for grouping the children, the duration:frequency ratio appropriate to each activity, and the teaching method itself must all reflect not only the age and sex of the children in the school, but also their movement potential, learning difficulties and other behavioural problems, and to some extent even their home environment.

It is with this sort of assessment and evaluation that the ensuing chapters are concerned. The next two chapters deal respectively with the primary motor aspects of physical handicap and the associated non-physical problems. An understanding of the motor aspects of physical handicap is relevant to the creation of a programme of physical education in the special school because, to a large extent, the handicap determines the nature of the activities to be included. Similarly, an ability to recognise the associated disorders and to compensate for them, whilst not being crucial to the choice of activities, is necessary for an evaluation of learning difficulties and for the assessment and selection of teaching methods.

REFERENCES

Department of Education and Science (1974) *Special schools for handicapped pupils*. List 42. H.M.S.O.: London.
Kane, J. E. (1974) *Physical education in secondary schools*: Macmillan: London.
Price, R. J. (1977) Integration and Physical Education. *British Journal of Physical Education*, 8, 5, 'Handicapped pupils' Section, iii–iv.

3

Physical handicaps and movement potential

The incidence of particular types of handicap within a school population is variable and, as a result, activity groups are often far from uniform. In this chapter it will be seen that this lack of homogeneity is even more acute if one considers the movement characteristics of these handicaps. It should come as no surprise to discover that different conditions manifest themselves in different ways. What is surprising, perhaps, is that there are marked inconsistencies as well within each condition. For example, it is not enough to know that a child has a cerebral palsy; it is necessary to know the nature and extent of his impairment and which body parts are affected. Only then can one begin to identify common elements among the movement potentials of different children with different handicaps and thus to structure groups and select appropriate activities.

Each major physical handicap is therefore examined from the following points of view:

(i) general background: the history and incidence of the condition;

(ii) aetiology: the factors believed to cause the condition;

(iii) classification: the types and degrees of impairment that occur within a condition;

(iv) movement manifestations: the effect of a particular handicap upon a person's ability to move;

(v) implications for physical education: the kinds of activities possible and/or suitable for a particular handicap (and vice versa).

The categories of handicap have been selected to reflect conditions that are significant either by virtue of their high incidence within the school population or because of certain intrinsic, peculiar characteristics. They are:

(i) Spina bifida (and other paraplegias);
(ii) Cerebral palsy;
(iii) Muscular dystrophy;
(iv) Others: haemophilia, asthma, epilepsy and cardiac dysfunction.

As a preliminary to this analysis an outline of normal motor development is given to serve as a background to understanding.

Normal development

Human life begins with the fusion of the male sperm with the female ovum. About two weeks later the embryo thus formed anchors itself to the wall of the uterus and its cells begin to differentiate in preparation for the specialist functions of the body systems. An epithelial layer called the trophoderm grows around the embryo and maintains the maternal blood supply. Simultaneously, an inner layer, the mesenchyme, grows in such a way that there is formed within it a central mass which is continuous with its own surface on one side (Fig. 1). Within this central mass are two hollow spheres each in contact with the other through a layer of columnar epithelial cells. The superior hollow is called the amniotic cavity and its connecting epithelial layer the ectoderm; and the inferior hollow is called the yolk sac and its connecting layer the endoderm. The area including and within the ectoderm and endoderm is called the embryonic disc from which develops the whole body. (The rest of the embryo is merely supportive.)

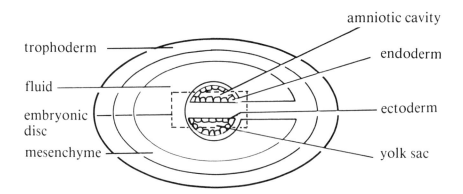

Figure 1 The situation of the embryonic disc within the embryo

As the cells within the embryonic disc continue to divide, the most recently formed of them are pushed out to form a new layer between the ectoderm and endoderm which is called the mesoderm. Within this layer a tightly packed rod of cells grows caudocephalically, forming the notocord. As it does so, it induces in the ectoderm a rapid cell differentiation which marks the beginning of the development of the nervous system.

At first this ectodermal differentiation takes the form of a neural groove which grows between two folds following the path of the developing notocord (Fig. 2). Eventually these folds increase so much that they fuse together and the new tube thus formed sinks down into the mesoderm. This neural tube and the neural crests which develop alongside it (Fig. 3) form the basis of the entire central nervous system.

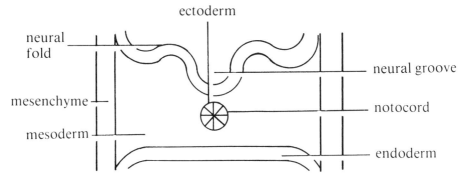

Figure 2 The developing neural groove in the ectoderm

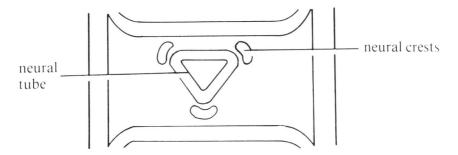

Figure 3 The appearance of the neural tube and crests

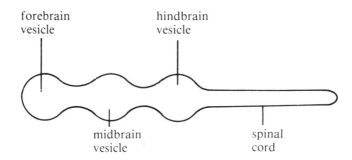

Figure 4 Differentiation into brain and spinal cord

Development does not proceed at a uniform rate, however, and accelerated growth is soon apparent at the cephalic end. As there are obvious physical restrictions upon this growth, convolutions begin to appear and a distinction between the spinal cord and the brain becomes apparent (Fig. 4). Development of the mature brain, through a continuing process of convolution, is represented schematically in Figure 5 and in tabular form in Table 13.

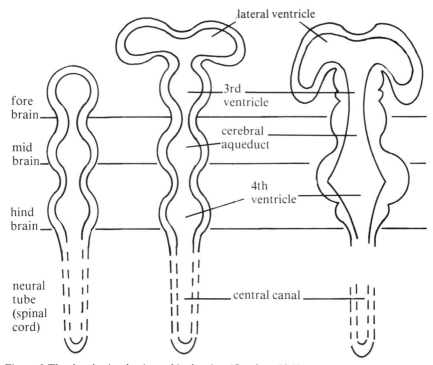

Figure 5 The developing brain and its lumina (Gardner 1968)

Table 13. Development of the brain from primary vesicles *(Barr 1972)*

Primary brain vesicles	Secondary brain vesicles	Mature brain
Rhombencephalon or Hindbrain	Myelencephalon and Metencephalon	Medulla Oblongata, Pons and Cerebellum
Mesencephalon or Midbrain	Mesencephalon	Midbrain
Phosencephalon or Forebrain	Diencephalon	Thalamus, Epithalamus, Hypothalamus & Subthalamus
	Telencephalon	Cerebral Hemispheres

Whilst this development is taking place at the cephalic end of the fetus, the rest of the body is forming as well. With every phase in this development, nerve fibres appear in the periphery establishing connections throughout the body with the central nervous system. The functions of this peripheral system are many and varied, although basically they are motor, sensory and visceral. For convenience, those fibres which convey impulses *to* the central nervous system (sensory neurons) are termed afferent, and those which transmit *away from* the central nervous system (motor neurons) are termed efferent. With the

31

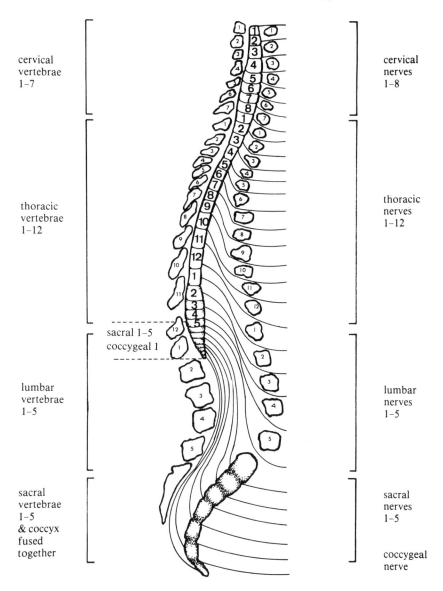

cervical
vertebrae
1–7

cervical
nerves
1–8

thoracic
vertebrae
1–12

thoracic
nerves
1–12

sacral 1–5
coccygeal 1

lumbar
vertebrae
1–5

lumbar
nerves
1–5

sacral
vertebrae
1–5
& coccyx
fused
together

sacral
nerves
1–5

coccygeal
nerve

Figure 6 Relation of neuromeres to scleromeres (Barr 1972)

exception of twelve pairs of cranial nerves, all these peripheral nerves connect with the central nervous system at the spinal cord, afferent or sensory fibres entering through the dorsal roots of the spinal nerves, and efferent or motor fibres leaving by way of the ventral roots.

Because of the delicate nature of fibres of the central nervous system, the normal fetus soon develops a protective covering of several layers' thickness. The brain is protected externally by the bony cranium and the spinal cord by its column of vertebrae and within this skeletal structure the whole system is protected by three skins or meninges and a cushion of cerebrospinal fluid.

The dorsal and ventral roots of the peripheral or spinal nerves are attached to the spinal cord by a series of rootlets. These pass through the bony case of the vertebral column by way of apertures or foramina. For each vertebra in the column there is one pair of nerves entering or leaving the spinal cord. There are thirty-one pairs of spinal nerves comprising eight cervical, twelve thoracic, five lumbar, five sacral and one coccygeal pair (Fig. 6). Although the spinal cord and the vertebral column begin their development equal in length, it is important to note that they do not remain so. Barr (1972) summarises this diversification as follows:

> Segments of the neural tube (neuromeres) correspond in position with segments of the developing vertebral column (scleromeres) until the third month of fetal development. The vertebral column elongates more rapidly than the spinal cord during the remainder of fetal life. The cord, which is fixed at its rostral end, gradually advances, and by the time of birth the caudal end is opposite the disc between the second and third lumbar vertebrae. A slight difference in growth rate continues during childhood, bringing the caudal end of the cord in the adult opposite the disc between the first and second lumbar vertebrae.

The distribution of spinal/peripheral nerves around the body is somatotopic; that is, those which are attached to the cervical region of the spinal cord serve the neck, arms and shoulders; those of the thoracic region serve the chest area; and those of the lumbar and sacral regions serve the abdomen and legs. Whilst this is very much a simplification (for example, most spinal nerves are attached to several cord segments), it does serve as a guide in the preliminary assessment of injury due to a spinal lesion.

The influence of the central nervous system upon movement
Apart from reflex activity, which is organised at a spinal level, all physical movement is subject to control by higher nerve centres in the brain (Fig. 7).

The medulla oblongata serves as a conduction centre for impulses passing between the brain and the spinal cord and also has a controlling influence over certain reflex actions. The cerebellum is responsible for the co-ordination of muscular actions, especially those concerned with the maintainance of normal posture, and is therefore of great importance to balance and equilibrium. The initiation, selection and control of voluntary movement is at the cerebrum, and it is here that movement experiences are registered, and motor programmes or vocabularies stored.

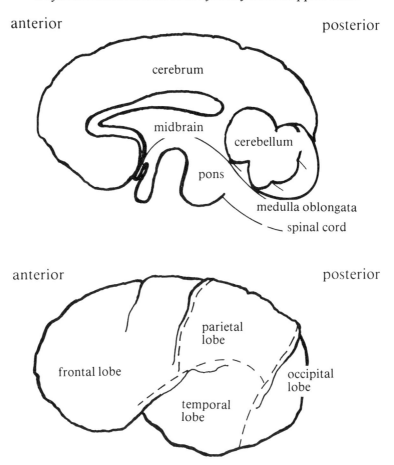

anterior   posterior

anterior   posterior

Figure 7 Superficial anatomy of the human brain: Sagittal section of the human brain showing the relative positions of the cerebrum, midbrain, pons, cerebellum and medulla oblongata (top). External view of the cerebrum showing the relative positions of the frontal, parietal, temporal and occipital lobes (lower).

The primary motor area is immediately anterior to the central sulcus or fissure of Rolando, and is represented somatotopically (Fig. 8). Impulses pass from the primary motor area down through the internal capsule (deep in the cerebrum) to the midbrain, and thence through the brain stem to the spinal cord to leave at whichever level is appropriate for the action(s) intended. Sensory nerves then relay back to the central nervous system information about the state of the body, posture, muscle tension, etc. It is by such feedback loops that all behaviour is monitored and the body position maintained or changed as required.

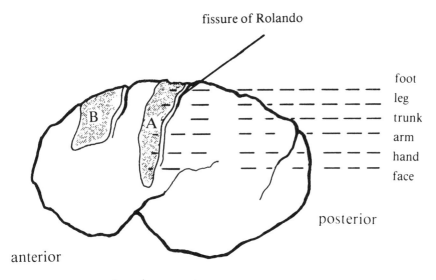

A. primary motor area
B. motor association area

Figure 8 External view of the cerebrum showing the relative positions of the primary and associated motor areas

The control of individual, purposive movements is particularly dependent upon such neuromuscular servoloops. All skeletal muscles (and all parts of these muscles) are equipped with nerve spindles, which are in effect monitors of length and tension within the muscle. The sensitive part of the spindle is kept in stretch by special nerve impulses issuing from the spinal cord through small nerve fibres called spindle efferents, which are mixed in with the ordinary large-diameter motor fibres in the spinal nerves. The tension in the sensitive part of the spindle is signalled back to the spinal cord through the spindle afferents which travel in the sensory nerves; and the impulses in these afferent fibres are delivered directly to the motor nerve cells innervating in the main muscle fibres. Under normal circumstances the tension of the spindle is maintained at approximately constant level irrespective of the length of the muscle in which the spindle lies, so that it can respond immediately to stretch. For smoothly co-ordinated, voluntary movements to be achieved the tension in the spindles must be continuously adjusted to keep pace with, or actually anticipate changes in length or tension in the muscle itself. To this end the spindle system is controlled by elaborate facilitatory and inhibitory systems throughout the spinal cord and brain stem.

Normal motor development
Essentially this is characterised by two sets of processes which are closely interwoven and dependent upon each other. They are:

(i) the development of a normal postural reflex mechanism which is not present at birth and which in time becomes highly complex and varied;

(ii) the inhibition of some of the responses of the neonate (which process may be brought about by maturation of the brain).

This latter process, sometimes referred to as a 'breaking up of the early total responses' (Bobath 1966), makes possible a resynthesis of parts of the total patterns in many and varied ways and, in association with the development of postural reflex mechanisms, allows for the performance of movements such as crawling and walking, and for the perfection of manipulative skills.

Three important consequences of this general description should be noted before the different handicaps are considered in detail.

Firstly, with regard to the development of patterns of movement, a distinction is made between motor behaviour which may be defined as 'primitive' and that which may be defined as 'abnormal'. Primitive movements are those normally seen at an early stage of a normal development but which in time disappear or are modified (e.g., the Moro grasp reflex and the crossed extensor kicking reflex). Abnormal movements are those which do not occur at any time during normal development.

Secondly, in the event of damage to the central nervous system, lesions at spinal level usually give rise to a loss of movement, i.e., a flaccid paralysis; whilst lesions in the brain (because reflex mechanisms at a spinal level remain undamaged) usually create a disturbance to the control of movement, i.e., a spastic paralysis.

Thirdly, with regard to the role of muscle spindles in the control of movement, if these are slack they fail to respond to stretch unless it is extreme. This occurs in hypotonia. If they are taut they respond unduly to any stretch, leading to excessive contraction of the main muscle fibres. This is what happens in hypertonia, and in particular in spasticity.

A description of the major, different handicapping conditions now follows.

Spina bifida

Children born with a spina bifida form a major part of the special school population. However within this population there are many degrees of neurological involvement, and consequently a wide range of movement potentials. Additionally there may be cerebral injuries, usually the result of an associated hydrocephalus, which can be very extensive.

It has been known since 1886 (Von Recklinghausen) that spina bifida is a type of myelodysplasia, that is the result of an arrestation in the development of the neural tube. About two weeks after conception the neural plate (the ectodermal layer of the embryonic disc) folds to form the neural tube (p. 29) and it is at this time that the abnormality begins to manifest itself. At birth it is readily detectable as a gap in the vertebral wall.

Unfortunately no one is yet certain why this happens. There is some

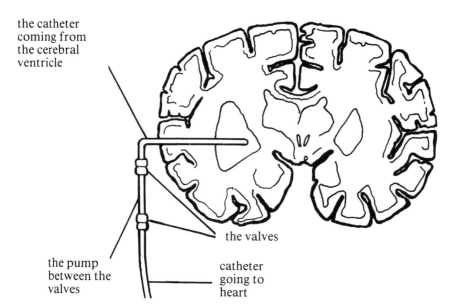

the catheter
coming from
the cerebral
ventricle

the valves

the pump
between the
valves

catheter
going to
heart

Figure 9 The Spitz-Holter shunt

evidence of familial involvement, in so much as the likelihood of a mother producing a second spina bifida child is high, but for the most part its causes are believed to be environmental. Climate, potato-blight and chemical impurities in water have all been the subject of recent researches, but to date the aetiology remains obscure.

The condition occurs all over the world with a general incidence of two per thousand live births, although there is much regional variation and in some places it is as high as four per thousand. In Great Britain Sharrard (1966) suggests that in some areas the incidence is as high as three per thousand, which means that a city with a population of five hundred thousand could have sixty new cases of spina bifida every year.

With such a high frequency, it has probably always been one of the most common handicaps, but until very recently this was not appreciated by the public because the majority of such children died in infancy. Death was brought about either because of the severity of the condition itself or because of associated hydrocephalus.

Hydrocephalus occurs in about seventy per cent of cases and is the result of a blockage in the ventricular system of the brain. In an uncontrolled state the cerebrospinal fluid, which continues to be produced despite the blockage, causes an enlargement of the head, extensive brain damage and a premature death. Its management by a procedure developed by an engineer and a surgeon has been a major breakthrough in the treatment of spina bifida (Fig. 9). The Spitz-Holter shunt, as it is known, comprises a one-eighth-inch diameter

rubber tube and a simple pressure valve. The tube is inserted into the central ventricular cavity of the brain to draw off excess fluid. The flow is controlled by the pressure valve (which can usually be felt beneath the skin behind the ear) and the excess passes down the tube into the jugular vein where it is dispersed into the blood stream. Whilst there are management problems involved (the valve sometimes blocks and the tube requires replacement at about one year, three years, five years and sometimes again in adolescence), this provision has greatly improved the prognosis of the spina bifida sufferer.

Classification
As with other spinal injuries, spina bifida is commonly classified according to the size and level of the damage. With a traumatic paraplegia (for example, a person who has broken his back in a fall or has had his spinal cord severed) one can state precisely where the lesion is situated. This is done by reference to the segments illustrated in Figure 6; each segment is identified by a letter, e.g. T6 indicates a lesion at the sixth thoracic segment, and L2 indicates one at the second lumbar segment. But with spina bifida the length and situation of the area of spinal cord involved may be large or small, cervical, thoracic, lumbar or sacral, and such accurate description is not possible. Further complicating the issue, the breach in the vertebral column may be posterior or, more rarely, anterior. There is little likelihood, therefore, that any two spina bifida sufferers will be the same, even though by far the most common combination is a posterior lumbar spina bifida.

Further classification is according to the severity or extent of the involvement of the injury.

SPINA BIFIDA OCCULTA
This is the least complex and the least grave, the only serious abnormality being the laminar defect of the vertebrae. None of the contents of the spinal cord is drawn out of place so, at birth at least, there is usually little or no neurological dysfunction (Fig. 10 i). Occasionally, however, the nerve cord adheres to the subcutaneous tissue (to which it has access through the gap in the vertebral wall) and damage occurs later in childhood as the vertebral column outgrows the spinal cord. Generally speaking, despite impaired sphincter control and some involvement of the muscles of the feet and legs, these children learn to walk quite well and do not need to use wheelchairs.

SPINA BIFIDA CYSTICA
There are usually considered to be three degrees of spina bifida cystica, all of which differ from the first type in that some of the contents of the spinal canal protrude through the gap in the incomplete vertebral wall. The name given to each reflects the nature of the contents of this protruding bulge or sac. In a meningocele the main contents of the subcutaneous sac are meninges but it is not uncommon to find nerve roots as well. In the meningomyelocele there is a

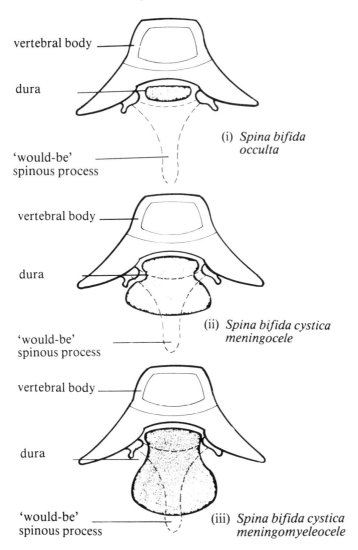

vertebral body

dura

'would-be'
spinous process

(i) *Spina bifida occulta*

vertebral body

dura

'would-be'
spinous process

(ii) *Spina bifida cystica meningocele*

vertebral body

dura

'would-be'
spinous process

(iii) *Spina bifida cystica meningomyeleocele*

Figure 10 Anatomical characteristics of the various degrees of spina bifida

part of the nerve cord itself within the sac. Although damaged, this portion of the cord is nonetheless structurally complete. In the meningomyelocystocele, the most severe form, the meningeal sac contains a part of the spinal cord which is badly malformed. Usually only the anterior half of the cord has a roughly normal anatomy (Fig. 10 ii & iii).

As the meningomyelocele and meningomyelocystocele are both the most severe and the most common, the rest of this section relates primarily to them, but it is also relevant, though to a lesser degree, to other cases of spina bifida.

Movement characteristics

The implications of spinal lesions for movement potential are much the same in any form of paraplegia. The major difference is in the nature of the lesion.

In traumatic paraplegia, whether the result of a knife wound, a spinal fracture or whatever, the lesion is usually confined to one segment. As a result it is a relatively straightforward task, through reference to a chart of myotomes, to ascertain which nerves are likely to be still intact and, in consequence, which parts of the body can still be moved. Extracts from such a chart are given in Table 14.

Table 14. a) Myotomes of the upper limbs *(Adapted from Sutton, 1973)*

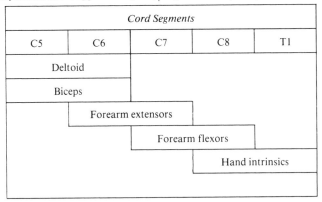

Table 14. b) Myotomes of the lower limbs *(Adapted from Sutton, 1973)*

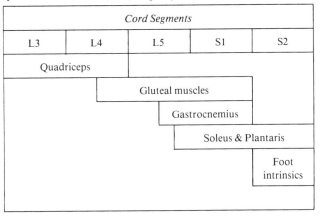

With spina bifida meningomyelocele there are likely to be several affected segments making accurate assessment of neurological dysfunction difficult. Furthermore it is quite common for parts of these affected segments (usually

the anterior segments) to remain undamaged. As a result, despite gross impairment, there might still be some residual sensation or muscular activity remaining. Unfortunately in most cases this is minimal and the usual consequence of a lumbar spina bifida cystica is flaccid paralysis of the legs and incontinence of the bowel and bladder. Depending on the level of the lesion certain of the muscle groups of the abdomen may also be involved.

The central nervous system above the damage, however, functions quite normally. As a result muscles above the lesion, e.g., the head, neck, arms and shoulders, are quite normal.

Considerations for physical education
With flaccid paralysis of the legs these children spend most of their lives in wheelchairs. Standing and walking are possible only with the aid of calipers and sticks. Physical education programmes are therefore centred upon (i) activities which can be pursued in wheelchairs, and (ii) activities in which the children can participate sitting or lying down on the floor. As these children have normal use of arms and shoulders, they can generally manoeuvre wheelchairs (and themselves about the floor) very well. The only activities which cannot be undertaken are those in which there can be no substitute for the use of legs, such as jumping and skipping. Most other forms of activity can be adapted quite successfully. But when a teacher is considering the appropriateness or otherwise of particular activities, there are certain other factors which might usefully be borne in mind.

Firstly, bones that have never borne weight and have no tonic muscle around them become very brittle and are easily fractured. Furthermore, paralysed limbs are anaesthetic. Even if a leg is broken (or bruised or cut) the child feels no pain and is therefore quite unaware of his injury. If wheelchair activities are introduced which are likely to be enthusiastically pursued, it may be advisable to ensure that children at risk wear calipers. If the children are to work on the floor or on apparatus, the teacher needs to ensure that there are no splinters in the benches, or uncovered hot radiators on the walls. Another consequence of anaesthetic limbs is that the owner tends to forget that they exist. As a result children tend to move about apparatus dragging their legs behind them quite oblivious to the damage they might be causing. The physical education lesson provides an excellent opportunity to teach these children to manoeuvre their bodies safely and efficiently, whether from apparatus to the floor, from the floor to a wheelchair, from a wheelchair to a bed, or whatever.

Secondly, in order to cope with the incontinence that most paraplegics suffer, appliances are worn, usually a plastic bag attached to the abdomen or the thigh. Strenuous physical activity not only tends to promote the flow of urine, but the appliances are notorious for the ease with which they come adrift. And a ball which bounces on a full bag, or a foil which misses its proper target can produce much the same effect!

Thirdly, although wearing a Spitz-Holter valve should not bar a child from

Through the imaginative use of even simple apparatus, children can be helped to handle their bodies efficiently and safely.

any physical activity, the shunt can become blocked. Effects can be quite dramatic with the development of severe headaches, drowsiness or vomiting, and therefore if a blockage is suspected the child should be taken to his usual hospital for treatment as an emergency.

Fourthly, to have said that paraplegics have normal control over their arms and shoulders is perhaps inadequate. In terms of strength, they may be slightly above average. This is not surprising when one considers that from birth their arms may have been their primary means of conveyance. But in terms of manual dexterity, hand-eye co-ordination and fine motor control they are usually inferior. Years of hospitalisation and of sitting in a wheelchair coupled with the fact that they have missed the movement exploration normal in early childhood, combine to produce a developmental lag. They have been deprived of a vast amount of sensori-motor experience and are not surprisingly retarded in this respect. The teacher must be patient and provide opportunities and encouragement for these children to make good this deficit.

Cerebral palsy

This condition (if it can be considered a single condition) affects at least as large a part of the special school population as does spina bifida. Indeed, there are several schools in England which are solely for cerebral palsied children. But whereas all spina bifida sufferers experience similar difficulties, albeit to differing degrees, cerebral palsy can manifest itself in a number of completely different ways, depending on the site of the cerebral lesion. In consequence,

generalisations are even more hazardous with cerebral palsy than they are with other conditions. All that can be said with safety is that for these children perhaps more than any others, individual child-centred approaches to teaching are essential.

Cerebral palsy, or infantile cerebral paralysis, consists of a number of different forms of motor disorder due to non-progressive cerebral lesions, and is characterised by lack of control and co-ordination of voluntary muscles. It was first described by Little in 1853 and, in consequence, spastic diplegia (the condition he described in most detail) is sometimes referred to as Little's disease.

Although incidence varies from one country to another (Table 15), in England it is generally considered to be slightly more than one per thousand.

Table 15. Comparative incidence of cerebral palsy *(Skatvedt, 1958)*

Researcher	Date	Country	Incidence
Phelps	1948	U.S.A.	4:1000
Perlstein	1955	U.S.A.	5:1000
Anderson	1954	Norway	1.9:1000
Scheel-Thomsen	1952	Denmark	1.5:1000
Asher & Shonell	1950	England	1:1000
Nilsonne	1952	Sweden	0.6:1000

There is some difference in incidence between the sexes with boys being affected more frequently than girls at a ratio of about 55:45, though it is not understood why this should be so. There is also a different proportional incidence in types of handicap. Spastics account for some 67–86% of the total, athetoids account for 8–21%, and the other types for the remaining 6–12% (Dunsden 1960).

Childhood cerebral palsies, according to Blencowe (1969)

> are manifest at or soon after birth and are caused by damage to the developing nervous system before or during birth, or in the early months of infancy.

It is not surprising, therefore, that most aetiological accounts group the numerous causative factors according to a temporal classification: prenatal, paranatal and postnatal. But although these are useful (and they are the ones that will be used here), their contribution to an understanding of the nature of the palsy is minimal. This problem is further complicated by the fact that hazards of widely different natures – genetic, toxic, vascular and asphyxial – are capable of producing similar neurological symptoms.

Virtually all traumata sustained by the mother-to-be, as well as numerous genetic anomalies, are theoretically capable of causing brain injuries and resulting in cerebral palsy. Probably the most frequent factor responsible for such brain damage is a temporary deficiency of oxygen supply to the fetus. Most tissues require oxygen, and in man the first organ to suffer from such a deficiency is the brain. Unfortunately, intrauterine anoxia can have many different causes, e.g., uterine haemorrhages, placental infarction, compression of the umbilical cord, premature separation of the placenta, degenerative placental changes in prolonged pregnancy, or reduced oxygen tension in the maternal blood. Fetal cerebral lesions may also be due to toxaemia of pregnancy or infection, to radio-active rays, maternal malnutrition, and even psychiatric disturbance.

Paranatal causes are similarly of numerous different kinds. Once again anoxaemic injuries are common, resulting from cerebral ischaemias during birth and from neonatal respiratory disorders. Mechanical birth injuries, perhaps a result of forceps delivery or Caesarian section, can also cause haemorrhaging. Alternatively the injury may be of a chemical nature as in the case of kernicterus. Another factor, though whether of cause or effect is usually uncertain, is that at least a third of all such cases are premature at birth, i.e., under 2.5 kg, and a further 8% are postmature, i.e., ten days late (Blencowe 1969).

Postnatal causes include cerebral inflammations or anoxaemia, and vascular lesions.

The most frequent causes of cerebral palsy are, therefore, perinatal vascular and anoxaemic brain injuries. As these lesions are also the main causes of neonatal death, it seems an obvious conclusion that cerebral palsy is the result of these same injuries at a sublethal degree. It is a disturbing paradox, therefore, that whereas improved prophylaxis has reduced neonatal mortality (better hygiene during pregnancy, more 'lenient' delivery, adequate oxygen supplies and the use of antibiotics being the main factors), there has been a corresponding rise in the number of children with sublethal lesions. Add to this the increasing numbers of people suffering from traumatic cerebral palsy as the result of car crashes and other such accidents, and it is understandable that there are so many of these children in our special schools.

Classification

Taxonomies of cerebral palsy have always been something of a problem. The same words are often used by different specialists to mean different things, and this has led to widespread confusion. Additionally, among laymen the term 'spastic' has become synonymous with all manner of handicaps, although technically, as Blencowe (1969) points out:

> The word 'spastic' . . . is simply an adjective employed for a special kind of disorder of muscle tone which may or may not be present (in cerebral palsy).

Skatvedt (1958) adopted Perlstein's classification, dividing cerebral palsies into spasticities, dyskinesias, and ataxias, whereas Dunsden (1960) identified the main types as spasticity, athetosis, ataxia, tremor and rigidity. Blencowe on the other hand refused to use the term spastic at all, and her classification was hemiplegia, quadriplegia, diplegia, the athetoid syndromes, and ataxia.

The classification adopted here is an attempt to accommodate the main features of each of the above, and the types of cerebral palsy are, therefore, described as follows:

(i) spasticity – including hemiplegia, quadriplegia and diplegia;

(ii) dyskinesia – including athetosis, tremor and rigidity;

(iii) ataxia.

SPASTICITY

This condition is the most common and is apparently the result of damage to the pyramidal tracts in the brain stem. It is characterised by excessive stretch reflexes and increased muscle tone. Further differentiation is usually made according to the distribution of the affected nerve supply. The term hemiplegia is used to indicate a paralysis of the limbs of one side of the body, e.g., the right arm and leg; a monoplegia is a paralysis limited to one limb; and a quadriplegia or tetraplegia is a paralysis of all four limbs. The term diplegia is used to refer to cases with paralysis of the legs and arms, though with greater involvement of the legs than the arms. (If only the legs are involved, the term paraplegia is used, although this is rarely the result of a cerebral lesion and is more commonly due to a spinal injury.)

DYSKINESIA

Otherwise known as the athetoid syndromes, these conditions are the result of extrapyramidal tract involvement, in particular damage to the basal ganglia, a group of motor nuclei central to the Island of Ryle in the cerebrum. The most common type of dyskinesia is athetosis, which is characterised by involuntary, incoordinate, uncontrollable, purposeless movements with varying degrees of muscle spasm or tension. Rather less common are dystonia, which is characterised by marked tension of the axial muscles causing unusual postural attitudes; tremor, which manifests itself through fine, uncontrolled pendular or otherwise rhythmic motions involving alternate agonist and antagonist muscle actions; and rigidity, which is a resistance to slow passive motion, usually intermittent, resulting from simultaneous contractions of agonists and antagonists.

ATAXIA

This term is used to indicate a disorder of the cerebellum. Symptoms of such a defect are firstly vertigo and disequilibrium, and secondly disorders of movement. These functions can be involved separately so that, for example, a person without any incoordination of the arms and legs may nonetheless be

unable to stand, or together in which case muscle coordination and balance are both affected. Amongst this group of disorders the most common in childhood are congenital ataxia and congenital ataxic diplegia; both of these are characterised by incoordination of voluntary movements and hypotonia, in addition to which in the former case there are balance problems and an intention tremor.

Movement characteristics

Ellis (1967) summarises the effects of cerebral palsy on motor development and movement as follows:

> (Cerebral palsy) shows itself in the infant and older children as abnormalities of posture and movement which may alter as a result of maturation, adaptation or treatment . . . Not only is motor development delayed but abnormal postures and patterns of movement are acquired . . . Not only is muscle tone frequently abnormal but also notoriously variable.

Whilst such general statements are useful as indications of the sort of problems that accompany cerebral palsy, they are inadequate on their own because of the considerable difference between spasticity, athetosis and ataxia. Each one of these conditions has to be considered separately.

SPASTICITY

The spastic child has a permanent hypertonus whose degree varies with the child's general condition, i.e., his excitability and the strength of stimulation to which he is subjected at any one moment. If contraction of several muscles, especially those around the proximal joints, is severe, the child may be more or less fixed in a typical posture. Some muscles may appear weak as a result of tonic reciprocal inhibition, and true weakness may develop in some muscle groups through long periods of disuse. Spasticity is of a typical distribution and changes in a predictable manner owing to tonic reflex activity. Movement of affected body parts is restricted in range and requires excessive effort.

In spastic diplegia the lower extremities are more severely affected than the upper ones, and the condition is usually of a fairly symmetrical distribution. Head control is good and speech unaffected, though eye movements are often poorly co-ordinated. Standing and walking are acquired late and only if the arms and hands are controllable as excessive use of righting and equilibrium reactions above the waist are necessary. These excessive movements of the head, trunk and arms are necessary to compensate for the comparative immobility and stiffness of the hips and legs. These children cannot shift their body weight automatically on to the standing leg to leave the other leg free to make a step, and the body weight tends to remain on the inside of the foot. They lack balance and rotation, and in walking seem to be falling from one foot to the other, consequently they are unable to stand still without holding

onto something. Most walk on tiptoe as dorsiflexion at the ankles would produce an increase of flexor tone throughout the lower limbs which would make standing and walking impossible and might cause them to collapse. Thus the lower limbs of an older diplegic will show a pattern of mixed flexor and extensor spasticity, i.e., co-contraction. Possible deformities resulting from frequent use of these abnormal patterns are kyphosis, lordosis, subluxation or dislocation of the hips, adduction and inward rotation of the legs, and talipes equinovarus, or equinovalgus foot deformities.

In spastic quadriplegia the whole body is affected and the distribution is very asymmetrical, one side being more involved than the other and the upper limbs more involved than the lower. If the spasticity is severe the child is helpless and immobile. Any effort to move produces associated reactions and results in increased spasticity, accentuating the problem. Once spasticity is fully developed the child is unable to right his head, maintain his equilibrium in any position or to use his arms and hands. If head control is fair (as in some less severe cases) the child may learn to use the head to neutralise tonic reflexes. This may happen in one of two ways: (i) if extensor and flexor spasticity are strong in supine and prone positions respectively, he may learn to sit by moving his head into a mid-position which allows sitting by creating a certain equilibrium between the two forms of spasticity; and (ii) if the child has a strong asymmetrical tonic neck reflex (ATNR) he may learn to use one arm for grasp and release by turning his head first to one side to reach out, then to the other to grasp the object. In time the moderate quadriplegic may acquire some of the righting and equilibrium reactions necessary for sitting and kneeling, but never for standing or walking. Without exception, therefore, the quadriplegic is confined to a wheelchair. Possible deformities resulting from the functional use of these tonic reflex patterns are scoliosis or kyphoscoliosis, flexor deformities of hips and knees, equinovarus and equinovalgus of the feet, and subluxation of the hip (usually just one hip because of the excessive use of the ATNR).

In hemiplegia there is a very marked asymmetry of postural and movement patterns. Consequently development is delayed in all activities which require balance of the trunk and the use of both hands. The child is slow to establish balance in sitting, standing and walking, and there is a tendency to fall towards the affected side. As there is flexor spasticity of the affected side (and a corresponding absence of protective extensor reactions) the child is for some time unable to put his hand out when he falls and has to learn to fall towards his sound side. In due course righting and equilibrium reactions may become hyperactive on the sound side so as to compensate for their absence on the affected side. In standing, the body weight is supported mainly by the sound leg, and as the child learns to walk, the affected leg gradually stiffens in order to be able to bear weight. Even though this weight bearing is only momentary, it can not be done without an extensor spasticity produced by the pressure of the ball of the foot against the floor. Consequently the child learns to walk on

his toes. At the same time, the flexor spasticity of the upper limb increases, largely as a result of associated reactions brought about by the efforts and activity of the sound side. Because of this asymmetry, the following contractures and deformities may develop: flexor deformities of the elbow and wrist, adduction of the thumb, scoliosis, and talipes equinovarus or equinovalgus of the feet with shortening of the Achilles tendon on the affected side.

ATHETOSIS

All athetoids show an unsteady and fluctuating type of muscle tone, but the amplitude of the fluctuations may vary very widely in the individual case. Such children lack sustained postural tone and therefore cannot maintain a stable position. Similarly there is insufficient postural fixation due to a lack of co-contraction (i.e., simultaneous contraction of agonists and antagonists) to give guidance and support to a moving part. The grading of antagonist activity during movement is poor, and contraction of one group of muscles leads to the complete relaxation of its antagonists (by reciprocal inhibition). As a result, movements are jerky and extreme in range, with poor control of middle ranges. Also because of this lack of co-contraction and extreme range of movement, there is hypermobility of all joints with a tendency to subluxation. Fluctuations of muscle tone are sudden and manifest themselves in some of the involuntary movements common to all members of the athetoid group. In an individual case, the following types of involuntary movement are observable: (i) intermittent tonic spasms – largely dependent upon a change of head position – these fix a child temporarily in certain extreme postures of total extension or flexion (the result of tonic labyrinthine reflexes) or in certain asymmetrical postures of extension in face limbs and flexion in occiput limbs (the result of asymmetrical tonic neck reflexes); (ii) mobile spasms – these involve the limbs in alternating movements of flexion and extension, pronation and supination, etc. are often rhythmic in nature, e.g., the 'athetoid dance' and the habitual pawing of the ground with the foot; (iii) fleeting localised contractions – these affect muscles or muscle groups anywhere in the body in quite an unpredictable manner, producing minor local twitches or grotesque and exaggerated postures and movements according to their strength. All of these involuntary movements are reinforced during any attempt at volitional activity.

Most athetoids are quadriplegics in whom head and arms are more involved than lower parts. A few hemiplegics show some distal athetosis, and rarely one sees a pure hemi-athetosis. Also many athetoids seem to have some element of ataxia, especially those with a very low postural tone. The ataxic element, however, is difficult to differentiate from athetosis if the involuntary movements are very marked.

Standing and walking depend upon the relative normality of the legs and the degree of head control and equilibrium that can be developed. Hands usually cannot be used for support and asymmetrical distribution of postural tone interferes with balance.

The athetoid child is not likely to develop any deformities as by definition he has too many movement patterns. Because of this hypermobility, there is a natural tendency towards subluxation. Deformities may arise, however, if the athetosis is combined with spasticity or dystonia.

ATAXIA

Lesions of the cerebellum or its tracts cause failure to maintain posture and errors of range, direction, force and rate of movement during action. More chronic lesions of these pathways give rise to various tremors, the chief feature of which is that they are absent at complete rest but appear when the affected part is unsupported or in action.

In congenital ataxia there is persistent hypotonia from birth, marked poverty of spontaneous movements and severe retardation of motor development. When these ataxics do sit or walk, they are unsteady and flat-footed with their legs wide apart. The arms are used to help maintain balance and, on reaching for anything, there is marked intention tremor and a general lack of coordination.

In congenital ataxic diplegia there is also a history of a lack of spontaneous movement and, in early infancy at least, hypotonia is a prominent feature. After a few months, however, there is a spastic increase in muscle tone and a paresis of voluntary movement, which, in addition, is poorly coordinated. When these children walk (and this is usually late) they are on their toes and not flat-footed, their legs are close together, sometimes 'scissored' and they are liable to flexor contractures at the hip and knees.

Considerations for physical education

From this analysis it is apparent that 'cerebral palsy' is more of a family name than a specific medical diagnosis, and that within it there are many different types of handicap, all similar in terms of their neurological origins, but all manifesting themselves in different ways and to different degrees through different parts of the body. To attempt to use these clinical syndromes as the basis upon which to group children for activities in school would appear to be impractical at best. A more useful classification is obtainable if one disregards the specific nature of these various conditions in favour of the more general principle that they all represent an inability to execute controlled, voluntary movement. For practical purposes, therefore, cerebral palsied children can be grouped not according to their clinical identity but according to their potential for independent movement. In this way three distinct groups become apparent:

(i) Ambulant children – those who can walk, albeit unsteadily, either without assistance or with the help of a rollator or similar walking aid. The very fact that these children can walk at all is indicative of an ability, in some measure, to control the head and arms. Some of them, of relatively minimal impairment, can walk and run quite well and are very active; these can be introduced

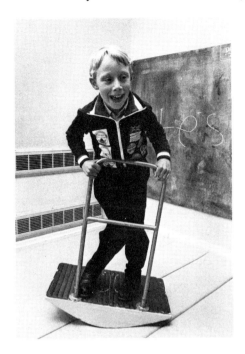

Where particular problems exist, time should be set aside for 'clinics' so that a child can benefit from the teacher's undivided attention.

to all of the usual range of games and other activities, even though they will experience difficulties with those that require them to jump, skip or move from one foot to another. Others, more seriously handicapped, either because of more extensive brain damage or because they have not yet achieved the level of control of the former group (a temporal consideration), can only stand or walk with considerable concentration. These need activities of a more sedate nature, providing opportunities for them to explore their movement potential unhurriedly, and thus to gain confidence and control without causing a breakdown in their ability to concentrate on what they are doing. For children at this stage of development, and many go beyond it, fast ball games and similar activities should only be used as an occasional bonus, as a sample of what can be achieved with time.

(ii) Independent wheelchair users – those whose inadequate control of their legs prevents them from walking but whose arms are sufficiently unaffected to enable them to control a wheelchair unassisted. These children are generally skilful enough in control of a wheelchair to join in activities with the paraplegics. There is unavoidably some involvement of the trunk and arms and so one should not expect the same standards of control or the same rates of improvement as with the paraplegics. But there is no reason why they should be excluded from any of the activities of the paraplegic. Indeed, because of the spastic tonus present in the legs of these cerebral palsied children (as compared

50

with the flaccid paralysis of the true paraplegic) there are some activities in which they are more able; in particular movements out of their chair involving changes of level, as in apparatus work.

(iii) Dependent wheelchair users – those quadriplegics whose control of arms and legs is limited to such an extent that not only is walking impossible, but also ordinary wheelchairs cannot be used either. Most of these children may learn to control an electrically powered wheelchair with a single, hand-operated steering unit (similar chairs have been built to facilitate foot or head operation), though it is conceivable that some of them even find this impossible. The co-ordination of voluntary movement is so poor in these cases that activities out of the wheelchair need to be conducted on a one-to-one basis and rarely extend beyond exercise of a physiotherapeutic nature. Even in their wheelchairs, whatever control they do have requires time and concentration for its expression. The exercise of this control is nonetheless valuable and opportunities should be provided for such activity. Games that do not demand speed of reaction can be played, such as skittles, table skittles, bar billiards and snooker (with appropriate modifications); and precision driving tests may also be valuable. Obviously the range of activities is somewhat limited, but there is a lot to be gained from encouraging these children to involve themselves in official duties as referees and timekeepers or simply as spectators.

Whatever the abilities of the children being taught, if they are cerebral palsied, certain points might beneficially be kept to the fore of one's mind:

Firstly, stressful and even pleasantly exciting situations tend to bring on muscle spasms, either of total flexion or total extension according to the individual case. As anecdotal evidence of the possible implications of such spasms there is the case of a teenaged girl, a spastic diplegic, in whom the 'giggles' always brought on a flexor spasm. When first of all she was learning to swim breaststroke, her giggling fits had rather drastic results, as total flexion took her head under water and completely inhibited any righting reactions. She had to learn either to control her giggling, or, failing that, to recognise its coming and turn onto her back. A flexor spasm in that position would bring her to her feet.

Secondly, each cerebral palsied child has virtually unique posture and movement patterns. Attempts to mould this into a 'normal' pattern may be ineffective. The child is more likely to benefit from opportunities to experience his own body form in a variety of different situations so that he may come to understand it, to recognise its limitations and thus to control it. An example of the significance of this to the physical education programme is to be found (yet again) in swimming. Many cerebral palsied children, who would have no hope of swimming if compelled to persevere with attempts at classical strokes, become quite proficient in their own way and manage to swim literally miles in comfort. Probably the best example of this is the one handed 'J' stroke in front crawl used by some hemiplegics. As they can only use one hand

51

effectively, to swim front crawl in the normal fashion would produce a curved path of travel. To compensate for this, at the end of each arm stroke they pull the hand across their body (thus completing a 'J' movement) and put themselves back on course.

Thirdly, the essence of the cerebral palsied child's problem is abnormal movement. Whether it is wise to ask him to pursue activities in which precision of movement is essential to satisfactory performance, as is often the case in track and field athletics, is open to debate. It might perhaps be better to concentrate on activities in which the movement element is subordinate to tactical ability or some non-personal 'constant', such as a goal or even the electrically powered wheelchair. Using the game of football as an example, the skill component is almost irrelevant provided that somehow the players manage to get the ball in the net. This is not to say, however, that a child who has a particular interest in athletics should be discouraged from participation in such activity. Given real enthusiasm, it is amazing what can be achieved even by the most severely handicapped.

Muscular Dystrophy

This is not nearly so common a condition as either spina bifida or cerebral palsy, but because it is progressive (and often indirectly terminal) it poses many problems for the educator; problems which are ethical as well as physical.

Aetiology

Muscular dystrophy is one of a group of diseases known collectively as myopathies. Within this category can be placed

> any disease or syndrome in which the patient's symptoms and/or physical signs can be attributed to pathological, biochemical or electrical changes occurring in muscle fibres or intestinal tissues of the voluntary musculature, and in which there is no evidence that the symptoms related to the muscles are in any way secondary to disordered function of the central or peripheral nervous system (Walton 1960).

More specifically, muscular dystrophy refers only to those forms of genetically-determined myopathy in which a degenerative process develops primarily in the muscles themselves. It is commonly defined, therefore, as a genetically-determined, degenerative, primary myopathy.

Despite the fact that the disease is the result of a genetic anomaly, the onset of clinical manifestations is somehow delayed and diagnosis is not normally made until the child is quite old and sometimes not until adulthood. This phenomenon of an abnormal gene remaining undetected at birth and exerting its effect progressively in post-natal life has been referred to as abiotrophy (Tyler 1960). Complicating this tardy diagnosis is the fact that several other

conditions are apparently similar, e.g., polymyositis and infantile or juvenile spinal atrophy. To confirm diagnosis of muscular dystrophy, the most useful investigations are muscle biopsy, electromyography and serum enzyme activity estimations; (such activity is almost always raised in cases of muscular dystrophy and yet normal in neuropathies). At present no primary bio-chemical abnormality has been demonstrated in muscular dystrophy and almost all of the abnormalities of metabolism that do occur may be accounted for by the decreased functioning of the muscle mass and the disintegration of muscle. Also, to date, no successful methods have been devised that either prevent, arrest or cure muscular dystrophy. Several treatments have been devised and investigated, including glycine, vitamin E, and multiple amino-acid therapy, but all have proved unsuccessful.

The characteristic pathological features of dystrophic muscle have been summarised by Walton as follows:

> Haphazard enlargement of some muscle fibres and atrophy of others giving a striking variation in fibre size in any specimen; migration of sarcolemmal nuclei into the substance of the muscle fibre often to form chains; fibre splitting is common; segmental necrosis of muscle fibres with phagocytosis of the necrotic remnants is seen in the more rapidly progressive forms of the disease; disintegrated muscle fibres are replaced by aggregation of nuclear remnants, by fibrous tissue and most often by fat; nerve fibres and muscle spindles appear to be unaffected.

Whilst it is apparent that unstriated muscle remains unaffected, the heart muscle is clearly involved in many muscular dystrophy cases. Consequently, persistent tachycardia is common and sudden death from myocardial failure is not infrequent. In some cases there is also an associated incidence of bone deformity.

Classification

Classically, there are five types of progressive muscular dystrophy:
    (i) Duchenne-type muscular dystrophy;
    (ii) Limb-girdle muscular dystrophy;
    (iii) Facioscapulohumeral muscular dystrophy;
    (iv) Distal myopathy;
    (v) Ocular myopathy.

Both the distal and ocular myopathies are extremely rare and like the facio-scapulohumeral muscular dystrophy, which is relatively mild in any case, they do not usually manifest themselves until adulthood. The Duchenne-type and the limb-girdle type, however, are both common in childhood. In fact Tyler and Wintrobe (1950) reclassified them jointly as 'childhood muscular dystrophy'. Consequently, it is with these two types that this text (and the schoolteacher) must be concerned.

DUCHENNE-TYPE MUSCULAR DYSTROPHY

This is the most severe type and was first described by Duchenne in 1855. The eponymous term 'Duchenne-type muscular dystrophy' is preferred to its alternative name 'pseudohypertrophic muscular dystrophy' not only because pseudohypertrophy does not occur in all cases with this type of muscular dystrophy, but also because it can sometimes be seen in other forms of muscular dystrophy as well. Genetic transmission is usually as a sex-linked recessive character with a high mutation rate (and rarely as an autosomal recessive), such that the disease almost exclusively manifests itself in the male. The onset of the disease is usually detectable within the first three years of life, although it may be as late as the third decade. Muscular involvement is symmetrical, affecting the pelvic girdle first and then the shoulder girdle. In addition, in about eighty per cent of cases, there is pseudohypertrophy, particularly of the calf muscles, but sometimes of the quadriceps and deltoids as well. The effects of the disease progress steadily and rapidly, leading usually to an inability to walk within ten years of onset. Deformities are similarly progressive with muscular contractures, skeletal distortion and atrophy. Abortive cases do not occur: once the progression has begun, it continues without abatement until death which usually comes in the second decade as a result of inanition, respiratory infection or cardiac failure, although sometimes, owing to antibiotic therapy, it is warded off until middle life.

LIMB-GIRDLE MUSCULAR DYSTROPHY

This is somewhat milder than the Duchenne-type and was first described by Erb in 1884. Its genetic transmission is usually as an autosomal recessive character (and only rarely as an autosomal dominant or a sex-linked recessive), and consequently it manifests itself in both sexes. The onset of the disease is generally later than in the Duchenne-type, usually being detected in the second or third decades, although it may be as early as the first decade or as late as middle life. Primary involvement is of either the pelvic girdle or the shoulder girdle with a spread to the other after a variable period of time. Muscular pseudohypertrophy occurs only rarely, and contractures and skeletal deformities only become evident late in the course of the disease. Abortive or relatively non-progressive cases do exist, though despite this variable rate of progress severe disability is usually present twenty years after onset. Most patients are severely disabled in middle life and die prematurely. Obviously, unless this disease expressed itself very early on in a child's life, it would have little effect upon his schooling.

Movement characteristics

Although there are obvious differences between the two childhood muscular dystrophies, if the onset of the limb-girdle type is early in childhood its progression will, more or less, follow the course of the Duchenne-type. The chronologically constructed description which follows is, therefore, that which

is typical of a Duchenne-type muscular dystrophy.

The first signs that a child is dystrophied are observed difficulty in running and climbing stairs, and sometimes difficulty in lifting the arms. The child falls frequently, displays an awkward, waddling gait and, when sitting up from backlying, tends to 'climb up his legs'. These features become progressively worse, usually from age four or five years up to nine or ten. During this time too his posture is increasingly characterised by lordosis.

By about seven, eight or nine years of age the child is usually so weak in the legs and falling so frequently that he has to resort to the use of a wheelchair. It is important to note that, as immobilisation tends to accelerate the dystrophic progress, this transfer is never hurried, and walking, even if only for short distances, is encouraged. There is also a tendency to develop foot and ankle deformities such as pes equinus, pes equinovarus and shortening of the ilio-tibial tract, initially because of the child's laboured gait, but then, more particularly, because of the immobility of wheelchair use. Unfortunately these deformities do not respond very well to physiotherapy and often require surgical treatment. But so as to avoid lengthy periods of immobilisation which would only further accelerate the dystrophic progression, as a general rule only the simplest operational procedures are performed.

As the weakness becomes more general and involves the arms and shoulders as well, the child finds increasing difficulty in pushing a wheelchair, and, at about ten to twelve years of age, he has to resort to an electrically powered chair. From this stage onwards the child's movement potential is extremely limited. He is unable to lift his legs or raise his arms from his lap without climbing his fingers up his clothing. He is incapable of shifting his position in his wheelchair and, should he slump forwards, is unable to right himself. In bed his immobility is almost complete and he has to be turned several times every night as even simple postural adjustments are impossible.

Considerations for physical education
Whilst the prognosis for these children is inevitably bleak, and the philosophy behind their participation in any form of physical recreation activity complex, they themselves usually greet almost any opportunity to join in physical education lessons with enthusiasm. Although these children are weak (and growing progressively weaker) and therefore very easily fatigued, that physical activity is beneficial is beyond question. Murphy (1964) emphasises this aspect of their physical management with the following words:

> It is apparent that physical therapy is most effective in correcting disuse atrophy and in improving the performance of patients in the activities of daily living . . . It is known that weakness . . . may be greatly and permanently increased after prolonged periods of bed rest . . . It is essential, particularly in the cases of the Duchenne-type of muscular dystrophy, that the patient should be kept active and encouraged to use his limbs as much as possible.

In the early stages, muscular dystrophy children can join in all of the usual primary school physical education activities with the possible exception of climbing. It is to be expected that they will fall over frequently (hence the doubts about climbing), but fortunately they seem to develop a knack for doing so without hurting themselves.

During the interim period in which they occupy the ordinary, push-type wheelchair, their mobility, not surprisingly, is inferior to that of the paraplegics and even the diplegics. However, in activities requiring co-ordination rather than strength or stamina, such as light bat and ball games, table skittles and snooker, they often excel. The reasons for this are manifold: firstly, their condition, unlike the spina bifidas and the cerebral palsies, is myopathic and not neuropathic, consequently, although their musculature is weak, its neurological control and co-ordination is unimpaired; secondly, unlike most other children with congenital handicaps, they have several years of normal sensori-motor experience behind them; and thirdly, each of the activities mentioned above can be successfully performed using only proximal movements as these muscles are the last to deteriorate.

By the time they need to use powered wheelchairs, however, their capacity for active involvement in any physical activity (other than swimming) may be negligible. For different reasons they are in much the same position as the severe quadriplegics. Consequently they can participate in similar activities: precision driving tests, table games and officiating duties. In addition, because they suffer no impairment of co-ordination and no muscular spasms, certain other modified activities are possible, such as crossbow archery and wheelchair hockey (with the stick fixed rudder-like to the forward end of their electric wheelchairs). The one activity in which they can participate fully without mechanical aids is swimming, but as this is also true for most other handicaps, it will be discussed in greater detail later on.

Haemophilia

This condition is the result of a congenital deficiency in one or another of the coagulation factors of the blood. Although there are believed to be thirteen of these, in ninety-five per cent of cases the deficiency is either Factor VIII ('classic' haemophilia) or Factor IX (sometimes referred to as Christmas Disease). Genetic transmission of this disease is as a sex-linked recessive trait carried in the asymptomatic females, so that it manifests itself in about one male in ten thousand, although some estimates put it as low as three quarters or even two thirds per hundred thousand (Duthie et al. 1972, and Biggs et al. 1957).

The normal blood coagulation system is conceived as a dynamic phenomenon initiated immediately blood is in contact with a surface other than vascular endothelium and leading to the ultimate formation of fibrin. If

Once in the water, even children whose movement potential on land is severely limited discover a freedom and enjoyment of movement which is a joy to behold.

there is a deficiency at any stage of this process coagulation or clotting is prevented. Haemophilia is thus characterised by

> a tendency to persistent bleeding following a breach in continuity of blood vessels (Kerr 1963).

Classification

Haemophilia is commonly classified according to severity, thus:

(i) Severe – a factor level 0–1% of normal There is evidence of abnormal bleeding from infancy and haemarthroses (bleeding into joints) are universal from an early age. These cases are prone to spontaneous haemorrhages i.e. those arising with no detectable precipitating cause.

(ii) Moderate – a factor level 1–5% of normal In these cases the haemorrhagic tendency is not so marked and spontaneous haemorrhaging is infrequent. Haemarthroses are still common.

(iii) Mild – a factor level 5–50% of normal These cases can cope with everyday and sporting traumata without undue haemorrhage. It is only tooth extractions, surgery and severe injury that reveal the potentially serious defect in their haemostasis.

Treatment at all levels, when it is necessary, is by isolation of the affected area from movement and by the infusion of coagulation factor concentrates derived from normal blood plasma.

Physical characteristics

From the time a severely affected child learns to walk, he is rarely without bruises on some part of his body. Haemarthroses are common, with the ankles, knees and elbows most frequently involved and the other joints less so. Between the first few haemorrhages a joint may revert to its former shape and function, but sooner or later chronic changes appear, eventually leading to a perpetually distorted appearance of the joint(s) often associated with deformity. The severe haemophiliac usually walks with a limp and shows a variety of joint changes and other consequences of bleeding.

Considerations for physical education

There is often a desire in parents and teachers alike to 'wrap these children in cotton wool'. Whilst the dangers of over-protection are not nearly so grave as the consequences of haemorrhaging, it is perhaps worth remembering that a haemophiliac has all the natural instincts for play and activity of any 'normal' boy. Although it is generally accepted that all body-contact sports and hard-ball games should be avoided as injury will almost certainly result, it does not follow that all other forms of recreational activity must similarly be barred. Even if all those sports are avoided in which there is a risk of some form of impact or collision (whether with another person or with a missile) or of an excessive strain or stress being placed on the joints, there are still many activities left from which to choose, e.g., archery, angling, table games including table tennis, and swimming. Even golf is played by some severe haemophiliacs, but almost all have suffered haemarthroses of arm and shoulder joints. The teacher's task is a difficult one. The haemophiliac child needs to be steered between inactivity and the risk of crippling injuries, and he should be made aware of the reasons for doing so.

Asthma

Asthma, or rather its treatment, is often a subject of controversy; primarily because it is misunderstood. Technically asthma is a 'paroxysmal attack of difficulty in breathing' (Roper 1969). Although it may be accompanied by physical conditions, e.g., certain allergies, it is most often psychosomatic, that is,

> arising mainly from overactivity of the autonomic nervous system which is influenced by the emotional state. (Roper)

That is not to say, however, that asthma is a condition which can be treated lightly. For the affected child, the cause of his suffering is not nearly so important as the effect which can be extremely distressing. Unfortunately, the apparent severity of an asthma attack sometimes causes parents (and others) to mollycoddle the individual, and such overreaction, if persisted in over a number of years, can serve to increase the instability of the emotional state and thus to reinforce the asthma.

Physical characteristics
The only physical characteristics likely to be abnormal, apart from the occasional breathlessness which is to be expected, are slight stiffness of the shoulder girdle and a developmental lag in motor ability; both of which are in some measure due to the child's underexposure to movement experiences in early childhood.

Considerations for physical education
Although there are doubtless some asthma sufferers who need very special consideration, many of these children are able to cope with normal schooling and are quite sound enough to participate in most physical education activities, including swimming, without any ill effects. There may be a need to withhold certain individuals from the more strenuous activities, but suitable alternatives are numerous. If an asthma attack is precipitated during an activity session, the child should be allowed to rest. *Under no circumstances* should a child be forced or coerced to work through a bout of asthma. Fortunately, many such children now carry a pocket-sized inhaler which very quickly stabilises their breathing.

Epilepsy

Although children who suffer solely from epilepsy are usually placed in ordinary schools or schools specially for epileptics (according to severity), the teacher in the special school for physically handicapped children needs to be alert to the problems associated with this disorder because of the frequency with which it accompanies other handicapping conditions.

Like paralysis or incoordination, epilepsy is a symptom of cerebral abnormality, but whereas these are the result of a destruction of nervous tissue, epilepsy is a positive symptom resulting from excessive excitation. Under certain circumstances, such as electrical stimulation, all brains are capable of initiating fits or convulsions, but in normal people there is a mechanism which prevents this. Epilepsy, which merely means a tendency to have fits, can be said, therefore, to depend on two things: a low convulsive threshold and a trigger mechanism. Although this trigger mechanism can be chemical, it is commonly an electrical discharge arising from abnormally irritated nerve cells situated in scar tissue in the brain.

Classification
There are two main kinds of epilepsy, general and focal, the former of which is again usually of two kinds, the petit mal or inhibitory type and the grand mal or excitatory type. Focal epilepsy, as the name suggests, is that in which only localised areas of the brain are irritated and, in consequence, only certain parts of the body or certain body functions are affected. Thus a focal fit arising in that part of the brain which represents the hand will result in jerking involving

only the arm; one involving the parietal lobe will result in bizarre sensations of tingling and so forth. General epilepsy, on the other hand, involves the whole body simultaneously. The inhibitory or petit mal variety is typified by a brief period of 'absence' or blank staring with scarcely any motor manifestation; whilst the excitation or grand mal variety produces a generalised convulsion – the child falls to the floor, lapses into unconsciousness, displays tremors and froths at the mouth.

In all cases, only passive first-aid is recommended. The convulsion is allowed to run its natural course (in some petit mal attacks it may even have passed undetected), and only in grand mal attacks is any active interference necessary. In these cases, to prevent biting of the tongue the child should be laid on his side with the head slightly below the horizontal, and to ensure a good airway the neck should be slightly extended and the jaw kept forward. After a major (grand mal) convulsion, most children feel a need to rest, but unless there was any injury caused by the fall that is the only dispensation required.

Considerations for physical education

Because of the unpredictability of epileptic attacks there is often concern about the extent to which such children should be involved in a physical education programme. Personal experience and conferment with others in the field indicate that they can be safely integrated into most groups for the pursuit of most activities with only a few provisos, namely (i) the teacher obviously knows which of his children suffer from epilepsy; he must be able (where this is possible) to recognise the signs that an attack is imminent; and he must know what action is necessary when such an attack does occur; (ii) an epileptic child in a swimming pool needs constant supervision on a one-to-one basis from a person trained and suitably clothed to go to his rescue; (iii) in the gymnasium (or elsewhere) the epileptic child should not be allowed into situations in which, should an attack occur, an attendant would be unable to prevent him from incurring serious injury, (e.g., activities on high level climbing apparatus).

Beyond this, the teacher should also be aware that most epileptic children take drugs to stabilise their condition, and, whilst in many cases the side effects are negligible, in some they include anaemia, unsteadiness and mental clouding. One encouraging note for the physical education teacher is the fact that epileptic attacks usually occur before or after activity, but only rarely whilst a child is actually performing.

Cardiac disorders

These require special attention, not because of any associated movement difficulty which the child may or may not have, but because of the unparalleled importance of the heart to continued living. The finer details of

cardiac disorders in children are in the realm of the consultant paediatrician. What the teacher has to ascertain is whether physical activity, strenuous or otherwise, and the excitement that accompanies competitive games, are likely to damage an already unstable heart.

Depending on the health of the autonomic nervous system, which controls the heart, a child may be safe to participate in the activities of a physical education programme. With some heart conditions the safety mechanism causing the body to collapse (or at least to stop working) if the heart is being overloaded functions normally, and activity is quite safe. With others, such as Eisenmenger's syndrome, this safety mechanism is faulty and under no circumstances should the child be allowed to overexert himself. Generalisations are taboo with heart disorders, and the teacher is advised to seek expert advice in every case.

Other less common conditions

Apart from the more common types of handicap which have already been discussed, the special school population consists of small numbers of largely different and comparatively rare physical handicaps. To attempt an examination of each of them in the same detail would be impractical. Instead, it is proposed to indicate certain key questions which the physical education teacher might ask about each, whether he is selecting children for participation in particular types of activity or devising programmes to suit the needs of specific children.

These questions are appropriate not only for evaluating major disabilities, but also short-term causes of immobility or incapacity. In the special school there is a tendency to concentrate almost exclusively upon the major handicaps; just as in the ordinary school the minimally handicapped, the injured and those recuperating after an illness are also often neglected. Unless children are actually ill, even if certain parts of their body are immobilised or dysfunctioning, there is no reason why they should not benefit from a modified form of physical education just as much as the able-bodied.

In any such case, the following questions need to be answered before the child is allowed to participate in any strenuous physical activity:

(i) What sort of a disorder is it? Is it neurological, muscular, orthopaedic, respiratory or cardiac? Given that the primary disorder is known, are there any secondary characteristics that need noting, such as brittle bones, vertigo, muscle spasms, epilepsy or the side effects of drugs and other medicaments?

(ii) Is the condition progressive or non-progressive, temporary or permanent? Answers to these questions may enable the teacher to prognosticate and to familiarise himself with the progress which these children should or should not be expected to make.

(iii) Which body parts are affected, in which way and to what extent? Are calipers, sticks, wheelchairs, appliances or prostheses used? Are the affected body parts to be rested or exercised?

(iv) Is there any possibility that participation in any given form of physical activity might aggravate a child's condition?

Whatever problems a particular child might have, if the teacher has answers to these questions, it should be possible to ascertain which activities are inappropriate and which, perhaps in modified form, are likely to contribute positively to the child's development.

Summary

In this chapter an attempt has been made to outline the more common physical handicaps in terms of their aetiology, physical characteristics and the way in which they affect movement. An attempt has also been made to relate these diagnoses to physical education.

It would appear, from what has been written so far, that, should a teacher decide to group his children for physical education purely on an age basis, he is likely to find in any one group an almost infinite number of variables, both in movement potential and motor ability. Not only are there numerous different handicaps, but also, within each one, there are different types or significantly different levels of severity or involvement. Whilst such a policy of non-selection might be tolerable in an educational gymnastics setting or in certain play situations associated with the nursery/infant classes of the school, it can only make the teaching of organised, structured activities an arduous and unwieldy affair.

It is suggested therefore that for most physical education activities some form of ability grouping is beneficial. It has already been demonstrated that to group children according to handicaps, e.g., a spina bifida group and a cerebral palsy group, is likely to be unsatisfactory, and so the most practical method would appear to be a system of cross-handicap grouping based upon movement potential and a broad-based age criterion. The following classification would seem to be appropriate, both in terms of homogeneity and feasibility; i.e., it is likely that within the average special school population these groups will be of a manageable size:

(i) Able ambulants These children can walk, run and jump quite freely and are normally active. They include the asthmatic group, the haemophiliacs, upper-limb thalidomides, children with fibrocystic disease, ectopia vesica and all other such conditions that do not seriously impair ambulation.

(ii) Unsteady ambulants These children are less mobile but nonetheless able to walk. They walk either independently (but unsteadily) or else using sticks, calipers or rollator. They include the milder spina bifidas, the less severe spastic diplegics, the hemiplegics, athetoids, ataxics, arthrygryposes, lower-limb amputees and severe haemophiliacs.

(iii) Independent wheelchair users These children, although unable to walk

(at least to any practical extent), have good control of head, shoulders and arms and sufficient strength in these members to be able to push a wheelchair over considerable distances and/or over difficult ground surfaces. This group normally comprises the spina bifidas and other paraplegics, and the spastic diplegics, but occasionally it is augmented by children from the ambulant groups whose legs are temporarily incapacitated as a result of injury or surgical treatment.

(iv) Dependent wheelchair users These children are either too weak or too poorly coordinated to be able to control an ordinary wheelchair. Unless they are in possession of an electrically powered chair, they are confined to static activities. This group includes the muscular dystrophies, the spastic quadriplegics and the severe athetoids.

With groups of this kind, a physical education teacher can devise a programme and select activities that are appropriate to the needs of all the children in the special school. Within these groups, however, there should always be a measure of flexibility; and even then, there are likely to be some children who require individual attention in one or more areas of development. It is to cope with this eventuality that time set aside for clinics is suggested (Chapter 2).

The next chapter deals with certain non-physical disorders which are commonly associated with motor impairment.

REFERENCES

Adams, R. D., Eaton, L. M. & Shy, G. M. (Eds.) (1960) *Neuromuscular disorders* The Williams & Wilkins Co: Baltimore.

Barr, M. L. (1972) *The human nervous system*. Harper & Row: New York.

Biggs, R. P. & Macfarlane, R. G. (1957) *Human blood coagulation* 2nd edition: Blackwell Scientific Publications, Oxford.

Blencowe, S. M. (1969) *Cerebral palsy and the young child*. Churchill Livingstone: Edinburgh & London.

Bobath, K. (1966) *The motor deficit in patients with cerebral palsy*. Little Club Clinics in Developmental Medicine No. 23: Spastics Society/Heinemann, London.

Chamberlain, G. (1969) *The safety of the unborn child*. Penguin: Harmondsworth.

Clarke, T. A. (1966) *The aetiology of minimal brain damage and its effect on motor ability*. Unpublished paper: Carnegie School of Physical Education: Leeds.

Dunsden, M. I. (1960) *Cerebral Palsy*. Education Research, 3 · 1 pp. 37–50.

Duthie, R. B., Matthews, J. M., Rizza, C. R. & Steel, W. M. (1972) *The management of musculo-skeletal problems in haemophiliacs*. Blackwell Scientific Publications, Oxford.

Ellis, E. (1967) *The physical management of developmental disorders*. Little Club Clinics in Developmental Medicine No. 26: Spastics Society/Heinemann: London.

Gardner, E. (1968) *Fundamentals of neurology*. W. B. Saunders Co: Philadelphia.

Hughes, J. T. (1966) *Pathology of the spinal cord*. Lloyd-Luke Ltd: London.

Henderson, P. et al. (1975) *Children with spina bifida at school: a booklet for teachers and students*. Association for Spina Bifida and Hydrocephalus: London.

Ingram, T. (1963) Ataxia and ataxic diplegia in childhood. In Walsh, G. (Ed.) *Cerebellum posture and cerebral palsy*, pp. 70–82. Spastics Society/Heinemann: London.

Kerr, C. B. (1963) *The management of haemophilia*. Australasian Medical Publishing Company Ltd: Sydney.

Mackenzie, I. (1963) A neurologist's view of cerebellar function. In Walsh, G. (Ed.) *Cerebellum posture and cerebral palsy*, pp. 63–69. Spastics Society/Heinemann: London.

Martin, M. C. (1967) *Spina bifida*. A paper presented to the Congress of the World Confederation for Physical Therapy: Sydney.

Murphy, E. G. (1964) *The chemistry and therapy of disorders of voluntary muscles*. C. C. Thomas Books: Illinois.

Perlstein, M. A. (1950) Medical aspects of cerebral palsy, (incidence, aetiology and pathogenesis). *Amer. J. Occup. Therapy*, 4, 2, 47–52 & 76.

Roper, N. (1969) *Livingstone's pocket medical dictionary* 11th edition. Churchill Livingstone: Edinburgh & London.

Soltan, M. C. (1964) Inheritance of muscular dystrophy. Unpublished thesis reported in Murphy, E. G. *The chemistry and therapy of disorders of voluntary muscles*. C. C. Thomas Books: Illinois.

Sharrard, W. J. W. (1966) Personal communication reported in Martin, M. C. (1967) *Spina Bifida*. A paper presented to the Congress of the World Confederation for Physical Therapy, Melbourne.

Skatvedt, M. (1958) Cerebral palsy: a clinical study of 370 cases. *Acta Paediatrica*, 46, Suppl. III, 1–101. Oslo University Press.

Sutton, N. G. (1973) *Injuries of the spinal cord: The management of paraplegia and tetraplegia*. Butterworth: London.

Tyler, F. H. (1960) Inheritance of neuromuscular disease. In Adams, R. D. et al. (Eds.) *Neuromuscular disorders*. The Williams and Wilkins Company: Baltimore.

Tyler, F. H. & Wintrobe, M. M. (1950) Studies in Disorders of muscle: 1. The problem of progressive muscular dystrophy, *Ann. Int. Med*, 32, 1, 72–79.

Von Recklinghausen, F. (1886) Uber die Art und die Entstehung der Spina Bifida, ihre Beziehung zum Ruchenmark und Darmspalte. Virchows Arch. Path. Anat. 165. In Hughes, J. T. (1966) *Pathology of the spinal cord*. Lloyd-Luke Ltd: London.

Walsh, G. (Ed.) (1963) *Cerebellum posture and cerebral palsy*. Little Club Clinics in Developmental Medicine No. 8. Spastics Society/Heinemann: London.

Walton, J. N. (1960) Muscular dystrophy and its relation to the other myopathies. In Adams, R. D. et al. (Eds.) *Neuromuscular disorders*. The Williams & Wilkins Co: Baltimore.

Walton, J. N., Canal, N. & Scarlato, G. (Eds.) (1970) *Muscle diseases*. Excerpta Medica: Amsterdam.

4

Associated disorders

The side effects of motor impairment are many and varied. Indeed it is a feature of most physical handicaps that they incorporate not one but several disorders. It is, for example, very rare that a cerebral palsied person suffers only from spasticity (or whatever), and equally unusual for a spina bifida child to have only paraplegia with which to contend. But, because these 'associated disorders', as they are known, are in themselves neither so obvious nor apparently so serious, they are often disregarded. In consequence, a child's inability to succeed at an activity may be attributed to his primary (irreversible) handicap when in fact it is one of these secondary (remediable) characteristics which is to blame. Obviously not all physically handicapped children suffer from all associated disorders, but where they do exist their effect upon learning and/or performance is considerable. The physical education teacher in the special school might profitably learn not only to recognise them but also to minimise their effect through appropriate forms of compensatory education.

The nature of these disorders is such that, commonly, they can be ascribed to one of two causes. They are either physically derived conditions, usually of a neurological origin, which have a direct effect upon performance; or they are the result of environmental circumstances, usually an experiential deprivation or an emotional instability arising out of the physical condition, and indirectly affect performance. There are, of course, many different disorders within each of these categories.

The first group of disorders, those which directly affect performance, are perhaps best analysed with reference to the type of systems-analysis model which was popularised by Welford (1960), Singleton (1967) and Whiting (1969). Implicit in the use of this sort of model is the belief that one's understanding of human behaviour can be increased if the sub-systems which combine to produce such behaviour are comparted and sequentialised (Fig. 11).

Basically the processes thought to underlie the performance of perceptual-motor skills are the following: firstly, stimuli from the display impinge upon the sense receptors; a perceptual process then selects relevant data from this display and mental or cognitive operations are performed upon these in an attempt to decide upon an appropriate response; effector mechanisms then select and activate the motor programmes appropriate to that response so that, finally, the response is made.

This chain of events is very much a simplification – the whole process is a

dynamic one and the feedback mechanisms are most complex – but it is adequate for present needs. A defect at any one of these stages is likely to produce an inappropriate response, even in an able-bodied performer. If the person attempting this response is already grossly physically handicapped, the likelihood of success is even more remote. Unfortunately deficiencies or abnormalities in all of these sub-systems are common.

The second group of disorders, those of environmental or experiential origin only indirectly affect performance, but they are no less important because of that. In the main, they are the psychological/attitudinal consequences of sensori-motor deprivation, of repeated failure and of frustrations brought on by limited powers of expression and an equally limited prognosis. The seat of these disturbances is cerebral, in cognitive and emotive centres, but their influence pervades all of behaviour.

Each of these possible areas of disorder, sensory, perceptual, cognitive, executive and emotional, will now be the subject of a more detailed analysis.

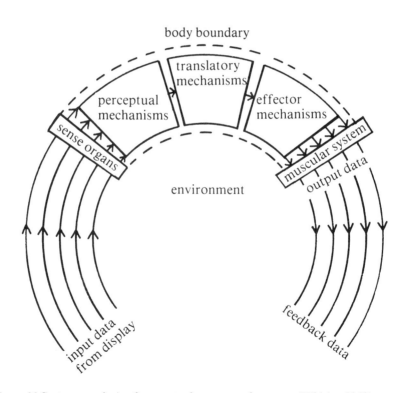

Figure 11 Systems analysis of perceptual-motor performance (Whiting 1969)

Sensory disorders

The sensory modalities important to physical activity include sight, hearing, touch and kinaesthesis, in each of which defects can occur.

Children who suffer serious defects in sight or hearing (i.e., blindness or deafness), or even less serious impairment (i.e., partial sight and partial hearing) where such conditions are dominant, that is, the most severe of a child's handicaps, are required to attend schools which cater specifically for these handicaps. The teacher in the special school for physically handicapped children is, therefore, only likely to have to contend with minor degrees of visual and auditory defect.

The visual defects that are commonly encountered are myopia and astigmatism, both of which can be corrected by wearing spectacles; defects of muscle balance and paralysis of eye muscles, which cause squints; and hemianopia, a neurological disorder which effects a reduction to the visual field, producing either tunnel-vision, peripheral vision, or the ability to see only that which is on one side, the last being not uncommon in cases of hemiplegia. Apart from the more obvious implications, these defects are variously responsible for difficulties in co-ordination, orientation, position in space, object identification and tracking.

For the partially sighted child in the special school for physically handicapped children, therefore, all activity areas should be relatively large and, as a safety precaution, should be free of non-essential equipment and unnecessary obstruction. Where possible, lighting should be uniform (e.g., strip lighting) so that there are no dark corners.

On the rare occasion that one encounters a totally blind child in the sort of special school with which we are presently concerned, every effort should be made to ensure that each child is given a thorough personal introduction to all teaching areas, and, under appropriate supervision, is allowed to feel his way around all apparatus and other equipment. This tactile feedback should be augmented wherever possible by verbal description.

Each new activity or skill should be described in detail and in a manner that is clear and concise. Too much information at any one time can be more confusing than helpful. In many situations, it is also useful if the blind learner can be given positive physical guidance in the performance of a new skill. In brief, the more modalities that can be involved in compensating for a deficit as total in its effect as blindness the better.

Auditory defects, especially in the physical education situation, are more influential upon learning, and therefore upon teaching method, than they are upon actual performance. A child who cannot hear can only respond to verbal or gestural instruction if it is given face to face and from not too great a distance. In addition, such a child is quite unable to orientate himself towards a sound source – a reflex response in those who can hear – and is therefore without a very useful feedback medium.

As far as performance is concerned, it should also be noted that a child who has sustained an injury to the semicircular canal or who has had a fenestration operation may experience difficulty in balancing. Swimming too may be dangerous but the decision to prohibit swimming should be taken by a medical consultant.

Minimal impairment of somatic or body sensation is, perhaps surprisingly, less common. Only in hemiplegics does there appear to be a significant incidence (about one third) and, even in these, such sensory loss is usually confined to the affected hand. Where such a defect does occur, it usually manifests itself through a loss of light touch sensibility, position sense and tactile discrimination.

The teacher's main concern in respect of body sensation, however, is likely to be the total anaesthesia of the paraplegic. Without any feeling whatsoever, the paraplegic's legs are not only a source of risk and embarassment, but also responsible for an incomplete body concept (Chapter 3).

Before moving on from here, it is necessary to consider the relationship between sensation and perception. Blencowe (1969) distinguishes between the two as follows:

sensation – the mere recognition of the arrival of a sensory impulse
perception – the integration of sensations into something meaningful.

From this it is to be assumed that one's perception of a given situation is only as accurate as one's sensory input system is reliable. It is most unlikely, therefore, that a sensory defect can exist without there being a consequential distorting effect upon the process of perception.

But it is not only sensory defects that are capable of undermining the efficiency of our perceptual processes. Perceptual skills, such as the ability to discriminate between information and noise or figure and ground, can also be underdeveloped as a result of an experiential deprivation.

Yet in neither case is the true cause of the error a perceptual disorder; it is rather the consequence of deficiencies in other areas (e.g., sensation or cognition) causing an intact perceptual mechanism either to operate wrongly through the receipt of inadequate or inappropriate information, or simply to function 'below par'.

Perceptual disorders

True perceptual defects are those resulting from damage to the occipitoparietal regions of the cerebrum, that area of the brain which is largely responsible for interpreting sensory input and giving it meaning.

Classically, there are three major symptoms of such brain damage: aphasia, agnosia and apraxia. Although traditionally they are supposed to be quite independent of one another, recent research (Gubbay et al. 1965 and Walton et al. 1962) indicates that their mode of operation is one of collusion. For the

'They're off!'
One doesn't have to be a superstar to experience the excitement of the big race.

sake of clarity of definition, however, there follows a brief description of each in turn, out of Blencowe (1969):

> Picturing the nervous system as an input-output system these disorders can be receptive or executive. Where speech is concerned, for example, a man can have a receptive aphasia (or dysphasia if it is not complete) in which he cannot recognise the meaning of the sentence he hears, or an expressive one in which he understands what is said, can formulate his ideas, but cannot utter grammatical sentences although his speech organs are not paralysed. [Similarly, there are] the agnosias, in which the patient can receive correctly the information, but cannot understand it, and the apraxias, in which he knows that he wishes to say or do but cannot formulate the necessary movements, even though he is not paralysed . . . Where sensation is unimpaired and 'mental images' are intact, inability to recognise an object perceived by one of the senses is known as agnosia. Apraxia, on the other hand, can in some ways be described as an agnosia for the performance of movements, but is properly described as an inability to perform certain subjectively purposive movements despite conservation of mobility, sensation and co-ordination.

In terms of the model in use here, it is only the receptive disorders that can be described as perceptual; the executive disorders are by definition executive. Nonetheless, it is clear from what Blencowe says that there is a great deal that can go wrong with man's perceptual mechanisms.

It has been said of these mechanisms that they are the means whereby 'incoming stimuli are transformed and organised into meaningful wholes' (Miller 1966). If they are faulty, it is possible for inappropriate meanings to be attached to sensory input, and thus for the selection of motor responses to be similarly haphazard.

Cognitive disorders

Although it may be quite false to assume that a physical handicap necessarily incorporates a mental deficiency, where brain damage exists of a general kind, as opposed to a lesion with a very specific location, it is likely that some mental/cognitive involvement will be apparent. In cerebral palsied children it has been estimated that over seventy-five per cent have an intelligence quotient below seventy-five, and in about seventy per cent of spina bifida cases, where there is associated hydrocephalus, unless the prophylactic measures outlined in Chapter 3 are taken very early, there is likely to be similarly extensive brain damage. One might expect, too, that those children exhibiting a maximal degree of motor deficiency would be those with the greater degree of mental sub-normality. This is, indeed, generally the case, but not always; in cases of athetosis, for example, the cerebral lesion, however severe, is local to the basal ganglia and consequently mental operations are usually unimpaired.

It is also important to note that, given normal cerebral 'equipment', an intelligence quotient may be depressed as a result of environmental factors, such as lengthy periods of hospitalisation in early childhood. Although this is technically not a mental deficiency but a mental retardation, it nonetheless has similar effects upon a child's cognitive and physical abilities.

Probably the most significant single feature of mental deficiency or retardation is that a child cannot think logically in a manner appropriate to his age. This has implications not only for the learning of technical skills but also for the development of tactical expertise. In simple terms, a child may have all the necessary motor responses available to him, but be unable to decide which is appropriate. More general consequences of a depressed intelligence quotient may include the inability to conceptualise the form of particular games and difficulty in remembering rules and objectives or even the significance of team colours. In a ball-game a child is more likely to pass to a person he recognises (e.g., a friend) than to pass to someone who is a teammate by sole virtue of the colour of his shirt. In gymnastics especially, and even in some more general movement education, teaching needs to be direct; such children may not be able to cope with too much freedom of choice.

An additional handicap is the child's short attention span; the inability to concentrate for even relatively short periods of time. This is sometimes a purely passive state, but it is often associated with distractibility, a defect associated with the cortical mechanisms that normally suppress stimuli considered to be unimportant to the situation in hand. In addition, forced respon-

siveness, the inability to select objects from the environment according to their meaning or importance to that situation at hand, can similarly cause a child to attend to the wrong stimuli in the display. In such cases, the individual uncontrollably reacts to any and/or every stimulus. Judgement and the estimation of probabilities is defective and so the consequence of actions cannot be forecast, and each new situation is met with fear, or, in some cases, with a dangerous indifference.

Each of these conditions may contribute to what Ebersole et al. (1968) describe as a sort of 'psychological rigidity'. This manifests itself as a resistance to a learning situation and is often wrongly identified as stubbornness. Such rigidity of behaviour is perhaps better understood if one represents a child's total field of activity in terms of three concentric circles (Fig. 12).

The outermost area (A) represents the activities in which a child feels competent to perform. The innermost area (C) represents the activities which a child feels, rightly or wrongly, that he cannot perform. The middle area (B) represents the area of rigidity. Even though the child is physically capable of

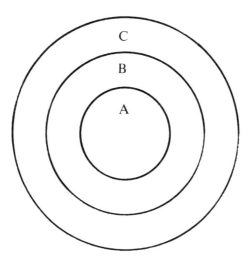

Figure 12 Diagrammatic representation of a child's relationship to activities of varying difficulty

success in these activities, he is reluctant to attempt them, either because he feels they are too difficult or because he has failed in these or similar activities before. As learning cannot take place without venturing beyond area (A), such a child needs a very gradual introduction to the activities within area (B), with the teacher ensuring that he regularly experiences success. Exposure to the activities in area (C) needs to be avoided until the child exhibits confidence in tackling the activities in area (B).

Executive disorders

In the past these have been somewhat overemphasised. Being executive or motoric, they manifest themselves in overt forms of behaviour, which are more readily observable than the previously mentioned receptive and cognitive disorders. But it should not be inferred from this that they are necessarily of greater importance. Indeed many so-called executive disorders are the result of less obvious perceptual or cognitive deficiencies.

Foremost amongst the executive disorders are the gross physically handicapping conditions with which this text is mainly concerned, spasticity, athetosis, paraplegia, etc., those disorders of paralysis, paresis, atrophy and inco-ordination which have already been examined in some detail. Also there are the executive aphasias, agnosias and apraxias, which likewise have already been mentioned. But in addition to these, there exist certain other characteristics of minimal neurological dysfunction that exert a general influence upon performance.

One such characteristic is 'disinhibition', the inability to refrain from producing an immediate, impulsive and often inadequate response. Strauss and Kephart (1955) suggest, as a causative factor, that

> instead of a choice among many responses [the child] has available only one response.

As a result, his behaviour is often inflexible and predictable; the same mistakes being made over and over again. This sort of inadequacy is only likely to be remedied if a child's movement 'vocabulary' can be increased; a thing perhaps best achieved through encouragement to discover different ways of doing things. As an illustration, a child who has only ever caught large balls will probably try to catch even tennis balls with the same broad placement of the hands and arms. If he is encouraged to play with balls of different sizes and weights he will come to appreciate that there are different responses appropriate to each.

Another such characteristic is 'perseveration', the apparent inability or unwillingness to transfer attention from one activity to another. In the motor impaired child this can manifest itself in very specific ways, namely: (i) a tendency to cling to the stimulus to which attention is first paid for an abnormally long period of time; (ii) a tendency to repeat the response made to that first stimulus even though it is no longer appropriate; and (iii) a tendency to return to the original stimulus/response on other later occasions. This reversion to a previously made response is particularly likely to occur if that response had been successful. Anecdotal evidence of this has been found in situations involving both mental and physical operations: a hydrocephalic girl in a mathematics class, having hazarded a guess at an answer to a question, was so delighted to discover that her answer had been correct, that the same

For some, just rolling a ball in a straight line demands great effort and concentration, and such achievements should be applauded as readily and as publicly as those of more talented children.

figure was offered as the answer to every other question. Similarly, a young epileptic boy (with some motor impairment) who was praised for making a high clearance kick in a game of football (when such a kick was an appropriate course of action) subsequently kicked the ball high and hard every time he received it. But as Oswin (1967) points out, perseveration is not restricted to learning or purposeful activities:

> When out of school, the child may become immersed in a purposeless activity e.g., rolling a small ball up and down a table for endless minutes, or scribbling on paper, or drawing everlasting boats or houses . . . [but] perseveration may be distinguished from just aimless fidgeting with objects by the somewhat intense appearance of the child's face as he does it. He may have the expression of someone fulfilling quite an important activity, no doubt, for him his actions are really of vital importance at that moment.

This last sentence is most important, crystallising the message behind the whole of this chapter so far. Many of the things motor impaired children do are apparently randomly executed and of no contextual significance. If the teacher can, in his mind, weigh against this apparent oblivion the effect of these associated disorders, whether sensory, perceptual, cognitive or executive, he might discover that behind the abortive responses of the motor impaired child there lies a very real though confused attempt to be successful.

Maladjustment

The term 'maladjustment' covers a whole host of behavioural disorders which, though commonly regarded as being produced by environmental constraints upon the normal, balanced development of personality, may also result from brain damage. Oswin considers that these disorders can be divided into two broad categories, 'outward behaviour problems' and 'inward behaviour problems' (Table 16). Although the table lists these problems separately, this is only done for ease of description. In reality, a child rarely displays his behavioural traits in isolation. More often than not he shows evidence of suffering from several types of behavioural disorder and each problem is likely to interrelate and interact with the others.

Table 16. Types of behaviour problems *(Oswin, 1967)*

The types of behaviour problem

Outward		Inward	
Destructiveness	Excitability	Emotional instability	Social immaturity
Distractibility	Spitefulness	Perseveration	Extreme goodness
Catastrophic reactions	Swearing	Unco-operativeness	Fear
Spitting	Unco-operativeness	Withdrawn-ness	Depression
Crying	Giggling	Laziness	Learning disorders
Hyperactivity	Disinhibition	(Inconsistency)	Distractibility

The reasons for this abnormal behaviour have been outlined elsewhere and include repeated failure, an inability to compete equally with peers, and the frustrations which accompany limited or uncontrolled movement. But whatever the cause, the effect can be considerable. In the words of Stott (1966), such a child

> may compensate by alternative forms of assertion or achievement which are socially disapproved . . . There is evidence of a neurological factor in certain forms of maladjustment and even in some kinds of delinquency.

Examples of maladjustment within the special school are innumerable, even though the majority of children compensate extremely well. An elaboration of just two of these examples will hopefully serve to demonstrate the diversity of these disorders.

Muscular dystrophy sufferers, by the time they are confined to electrically powered wheelchairs, are extremely weak in all four limbs. Virtually the only active movements left to them are those involving the head and neck. All children, at some time or another, feel they have been unjustly treated and feel a need to express these feelings. The normal child might choose to do this through taking a quiet walk, participating in a game of football, arguing verbally or even using physical violence. Whichever course is taken, it is un-

likely that the state of tension will persist. In the case of the muscular dystrophied child the alternatives are fewer. Either no action is taken, in which case the tension wells up inside, or a verbal attack is launched (a form of offence in which most such children become highly skilled), or the electric wheelchair is used as a tank or battering ram! One such child was once over-heard swearing vehemently over the school telephone by the teacher on duty who, feeling it necessary to apologise to the 'recipient' on behalf of the school, interrupted the monologue. The guilty party immediately explained that there was no-one on the other end other than an imagined adversary. He had had a bad day and felt a need to 'take it out on someone'.

Moderate haemophiliacs, on the other hand, are potentially very active children. They are normally strong and usually well coordinated. Un-fortunately it is not permissible for them to participate in many physical ac-tivities (for reasons which have already been explained). Some such children accept their lot, albeit reluctantly, and seek alternative forms of recreation. Others refuse to do this, take advantage of every opportunity in unsupervised play to do those things they know they should not, and consequently are frequent attenders at local hospitals. Yet others, fortunately a minority, turn their handicap to advantage through the use of aggressive, even violent forms of behaviour upon peers who are unable to retaliate because of their attacker's haemophilia!

In view of such problems, the teacher needs to structure his relationships with the children in such a way that they are all treated as individuals. They have most of the likes, dislikes, fears and ambitions of normal children, but the physical, psychological and emotional problems with which they have to contend make learning and growing up a very arduous task. What might be an ordinary achievement for one child, might also be a very significant milestone in the life of another. Similarly, a misdemeanour of any particular sort might be inexcusable for one child, yet almost to be expected from another. Punish-ment and reward need to reflect far more than the nature of the achievement; and this is particularly true in physical education.

Summary

In this chapter an attempt has been made to outline some of the less obvious disorders associated with learning difficulties, performance inconsistencies and behavioural problems.

For the clumsy or minimally impaired child, in whom these disorders might constitute the whole problem, techniques have been devised to help the teacher to identify these areas of deficiency and to correct them with 'tailor-made' training programmes. Noteworthy researchers in this field have been Kephart (1960), Cruickshank (1961) and Cratty (1969).

But for the severely physically handicapped child, in whom these disorders merely exacerbate a more gross movement difficulty, the teacher does not have

Weight training: particularly for children confined to wheelchairs the developing of strong arms and shoulders is imperative.

Weight training: with younger children sandbags are both lighter and safer than the more conventional metal weights

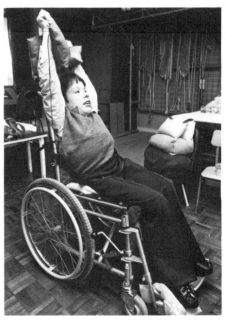

such detailed programmes to follow. The choice of activities to be included in his programme is necessarily determined by the nature, extent and degree of the physical disabilities of his children. It is in determining the teaching methods and techniques he is to employ that these associated disorders might profitably be taken into account. Consequently, even though the programmes which exist for minimally handicapped children may not always be appropriate, the principles which underlie them most certainly are.

Drawing upon the recommendations of several researchers in this field, the following points would appear to be worthy of consideration in the development of any programme of compensatory education:

(i) The programme should be well structured with all aspects of the curriculum reinforcing one another. Generally speaking, large muscle control is gained first, followed by a gradual acquisition of fine muscle control. The sort of activities incorporated into the programme at any one time should reflect this fact.

(ii) Lesson plans should follow a regular routine, so that the children feel secure, and should incorporate only a gradual increase in complexity. The length of any one lesson should be neither so long as to exhaust the children prematurely (either physically or mentally) nor so short as to be ineffectual upon their learning processes.

(iii) Lesson content should reflect an attempt to account for the children's total development, an awareness of the varied receptivity of the children to activities of differing degrees of difficulty and/or novelty, and an endeavour to compensate for the weaknesses of the children by developing their strengths.

(iv) Teaching method should be flexible, adapted to the needs of individuals within the group, and based upon evaluations of how their brain damage (or other disability) has affected their ability to learn. For most children a reduction in extraneous environmental stimuli coupled with an increased stimulus value in teaching materials, visual aids, etc., is generally most helpful.

(v) Particularly for children who lack confidence and are reluctant to tackle anything new the number of stages in a given project should be increased to provide more opportunities for them to experience success. Children should be encouraged to face up to stress by the gradual introduction of problem solving situations to their lessons. When a child experiences success in novel or (ostensibly) difficult situations, confidence increases rapidly, bringing with it a desire to learn more and a willingness to engage in a wider variety of activities.

(vi) It is not without just cause that the phrase 'the fun principle' has been coined. One of the physical educationist's most valuable assets is the fact that moving can be fun and fun breeds involvement. If children can be helped to enjoy movement, then the battle is half won.

The remaining chapters relate these associated disorders and the major physical handicaps upon which they act to those activities which, by convention, are considered to be a part of the physical education programme.

REFERENCES

Arnheim, D. D. & Sinclair, W. A. (1975) *The clumsy child: a programme of motor therapy.* C. V. Mosby: St. Louis.

Blencowe, S. M. (1969) *Cerebral palsy and the young child.* Churchill Livingstone: Edinburgh & London.

Cratty, B. J. (1969) *Motor activity and the education of retardates.* Lea & Febiger: Philadelphia.

Cruickshank, W. M., Bentzen, F. A., Ratleburg, F. H. & Tannhauser, M. T. (1961) *A teaching method for brain injured and hyperactive children.* Syracuse University Press.

Ebersole, M., Kephart, N. C. & Ebersole, J. B. (1968) *Steps to achievement for the slow learner.* Merrill: Ohio.

Gubbay, S. S., Ellis, E., Walton, J. N. & Court, S. D. M. ((1965) A study of apraxic and agnosic defects in children. *Brain*, 88, 295–312.

Kephart, N. C. (1960) *The slow learner in the classroom.* Merrill: Ohio.

Miller, G. A. (1966) *Psychology, the science of mental life.* Penguin: Harmondsworth.

Morris, P. R. & Whiting, H. T. A. (1971) *Motor impairment and compensatory education.* Bell: London.

Oswin, M. (1967) *Behaviour problems amongst children with cerebral palsy.* John Wright: Bristol.

Shivers, J. S. & Fait, H. F. (1975) *Therapeutic and adapted recreational services.* Lea & Febiger: Philadelphia.

Singleton, W. T. (1967) Ergonomics in systems design. *Ergonomics*, 10, 5, 541–548.

Stott, D. H. (1966) *Studies of troublesome children.* Tavistock: London.

Strauss, A. A. & Kephart, N. C. (1955) *Psychopathology and education of the brain-injured child.* Grune & Statton: New York.

Walton, J. J., Ellis, E. & Court, S. D. M. (1962) Clumsy children: developmental apraxia and agnosia. *Brain* 85, 603–612.

Welford, A. T. (1960) The measurement of sensory-motor performance: survey and re-appraisal of twelve years' progress. *Ergonomics* 3, 3, 189–230.

Whiting, H. T. A. (1969) *Acquiring ball skill: A Psychological Interpretation.* Bell: London

5

The physical education programme in the special school

The main intention of this book is to outline those areas which a teacher in a special school might profitably consider in the introduction of a programme of physical education to physically handicapped children. In Chapter 2 the situation in special schools in England and Wales was investigated; in Chapter 3 each of the major handicapping conditions was analysed in turn in order to assess movement potential; and in Chapter 4 certain associated behavioural disorders were outlined, and their possible effect upon the teaching/learning situation was noted. It now seems appropriate to reflect upon all these aspects collectively and within this frame of reference to consider the actual content of such a physical education programme.

The activities commonly associated with programmes of physical education are virtually innumerable. Within certain broad limits the selection of one activity in preference to any other is relatively arbitrary, and need only reflect the interests and coaching expertise of the staff and the facilities available for use by the school. The important considerations relate not so much to the activities themselves as to what is hoped to be achieved through those activities. In other words the choice of activity depends on what the teacher wants to achieve, and it is appropriate only in so far as the teacher can achieve both his general, long-term aims and his specific, more immediate objectives through that activity. The most important of these aims and objectives would appear to be the following:

(i) To encourage movement, and thus to promote fitness and health, and possibly to ameliorate a physical disability;

(ii) Through recreation and play to render such movement enjoyable and interesting and thus to motivate the children towards further activity;

(iii) Through such fitness, health and recreational/social experiences to foster self-confidence, camaraderie and independence;

(iv) To develop strengths in each child according to his individual needs, so that he might better compensate for the inadequacies of his disability;

(v) To develop skills in the children which, hopefully, will benefit them not only in a recreational context, but also functionally through increased competence in daily living skills;

(vi) To ensure that, through such a programme, nothing is done that might cause deterioration in a child's condition.

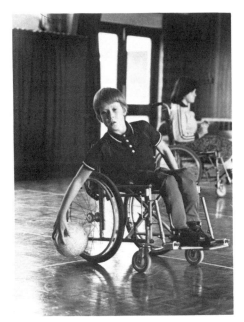

An essential skill for the chairbound ball-player is the ability to pick up a ball without stopping, usually achieved by rolling the ball round the rim of the wheel as the chair passes by.

With practise, gathering up the ball in this way can be done at great speed and the skill can be incorporated into a variety of game situations.

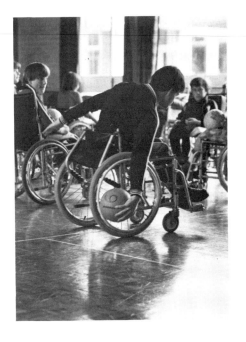

The Physical Education Programme in the Special School

Traditionally, school physical education comprises three elements, namely, (i) 'P.E.', which includes gymnastics, movement training, skill acquisition, etc. (As was pointed out earlier, it is accepted that the term 'P.E.' is something of a misnomer. Its use is defended, however, on the grounds that it is a term in common usage in schools throughout the country and is conceptually distinct from the rest of the physical education programme.) (ii) Games, both team and individual games; and (iii) swimming, which commonly includes all aspects of watermanship, such as canoeing and water polo. One might also add (iv) outdoor pursuits, including hill walking, orienteering, riding, skiing and campcraft.

Each of these types of activity can provide the physical, psychological and socio-emotional benefits outlined in Chapter 1 and, despite the physical handicaps of the children, they can all be incorporated quite successfully into the physical education programme of the special school. Additionally, there are activities of a more elementary kind, such as training in static balance, walking, control of a wheelchair and dressing, which also require special emphasis. Thus, unlike the conventional physical education programme which tends to be almost exclusively recreation orientated, a large part of the special school programme is functionally biased. However, as the majority of children stay in the same school for ten to twelve years, their needs change and, as a result, the physical education programme tends to shift its emphasis accordingly.

During the nursery and infant years (3–7) the needs of the children derive from two main factors, (i) at this early age they are still learning to cope with and to synthesise the various locomotor and co-ordination problems of their handicap; and (ii) partly because of the restrictions imposed by their handicap and partly because of lengthy periods of hospitalisation (and sometimes overprotective attitudes of parents as well), they have missed an incalculable amount of sensori-motor experience which the able-bodied child acquires through play and exploration of his environment. The physical education programme must take full account of each child's own special problems.

Although primary re-education of neuromuscular function is in the hands of the physiotherapist, well-structured play situations can reinforce her efforts and provide stimulating and challenging opportunities for all manner of sensori-motor learning: balance, sliding, climbing, rolling, crawling, swinging, throwing, paddling, splashing, etc.

By the junior and middle school years (7–12) the children have probably come to terms with their major locomotion and co-ordination problems. They are aware of their strengths and weaknesses and are learning to compensate accordingly. But at this age they are still largely egocentric and find it difficult to relate meaningfully to others in a team. It is therefore probably best at this stage to concentrate upon individual activities and so to consolidate the multifarious activities to which the children were introduced in their nursery years.

The physical education programme at this stage, therefore, serves to widen

and refine the movement vocabularies of the children, and to prepare them, through interaction with others in relays, minor games, etc., for the social games to be played in adolescence and adulthood.

During the remainder of the school years (12–16) the children not only mature physically but socially and intellectually as well. The teacher can introduce them (with some success now) to major team games and more sophisticated individual pursuits such as fencing and archery. He can also begin to rationalise with the children by introducing them to the theoretical aspects of his subject and relating the benefits of physical exercise to the needs of their handicaps. He can explain to them that both now, while they are at school, and in adulthood, when school staff no longer look after them, physical recreation is valuable both in maintaining physical fitness, and in providing a social outlet – something which for the young disabled adult is often very difficult to find.

Through the physical education programme in the senior school, therefore, the children can be introduced to various ways of maintaining physical fitness, perhaps even of obviating the need for certain physiotherapeutic regimes. They can also be introduced to recreational activities through which they may find enjoyment, personal satisfaction and physical well-being. The teacher should be able to provide the names of clubs and other groups in his area where the disabled can find opportunities to pursue their recreation after leaving school.

At all stages and in all activities the programme should concentrate on abilities and strengths in an attempt to compensate for deficiencies and weaknesses. Even in group activities, the needs of the individual are to be considered first and foremost. Teaching cues can be highlighted to facilitate attention and learning processes, and irrelevancies and distractions must be minimised. The programme should be structured so that the teacher's immediate objectives are clear to the child and, equally important, are seen to be achievable.

General guidelines are offered now on each of these three areas, although a fuller evaluation, with particular reference to lesson content and teaching method, is given in later chapters.

Physical education

Body awareness, movement experience and gymnastics are fundamental to any programme of physical education. For the able-bodied child, they increase his awareness of his bodily potential, improve co-ordination and balance, strength and mobility, and train him in agilities and motor skills. But the teacher has an advantage: in the main, these children are developing such qualities anyway as a natural part of growing up, and the foundations of his skills have been consolidating since birth. The physically handicapped child on the other hand is not so fortunate for he does not possess this sound basis upon which to

For chairbound and ambulant alike, throwing and catching should be mastered standing still before they are attempted on the move.

develop new skills, nor has he got an adequate physique with which to work.

The P.E. lesson provides an opportunity whereby, through conventional (if slightly modified) educational gymnastics, each child can be helped to come to terms with his bodily limitations, and to explore his potential.

It begins at the nursery and infant stage, not as a formal lesson but as guided play. The children are provided with opportunities to move in different directions, on different surfaces, in different ways, with different body parts; and are given opportunities to handle objects such as balls, bean bags, ropes, hoops and trolleys. They are encouraged to be active and adventurous. At all times however this should be in a controlled environment where they are directed towards activities appropriate to their condition, and helped to recognise those that are not.

In the junior to middle school years the P.E. lesson proper is introduced. Warm-up sessions, movement sequences, apparatus work, etc., all familiar elements of the normal P.E. lesson, can be employed. Some children may wear calipers, some may need sticks or rollator, but with suitable help from the teacher all can be fully involved.

Educational and formal gymnastics, and direct teaching and learning by discovery are all useful. No two children's needs are the same, and in any group some will respond to one approach, some to another, and the versatile teacher will choose whichever is appropriate for any particular child at any given time. For example, when shown a piece of climbing apparatus, a child with no brain damage might be asked how many different ways can be found to move from A to B, whereas an ataxic child or one with perceptual

difficulties might first need to have his attention drawn specifically to such features as a good handhold or a shaky footing, or even to be physically helped through a movement sequence. Similarly, should a teacher wish to introduce a completely new skill to a group of children a few minutes' direct teaching with a few selected pupils might be desirable.

Underlying the whole of this aspect of the physical education programme is the fact that apart from its recreative role, it is of real functional significance in that it can contribute extensively to the mastery of daily living skills. Personal independence is a most important aim and sufficient time needs to be allocated at the beginning and the end of the lesson for those children who are able to dress and undress themselves. Similarly, within the lesson, provision might usefully be made for walking practices, training in the transfer of body weight (e.g. from a chair to the floor, from floor to standing, or from a chair to the bath), and for learning essential wheelchair skills such as manoeuvring, kerb-jumping and capsize drills. An element of competition, both inter- and intra-personal, can be introduced as a further stimulus if necessary.

Games

Games are generally considered to be pure recreation, but in the lower school and for children with learning difficulties, games playing is of more widespread value. As Coleman (1971) wrote

> Learning through games has a number of intrinsic values. One of these is the attention-focusing quality. Games tend to focus attention more effectively than most other teaching devices, partly because they involve the student actively rather than passively.

In the lower school, games are used to reinforce 'P.E.' and physiotherapy, to assist conceptual development and to provide an element of fun. They might include playground activities such as hopscotch, tig, games of pretence, mime, dance and simple ball games. In the middle school, improvement in motor skills allows more sophisticated games to be played. Competition is introduced, rules become important, and the notion of co-operation through team play is developed.

For older children, whose range of motor skills is more or less complete (though still in need of refinement), games are almost exclusively recreational. For reasons already given, the pursuit of recreational activities both in school and in adulthood is highly desirable, and the teacher can play an important part in promoting an interest in them. The range of activities available is very wide, but particular consideration needs to be given to the following:

(i) resources—the facilities, equipment and coaching expertise available;

(ii) motivation—the interests of the children as adolescents under instruction;

(iii) personal suitability—the extent to which the activities can suit the

Basketball can also help to improve balance, hand-eye coordination and control of a wheelchair.

performance capabilities of the children concerned;

(iv) community relevance—the opportunities the children have to continue such activities once they have left school.

One very popular game among both able-bodied and disabled is basketball, and it seems to be quite possible for most schools to introduce the game without any major upheavals of staff, facilities or pupil groupings. Most schools have a gymnasium or suitable hall and, if they cannot provide backboards and rings (now available as collapsible, stow-away items), there are various alternative forms of goal which, in the early stages at least, are quite adequate (see (iii) below). The information collected also suggests that the size of groups (and the proportion of such to members of staff), which is common in schools at the present time, is similarly appropriate to the introduction of the game (see Chapter 2).

The following list of significant factors in the popularity and suitability of basketball might also be a useful guide in the selection of other activities:

(i) It can be played by ambulant and wheelchair users alike. The ambulant version is very fast and therefore not suitable for people who use sticks or

crutches, but these are usually quite willing (and able) to compete in wheelchairs.

(ii) The height of the basket is variable, as is the size and weight of the ball, the size of the court, and the number in a team. Consequently, the game can be introduced at an early age, and conditions adjusted as the children grow.

(iii) Apart from mini-basketball many variations or progressive practices can be used in schools (e.g., captain ball, bench ball) in which children with muscular dystrophies, who cannot manage the full game, can participate quite well.

(iv) The rules of basketball can be adapted or modified not only to make the game accessible to all children, but also to emphasise particular aspects of play such as passing or dribbling; and this can be done without grossly altering the character of the game. (The staff who introduce the game need not necessarily be experts themselves.)

(v) Being a fast-moving game, whether in a wheelchair or on foot, it is beneficial to cardiorespiratory and neuromuscular fitness.

(vi) Almost every gymnasium or sports hall in the country is equipped for basketball, and, in a modified form, it can even be played in a general purpose hall, on grass or in the playground.

(vii) Opportunities exist throughout the country for participation by able-bodied and disabled, novice and expert, young and old alike.

(viii) Competition is available locally, nationally and internationally, again for able-bodied and disabled alike.

(ix) For the less active it is a good spectator sport and also provides an unusually large number of opportunities for individuals wishing to take on officiating duties.

(x) Being commonly played in a sports complex offering other activities and refreshments, it is also useful as a social outlet.

But, despite these numerous favourable qualifications, basketball has its inadequacies because there is an unavoidable emphasis on catching, throwing and locomotion and, what is more, on doing these things accurately and quickly, means that there are certain children for whom it is unsuitable.

The ataxic or otherwise poorly co-ordinated child, though ambulant, is very unsteady and usually has certain perceptual difficulties. Even if such a child manages to catch a ball – an achievement in itself – he needs time (preferably without harassment) to organise his perceptual field sufficiently to decide what to do with it. The only practical and wholly satisfactory solution is to allow such children to play the game amongst themselves, so that all of the players have similar problems. Unfortunately, there are rarely enough of these children in any one school to make this possible. Where it is possible, assistance in perceptual organisation (e.g., by using a brightly coloured ball, easily distinguishable team colours, etc.) and giving the player with the ball time to think (e.g., by introducing a one-yard encroachment prohibition law) are likely to be beneficial.

The spastic quadriplegic is so poorly co-ordinated, and the child with advanced muscular dystrophy so weak, that almost any fast ball game is impossible. For these participation in basketball is extremely limited. (If the goal or basket is lowered almost to ground level thus eliminating high level play, given electric wheelchairs, they learn to become fine guards, intercepting passes and setting excellent screens with their chairs, but by this time the game bears little resemblance to basketball!) However even for these, basketball makes more provision than most as children who cannot play can perhaps officiate. The game is controlled by two referees, a timekeeper and a scorer (who usually needs an assistant); and each team usually has a non-playing coach. These, and spectator-participation, are very real alternatives, especially for those of average or above average intelligence.

Swimming

The fact that almost every special school in the country possesses (and uses) a pool of some sort is indicative both of the acknowledged values of hydrotherapy and of a growing recognition of the benefits, both physical and psychological, of swimming generally. As a team of Her Majesty's Inspectors discovered recently whilst researching into this provision

> (Swimming) is one of the longest established and most valuable activities for the physically handicapped with its origins in the early use of hydrotherapy in the treatment of paralysis . . . The value of swimming for educational, recreational and survival purposes is as relevant for physically handicapped as for normal children . . . There was no doubt that the sense of achievement, as well as the enjoyment in learning to swim gave added self-confidence to the boys and girls; this was believed by the staffs of the schools to be an additional factor in encouraging pupils to tackle problems as they arose elsewhere (D.E.S. 1971).

Probably the most important single recommendation for including swimming in a school physical education programme is that it is the only activity in which it is possible for all the children, irrespective of handicap, to move quite freely without calipers, sticks or wheelchairs. On land gravity takes its full effect but in water the children derive considerable assistance from buoyancy. Indeed, according to Froude's Law of Impedence (1898), water is seven hundred and ninety times as supportive as air (McMillan, 1973). In consequence, even those with advanced muscular dystrophy and severe spastic quadriplegia experience an independence of movement they could not possibly have in any other way.

With water at 30–31°C (86–88°F) (although 35°C – 94°F – is recommended for hydrotherapy proper), swimming is not only enjoyable and invigorating, but also within the capabilities of most children, irrespective of handicap. The water temperatures are somewhat higher than is normal because of the

Even though hydrotherapy pools are often irregularly shaped, short in length, shallow and uncomfortably warm, they do make excellent teaching pools.

stimulating effect this has upon blood circulation. In the words of the Department of Education and Science Report (1971):

> In water sufficiently warm to bring about muscle relaxation . . . it was interesting, even dramatic to see the transformation from the jerky and spasmodic movements of a child by the side of the pool to his smooth and relaxed movement in the water.

Temperatures too warm for vigorous activity (or even pleasurable swimming) are tolerable for hydrotherapy because, for the most part, these exercises are of a static nature.

With the more severely disabled, it is usual to have at least one member of staff in the water and one on the poolside at all times. Although it would be ideal to maintain a one-to-one relationship (in the early stages of learning at least) this is not always possible. However epileptics always need very careful supervision when they are in the water, but asthmatics and haemophiliacs for example can be supervised much as they would be in an ordinary school. Obviously age, swimming ability and severity or type of handicap are all factors that might influence the size of the group, but suitable numbers of staff must be available for every group in the pool.

The content of the swimming programme depends upon the age, intelligence, and maturity of the children; the severity and types of handicap within each group; and, of course, competency at swimming. Whilst some children with very severe handicaps might not be able to progress as far as other more able children, the programme can be devised, according to age and

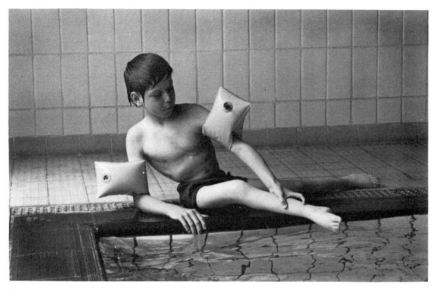

Even at the poolside, children whose legs are paralysed need to exercise caution lest they injure themselves.

ability, in the following way: the youngest children first of all, are encouraged to play, near or in the water. As most modern pools incorporate a ramp or shallow pool it is generally possible to introduce the children to deep water by degrees, without discomfort or fear. Once in the main pool they are allowed to explore and experiment, encouragement to do so being provided in the form of simple games. As their confidence increases they are encouraged to move about. After this swimming instruction can begin. Later, for those who are proficient swimmers activities such as water polo, canoeing, and survival and life-saving techniques can be introduced.

Structuring the programme

One of the advantages physical education has over its rival disciplines in the school curriculum is that it is so closely allied to recreation. All recreational activities, by definition, have certain values that make them interesting, absorbing and enjoyable to the performer. But, as it is never possible to include them all within one school programme, the curriculum planner has to be selective. However, there are dangers in being over-restrictive, a dichotomy which has been nicely highlighted by Munrow (1972):

> What we are urging is, on the one hand, the avoidance of an indiscriminate proliferation of activities but, on the other, a deliberate choice of programme which is as wide in its potential appeal to individuals as we can achieve. The task is more complicated than the mere working out of a

comprehensive skill classification, for individuals are not just input-decision-output machines, satisfied by the extent to which their neuro-muscular equipment fits the requirements of a particular activity. They will also respond because the activity in question suits their temperament.

A programme has to be devised which is (i) compact enough to be manage-able (even within the confines of the special school), (ii) suitable or adaptable to the needs of children with widely varying degrees of disability, (iii) likely to suit a variety of tastes and temperaments, and (iv) adequately comprehensive.

Of the first three criteria enough has been said already, and in any case these problems are not peculiar to physical education. But what are (or should be) the components of a programme of physical education? Just what is it, beneath the superficial preoccupation with playing games, that the physical education teacher is trying to achieve? There have been several attempts at this sort of analysis, all more or less valuable. The list that follows comes from Arnheim and Sinclair (1975) and is offered purely as an example:

Selection of motor tasks is based on the challenge they offer and on the particular category of movement development that the child needs. More specifically, twelve task categories are employed:
  (i) tension release,
  (ii) locomotion,
  (iii) balance,
  (iv) body and space perception,
  (v) rhythm and temporal awareness,
  (vi) rebound and airborne activities,
  (vii) projectile management,
  (viii) management of daily motor activities,
  (ix) selected play skills,
  (x) motor fitness,
  (xi) aggression management,
  (xii) water submersion.

Let us temporarily accept these twelve criteria are the only elements the physical education teacher has to incorporate into his programme. Obviously not all these characteristics are to be found in a single activity. But any given activity is likely to include several of them. The teacher's dilemma therefore is in the selection of that number and variety of activities which will be most satisfactory from all points of view. So how does he go about it?

One suggestion can be found through further reference to Munrow:

A workmanlike approach would be to construct a programme, varying as widely as was practicable according to one criterion (say 'balance' using the twelve category grouping outlined above) and then, during its practical working, to scrutinise its suitability for various temperaments, shapes and sizes and (subject to the practicalities of facilities and staff) to substitute or

supplement, where necessary. If one criterion determines the original spread of activities and if it is recognised that these may be modified by the other criteria . . . then our 'best-fit' programme should not prove defective in any fundamental respect.

In this way, it should be possible for the teacher to build up a series of matrices which would show at a glance the extent to which a given combination of activities is balanced or, if it is deficient, in which way(s) it is so. An example is given in Table 17 although it should be stressed that the details within the example have not been validated.

Table 17. Matrix showing the task categories involved in a given range of activities

	Tension release	Locomotion	Balance	Body & space perception	Rhythm & temporal awareness	Rebound & airborne activities	Projectile management	Management of daily motor skills	Selected play skills	Motor fitness	Aggression management	Water submersion
Archery		✓					✓		✓			
Basketball	✓	✓	✓				✓		✓	✓	✓	
Gymnastics		✓	✓	✓	✓	✓		✓		✓		
Riding			✓	✓	✓							
Swimming		✓	✓	✓	✓					✓		✓
Table Tennis	✓				✓	✓	✓		✓	✓	✓	
Trampolining			✓	✓		✓			✓	✓		
Water Polo	✓	✓	✓	✓				✓		✓	✓	✓
Weight Training				✓	✓			✓		✓		
Slalom	✓	✓	✓		✓			✓		✓		

Using Table 17 as a hypothetical case, it can be seen that through basketball, gymnastics and swimming, something is being done in all twelve areas. But there are of course many facets to each of these and there are always personal and environmental factors to consider. Nonetheless, used sensibly, this sort of

analysis might prove extremely useful both to the teacher setting up a programme of physical education for the first time and to the experienced teacher wanting to reassess the programme he is offering.

If a suitably balanced programme cannot be devised using conventional activities, there is always the possibility of adapting such activities to the particular needs of the children under instruction. For any given activity there are always a variety of ways in which this can be done, depending as ever upon the nature of the disability. These include

(i) Substitution of a different body position for that normally used;

(ii) Substitution of slower movements for faster movements such as walking for running;

(iii) Modification of the equipment, e.g. through orthopaedic handgrips, etc.;

(iv) Development of new techniques such as the hemiplegic's 'J' stroke in swimming;

(v) Utilisation of aids such as the hook attachment used by some quadriplegics in archery for drawing and releasing the bow string;

(vi) Reduction of size of playing area and/or magnification of goal size, etc.

The next four chapters look in more detail at the actual content of the physical education programme, i.e. 'P.E.', games, swimming and outdoor pursuits, with particular attention being paid to teaching method.

REFERENCES

Arnheim, D. D. & Sinclair, W. A. (1975) *The clumsy child: a programme of motor therapy.* C. V. Mosby: St. Louis.

Coleman, J. S. (1971) Learning through games. In: Avedon, E. M. & Sutton-Smith, B. *The study of games.* John Wiley: New York.

Department of Education and Science (1971) *Physical education for the physically handicapped.* H.M.S.O.: London.

Geddes, D. (1974) *Physical activities for individuals with handicapping conditions.* C. V. Mosby: St. Louis.

Houghton, W. (1967) *Educational Gymnastics.* Inner London Education Authority.

McMillan, A. (1973) *The Halliwick Method.* Unpublished paper presented to an International Sport and Leisure Conference at Linkoping, Sweden.

Munrow, A. D. (1972) *Physical education: a discussion of principles.* Bell: London.

Shivers, J. S. & Fait, H. F. (1975) *Therapeutic and adapted recreational services.* Lea & Febiger: Philadelphia.

6

The locomotor/body management component of physical education

A distinction was made earlier between that which is commonly referred to as P.E. and those more structured activities we call games. Traditionally, both have a major part to play in the physical education of children, even though in many instances they overlap or are virtually synonymous. But whatever one calls the P.E. part of the programme (and that is certainly easier on the tongue than 'the locomotor/body management component') the distinction is a real one. On the one hand there is the part of the programme that concentrates on body management for its own sake, and on the other, the area of activity through which such bodily skills are applied to the pursuit of various recreational activities or games. This chapter focuses attention on the former, which Cratty (1975) has described as 'improving basic physical abilities'.

However, the fact that a distinction is made between the training of abilities and the pursuit of major recreational activities should not be misconstrued. Even in basic activities the 'fun principle' still applies (Chapter 4) and innumerable minor games have been devised over the years to make these exercises more interesting and enjoyable. Some examples of minor games are given, but teachers and children should be encouraged to invent their own; it can be a source of great pride and a valuable motivating force for children to recognise a particular activity as their own.

In Chapter 5 reference was made to the classification by Arnheim and Sinclair (1975) of areas of physical education. As this appears to be as comprehensive as any, their categories form the basis of this chapter. However the section on water environment is dealt with in Chapter 8.

Because of the wide range of individual differences encountered within the special school population, the activities listed will not be related to any particular age group. For the most part it will be obvious that certain activities are unsuitable for those with particular handicaps but special comment is made where appropriate.

Locomotion

Movement is one of the principal activities with which the physical educationist is concerned, and he has an obligation to provide as wide a range of movement experiences as each child's particular condition will allow.

Physically handicapped children have probably spent an inordinately large part of their infancy suffering some sort of movement restriction: the physical education programme is the medium par excellence that can provide suitable compensatory experiences.

In the early stages of development certain locomotor skills can usefully be acquired by ambulant and nonambulant children alike. For the ambulant child their significance is developmental (in so far as they precede walking and running) and acquisitive (in so far as they contribute to an otherwise incomplete battery of movement skills), but for the nonambulant child their significance is more fundamental. A wheelchair is only valuable so long as a child's goal is accessible from it – and it is surprising how often this is not the case. Even in purpose-built premises, a child who is normally confined to a wheelchair has to move himself several times a day, if only from his bed to his wheelchair or from his wheelchair to the toilet or bath, and vice versa. If the child has a variety of movement patterns at his disposal these and other day-to-day tasks can be made that much easier.

ROLLING

This is done most commonly and most usefully about a longitudinal axis (side rolling), although some children also manage to roll about a lateral axis (forward and backwards rolls).

Activities Rolling to left and right along a mat with hands by the side, above the head, with one hand by the side and the other above the head; rolling in a straight line with the eyes closed; following a sound source; rolling like a ball.
N.B. Repeated rolling is not advisable for children with flaccid paralysis of the legs. One complete turn is all that is likely to be needed in any practical application of this skill, and even one turn is enough to demonstrate that special care and attention needs to be given to limbs over which one has no control.

CRAWLING

The exact nature of the crawling task selected for any particular child must obviously reflect the nature and extent of that child's handicap. Some children can crawl or shuffle along in many different ways, whilst others find extreme difficulty in just moving at all. However, provided every child manages to find at least one way of getting from A to B the teacher's task is relatively uncomplicated and the child is on the way to independence.

Activities Crawling on the hands and knees (forwards and backwards) using opposite arm and leg alternately; 'seal walking' (forwards only) with both arms being extended together dragging the rest of the body behind them; hand walking (forwards only) with the legs dragging behind; shuffling (forwards and backwards) by sitting upright, taking the body-weight on the arms and swinging the trunk through to sit forward or backward.

CLIMBING

Moving from one level to another, either transferring from the floor onto a chair or taking oneself up or down steps, is useful to ambulant and non-ambulant children alike and promotes confidence in the child's ability to handle his own body.

Activities These are as numerous and varied (or as limited) as the facilities in the school. At best use can be made of gymnasium equipment such as benches, boxes, wall bars, ladders; playground equipment such as climbing frames; and in adventure playgrounds, mounds, ladders, trees and steps.

SLIDING

Although there is little active body movement involved, sliding does provide a unique and exhilarating movement experience. If the slide is suitably positioned it can be used as a reward for efforts made in other ways: for example, if the slide is set into the side of a small hill or mound, children have to climb, crawl or otherwise carry themselves to the top in order to 'qualify' for a go on the slide.

N.B. If the slide is to be used by children with paralysed or otherwise fragile legs, suitable precautions need to be taken to ensure their safe landing.

For the ambulant child

WALKING

This is the simplest form of upright movement because at least one foot is always in contact with the ground. Most of these exercises can be accomplished using sticks or crutches if necessary.

Activities Walking forwards, backwards and sideways (to left and right); walking quickly, walking slowly; walking with high steps and with low steps, with heavy steps (i.e., flat-footed) and with soft steps (i.e., on the toes); unilateral walking (same arm and leg forward) and cross-pattern walking (opposite arm and leg); walking while pushing a trolley or rollator; walking upstairs, walking downstairs; walking on different surfaces (floorboards, mats, grass, concrete, etc.); walking uphill, walking downhill.

Games Most young children enjoy marching. Follow-my-leader in Indian file, with each child imitating the gait of the leader is also successful.

RUNNING

This differs from walking (and is consequently more difficult) because at no time are both feet in contact with the ground at the same time. Children who use sticks or crutches can learn to run (usually either 'two point' running with both crutches forward together and both legs swinging through together, or 'three point' running with both crutches forward together followed by one leg at a time) although this should not be encouraged if it is likely to interfere with

the efforts of the physiotherapist to establish a particular (conflicting) pattern of movement.

Activities Running forwards, backwards and on the spot; running straight and running a zigzag course; running with different height and length of stride; running up and down inclines; running upstairs (preferably *not* downstairs).

Games Running races (distance variable), games of tig.

JUMPING

Jumping, hopping and skipping are all extensions of the walking-running progression in that at some point in their performance neither leg is in contact with the ground (i.e., the body is momentarily airborne).

Activities Straightforward jumping, first of all free of obstacles and then, by gradual stages jumping over obstacles (lines on the floor, canes, rolled-up mats, etc.); jumping off one foot and landing on the same foot, the other foot or both feet; jumping off both feet and landing on both feet or on one foot; jumping forwards, backwards or sideways; jumping from one level to another (up or down); jumping for height and jumping for length; jumping in sequence (e.g., hopping, bunny jumps, etc.); combinations of jumps.
N.B. All jumping activities should be attempted standing still before being executed on the move. Appropriate safety precautions should be taken with all jumping activities involving height or changes of level.

Games Hurdles, Sargeant jump (standing high jump), standing long jump, hop-scotch, skipping, leap-frog. It is upon this foundation that more traditional forms of gymnastics, vaulting, somersaults, etc., can be built into the programme.

For the chairbound child

SELF PROPULSION

For the child who is able to propel a wheelchair unaided, mastery of the chair is an important factor in his independence. Unfortunately, even today very few buildings are designed to accommodate a wheelchair, just as very few paths or pavements are really as level and as smooth as they appear to those who can walk. As a result, there is far more to the teaching of chair control than might at first appear to be the case.

Activities Control of the wheelchair both forwards and backwards (some paraplegics even manage to make the chair move sideways by holding the wheel rims and rocking the chair bodily, but this demands strength and balance and is not recommended until an advanced stage of chair control and body management has been achieved); control of the wheelchair uphill, downhill and on a camber; control of the wheelchair over difficult terrain

a)   Spastic paraplegic

b)   Flaccid paraplegic

Figure 13 Mounting a wheelchair from the floor

(grass, shale, gravel, etc.); ability to manoeuvre the wheelchair up a kerb or step (by lifting the front castor wheels off the ground and onto the step and then rolling the large rear wheels up the kerb) and down again (rolling down backwards on all four wheels or, if balance and chair control is adequate, rolling down forwards with the front wheels off the ground); ability to manoeuvre the wheelchair through doors and gates.

N.B. Any movement education, whether with ambulant or chairbound children, carries in its wake the possibility of accident. Just as ambulant children have to learn to cope with falling over or how to land when jumping from a height, so too do children who spend the bulk of their lives in wheelchairs have to come to terms with the possibility of falling out or of overturning the chair. With some children, particularly the young or poorly co-ordinated, it is advisable that they wear a safety harness. But for older, more active children it is as well to familiarise them with the implications of a spill *before the event*, by acquainting them with some sort of capsize drill.

The drill should be introduced gradually so as not to create anxiety, and might incorporate the following stages:

(i) If the teacher is able (and he should be as competent in a wheelchair as his pupils) he should first of all demonstrate the complete drill; this shows the children what can be achieved with practice and reassures them that they are in knowledgeable hands;

(ii) The teacher *carries* child and chair through a simulated fall in slow motion;

(iii) Attention is drawn to the need to protect uncontrollable and fragile

Simulating a tumble: a) note the head tucked into the chest to guard against banging it on the floor.

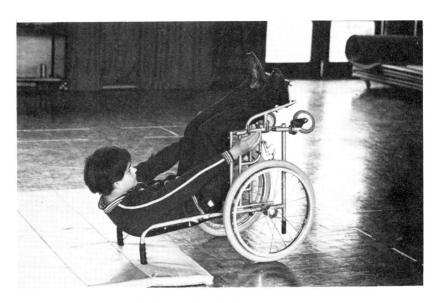

Simulating a tumble: b) firstly, apply the brakes.

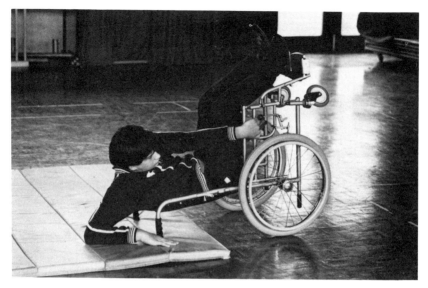

Simulating a tumble: c) secondly, with one hand, reach across the legs to grasp a permanent (fixed) part of the chair and with the other hand reach back and place it on the floor.

Simulating a tumble: d) thirdly, push up from the floor, moving the hand on the floor closer to the chair with each push. On regaining an upright position, release the brakes.

legs, and to the advisability of tucking the head into the chest so as not to bang the back of the head on the floor;

(iv) Apply the brakes. If the chair has been turned on its side, the child should roll onto the floor, sit up and then stand the chair up; the child should then re-enter the chair by whichever method is best suited to the individual: the paraplegic usually re-enters backwards by sitting on the footplates and then, placing the hands on the seat behind him, by lifting himself up onto the seat; whilst the spastic diplegic kneels on the floor facing the chair, and climbs up the chair and turns to sit on the seat (Fig. 13);

(v) If the chair has gone over backwards, the same procedure can be adopted as in (iv); alternatively, having put on the brakes while the chair is on its back some children learn to right the chair without getting out;

(vi) Ultimately, when the children are able, full capsize drills can be rehearsed (using mattresses or sponge blocks on the floor).

Apart from the obvious safety implications of this sort of drill, it also lends confidence to other situations, e.g., learning to tackle steps and to balance on rear wheels, a not altogether useless stunt which many children come to regard as a 'rite de passage'.

Games Apart from ordinary races, by far the most popular extension of these activities is the slalom competition. This involves steering the chair around a set course of obstacles (ramps, steps, garages, etc.,) as quickly as possible. Such competition against the clock can be against one's self as well as against one's friends with the final score being actual time taken from start to finish and penalties (time faults) added for knocking over obstacles, deviating from the course, etc. (Fig. 14). Alternative movement experience can also be gained through the use of scooter boards, go-karts, etc.

POWERED WHEELCHAIRS

For the child who is confined to a battery powered chair the above activities are equally appropriate, although participation is never possible to the same extent. Nonetheless, for children whose own motor performance is so tragically inadequate, the level of independence which can be achieved and the level of skill which can be demonstrated through control of these chairs is a source of great satisfaction.

Motor Fitness

Traditionally 'fitness' has always been at the hub of the physical education programme occupying, with the acquisition of skill, a prestigious place at the head of most teachers' list of priorities. Despite this, the concept of fitness is often misunderstood.

In its most general sense it refers to 'an individual's capacity to survive and live effectively in his environment' (Barrow and McGee 1971). As such, motor

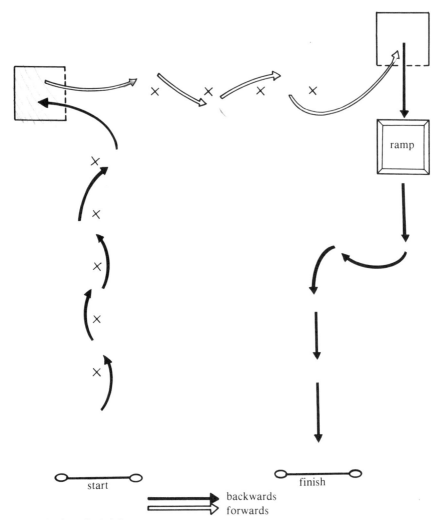

Figure 14 A typical slalom course

fitness, or physical fitness, is but one part of a multi-dimensional concept of fitness which includes psychological, emotional and social as well as physical wellbeing. What is more, in so far as fitness is measurable at all, it varies with the age, sex, body-type and life-style of the individual. But it is with motor fitness that the physical education teacher is principally concerned, even though an alteration to the state of any one of these subsystems will doubtless have some effect upon the others as well.

Motor fitness is commonly considered to be an aggregate of the following: strength, endurance, cardiovascular efficiency, flexibility, balance, speed and

101

agility. As locomotion and balance are treated elsewhere in this chapter, this section will concentrate on strength, endurance, cardiovascular efficiency and flexibility.

Strength and endurance

Although these are essentially different, they are brought together in this section because the exercises and activities to be described are appropriate for both. The difference in training for one as opposed to the other is more a matter of mode of execution than the nature of the activity itself. For example someone building up strength by doing press-ups would need to overload his muscles by placing a weight across the shoulders, even though he would then be able to do fewer repetitions at a time; a person concentrating upon endurance, on the other hand, would not overload his muscles to the same extent and would probably do without the weight, but he would attempt to continue the exercise for much longer.

An important consideration in this respect is that recent research indicates that people are inherently better equipped to perform in one way (in strength or in endurance activities) than in the other.

This inherent quality is based upon the type of muscle fibres which predominate in the neuromotor make up, fibres which are more productive of brief powerful efforts (suitable for feats of strength) or fibres which result in more efficient contractions engaged in over time, as in endurance activities (Cratty 1975).

Neither strength nor endurance training is likely to be necessary for the normal child. In younger children, physical strength and endurance seem to be of a more general nature and not until adolescence does there appear to be any point in attempting to develop specific qualities. This is not the case, however, for children whose muscles have atrophied through disuse or disease. For them, there is considerable value in such exercise, not only for the pursuit of recreational outlets, but also, more importantly, for the accomplishment of the activities of daily life. Unless the child needs to concentrate on either strength or endurance for a particular reason, a middle of the road regime is probably suitable for both.

Activities For legs – any locomotor activity (running, jumping, hopping, etc.), leg-raising (lying on the back, lift the legs off the floor), squats (standing with feet shoulder-width apart, squat down to the floor keeping the back straight and stand up again);

For arms – pushing a wheelchair, press-ups (lying on the floor face down, place hands on the floor beneath the shoulders and push up to straight arms, if possible keeping the body straight, *alternatively* sitting in a wheelchair between two parallel bars just above shoulder height, with one hand on each bar, lift up to full arm extension and lower back into the wheelchair), chin-ups (hanging

from a beam by the hands, pull up to touch the beam with chin or chest), ladder walk (hanging from a horizontally suspended ladder, hand walk from one rung to another);

For trunk – sit-ups (back-lying on the floor, sit up without using the arms), back-lifts (lying face down on the floor, lift head and shoulders as high as possible without using the arms).

Cardiovascular efficiency

This is a measure of the ability of the heart and lungs to deliver oxygen to the body and is generally considered to be a very good indication of a person's overall level of physical fitness. Any exercise intended to improve cardio-vascular efficiency must therefore place sufficient stress upon the heart and lungs to produce beneficial changes in the body. Such activity is said to be 'aerobic' (Cooper 1970).

Activities As most activities of an aerobic nature are those involving some basic form of locomotion (e.g., jogging or pushing a wheelchair) over an extended period of time (10–12 minutes), those activities mentioned earlier in this chapter are typical.

Flexibility

This is a measure of the degree to which a joint can be put through a particular range of movement. Although too much flexibility at a joint is sometimes accompanied by a tendency to subluxation or dislocation, and too little by stiffness and difficulty in the performance of even simple motor tasks, a moderately extensive range of movement at a joint is beneficial to most ac-tivities. This applies equally to throwing a discus and putting on a cardigan.

Activities For legs – cross-legged sitting (sitting upright with legs crossed, apply gentle downward pressure to knees with the hands), kneeling (with feet plantar-flexed, sit back on the calves and walk hands along the floor in a backwards direction), hamstring-stretch (sitting on the floor with the legs out straight forward and apart, lean forwards to place hands on the floor as far forward as possible);

For trunk – toe-touching (standing with feet astride, bend over forwards to touch feet with hands), back-extension (lying face down on the floor, lift head, shoulders and legs as high as possible), floor-touching (sitting in wheelchair, lean over sideways to touch the floor or the bottom of the left wheel with the right hand and vice versa);

For shoulders – arm-circles (with the arms out to the sides, trace large circles with the hands), 'wing-stretcher' (fingertips on shoulders and elbows pointing horizontally out to the sides, push elbows back together), shoulder-stretch (passing one hand over the shoulder and one hand under the shoulder, attempt to link hands behind the back).

N.B. Because of the repetitive nature of these activities it is not advisable to devote whole lessons to them, generally speaking a balanced fifteen-minute session is adequate.

Games Almost all physical recreation activities have some effect upon motor fitness, but two activities in particular have been developed specially with this in mind:

Circuit training – introduced in the 1950s by Morgan and Adamson (1961), this system enables the trainee to move from one activity to another without rest by exercising different body parts in rotation. For example, a nine-unit circuit might incorporate different exercises for legs, trunk and arms thus: (a) squats, (b) sit-ups, (c) chin-ups, (d) hamstring-stretch, (e) back-lifts, (f) press-ups, (g) leg-raises, (h) toe touching and (i) ladder walk.

Weight training – this is an extension of the circuit training principle to incorporate activities involving the use of weights.

Rhythm and Temporal Awareness

Many of the activities outlined so far are repetitive. Where a child finds such an activity difficult giving it a rhythmic base can prove helpful. Conversely, where a child has a poor sense of time, the repeated execution of simple motor activities in cadence can also be beneficial.

Additionally, where such a rhythm and temporal awareness can be re-inforced through music (whether sung by the children or played on a record), a little colour is added to an otherwise flat sequence of movements.

Activities Military drill – most children love to march. A natural extension of this is the enjoyment and satisfaction that comes from the performance of exercises (standing, sitting or lying) in unison with others.

Jazz gymnastics – these are keep fit exercises performed to music. These are particularly popular with adult groups, but are enjoyed as well by children of all ages in school.

Folk dancing – most traditional dance forms, reels, polkas, etc. have quite a variety of basic steps, all of which are performed to a strong, constant beat. As such, they are valuable not only because they assist in the development of rhythm, but also because they aid concentration, co-ordination and motor control. And if one equates one positive push of the wheelchair with one dance step, most of these dances (or variations of them) are just as possible for chair-bound children as they are for ambulant children.

Balance

Balancing is not just a knack, useful in the performance of tricks, handstands, feats of juggling and the like. It is an essential prerequisite to sitting, standing, running, and most other postural and locomotor skills. In many motor-

Balancing on two wheels: a not altogether useless stunt which many children come to regard as a 'rite de passage'.

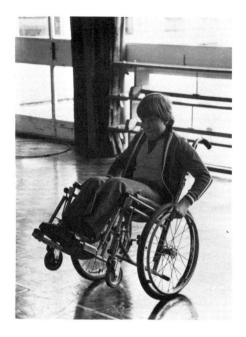

impaired children the 'sense' of balance is defective, but this does not necessarily mean that it is irremediable.

As a rule, balance is improved by 'placing the child within a situation which requires that he exercise precision when attempting to relate to gravity in some way' (Cratty 1975). Depending on the extent of the disorder in an individual case, the degree of difficulty implicit in any remedial balance task may be adjusted in several ways, (i) the base of support may be made smaller, (ii) the supporting surface may be made less stable, (iii) use of the arms may be restricted or prohibited, and (iv) use of the eyes may be restricted, impaired or prevented.

Activities Static – 'V' sit (sitting upright on the floor with hands clasping ankles, thus holding the legs in the air), standing still (on tiptoes/with eyes closed/with hands on head/etc.), standing on one leg (as above), standing on a narrow beam (as above), standing on a balance board (as above), head-stand (hands and head on the floor, legs in the air), elephant-stand (hands only on the floor, knees supported against elbows), hand-stand (hands only on floor, arms, trunk and legs extended straight upwards);
N.B. For those with extensive balance problems, exercises calling for continuous readjustment are useful, e.g., sitting a young child on a large inflatable rubber ball and moving it just enough to force the child to readjust his position, or with the child sitting, kneeling or standing on a mat applying just enough pressure on the chest or back with the hands that, unless he adjusts his position, he falls over.

Moving – walking, running, hopping, jumping exercises (eyes closed/hands on hips/hands on head/etc.) on a narrow line taped to the floor, on a balance beam or on a discontinuous surface e.g., stepping stones.

Games Balance board contests, walking on stilts or pogo-sticks, hop-scotch, etc. Balancing on rear wheels of a wheelchair (close supervision needed in the early stages – see locomotion above).

Body and space perception

Body perception is directly affected by cognitive, affective and psycho-motor learning and has a direct relationship to the individual's understanding of space . . . The three areas of body perception that have been found to be most important are body knowledge, body image and body-space relationships (Arnheim and Sinclair 1975).

Body knowledge
A child's knowledge of what his body is, what it can do and what it cannot do begins at birth and is modified by every new achievement (and failure to achieve) throughout childhood and adulthood. Beginning with gross body movements and a crude control over his sensory apparatus, the able-bodied child gradually acquires an understanding of body planes, body movement and co-ordination, laterality, directionality, etc., until ultimately he has at his disposal all the faculties and physical propensities of the mature healthy adult. For the handicapped child on the other hand, at some stage there comes the realisation that his body is not normal. From that moment on, he has to come to terms with what he can do and what he cannot do.

Body image
Whereas body knowledge is finite (one either can do something or one cannot) the body image is more vulnerable, representing the product of *all* one's experiences: not only one's physical and mental achievements, but also the attitudes and values which the child (and others) bring to bear upon those achievements. Consequently, a child who knows himself to be handicapped might come to identify himself with the inadequacies and weaknesses of all handicaps, even though his own disability is quite specific.

The extent to which a child is able to relate meaningfully to his environment is dependent upon the extent to which his body image is an accurate reflection of his actual body capacity, i.e., his body knowledge.

Body-space relationships
The relationship one has with one's environment is but an extension of one's body knowledge and a contributing factor to the make-up of one's body

'O'Grady says "Put your hands in the air".'
Games of this kind are very popular with younger children and very useful as an aid to body-knowledge and the development of meaningful body-space relationships.

image. If a child fixes his gaze upon an attractive object, puts his hand out to grasp it, but finds that his hand will not go where he want it to go, obviously the relationship that child establishes with his environment will be unsatisfactory. Similarly, if a child's eyes are feeding him incorrect information (as in the case of myopia) even with proper motor control his relationship with his immediate surroundings is likely to be confused. Only when a child can accurately assess his capabilities and inadequacies and relate them meaningfully to his environment, making realistic judgements as to distances, sizes, position in space, etc., can he begin to function efficiently.

Activities Touch your right ear/left knee/etc., bend your right leg/left arm/etc., shake your head/left foot/right hand/etc., point at the door/the ceiling/the floor/etc., fetch me that beanbag/football/etc., 'Is it further to X than Y?', 'Is A bigger than B?' etc. etc.
N.B. Apart from single activities of this kind, an educational gymnastics/movement exploration approach is ideally suited to assist perceptual development of this sort.

Games 'O'Grady says . . .' – the teacher or a child from within the group faces the rest of the group and issues the command 'Put your hands on your head' or 'O'Grady says put your hands on your knees'. Children should respond only if the command is preceded by 'O'Grady says . . .';
   Obstacle races – any form of 'commando course' which involves children in

climbing through tyres, under nets, over benches, etc., is an invaluable and most enjoyable aid to this sort of development;

Pirates – with a randomly situated assortment of apparatus, mats, benches, etc. a game of tig is played with no-one allowed to touch the floor.

Rebound and airborne activities

The sort of activities normally associated with the use of trampoline, trampette and springboard are only of any real value to the child who has a reasonable amount of tonus in the muscles of the legs. Although to use a trampoline it is not necessary for a child to be able to walk, the use of trampette or spring-board demands an ability to walk, run and jump. The experiential value of bouncing a child with flaccid paralysis of the legs scarcely compensates for the dangers inherent in the possibility of fractures to the legs or jolts to the spine.

For those who can benefit from these activities, however, they arc an in-valuable aid to the development of confidence, motor fitness and body-spatial awareness, as well as being a thoroughly enjoyable experience.

Activities Elementary – bouncing/jumping on feet, jumping for height/ shape/etc.;

Intermediate – bouncing on feet/knees/seat in combination;

Advanced – development of bouncing sequences incorporating twists/ turns/face drops/somersaults/etc.

N.B. The trampoline can be extremely dangerous if it is improperly used. At all levels of ability it is recommended that the following procedures should be adopted:

(i) The trampoline should never be left unattended. When it is not in use, it should be folded away.

(ii) Children should not wear outdoor shoes or calipers (unless suitably padded) on the trampoline as this causes damage to the webbing.

(iii) There should be at least one able-bodied spotter on each side of the trampoline to prevent accidents.

(iv) Safety pads should be used to cover the metal frame and the springs which support the bed.

(v) Before dismounting from the trampoline the performer should come to a complete stop. Under no circumstances should a child be allowed to bounce from the trampoline to the floor.

Projectile Management

Although there is little scope for the practical application of projectile management skills to the problems of daily living, such activities provide a most useful adjunct to any programme aimed at improving body-space relationships, hand-eye co-ordination etc., as well as providing the key to participation in an immeasurable variety of recreational activities.

Throwing

The ability to throw is fundamental both to team games such as basketball, rounders, etc., and to the pursuit of field athletics, javelin, discus, shot, etc. With young children particularly, opportunities should be provided for a wide range of throwing activities, performed standing or sitting still in the first instance, and then at a later stage performed on the move.

Activities Throwing bean-bags/large balls/small handballs/quoits/etc., with one hand/two hands, overarm and underarm; throwing for height/distance/accuracy (e.g., at a target on the floor or on the wall).

N.B. Because of the time taken in retrieval, most basic throwing skills can be profitably practised in pairs, although one cannot overstress the safety precautions necessary in any throwing activity involving missiles which are heavy, hard or sharp.

Catching

This is the obvious complementary activity to any ball-throwing skill (*not* darts, shot, javelins, etc.) and can be practised in much the same way. As a general rule, children find most success if they begin with large balls using both hands and then move on to bean-bags and small balls, firstly using both hands and then using just one hand. Similarly, catching is more likely to be successful if it is first attempted over short distances and only gradually introduced over greater distances. It is worth remembering in this respect that greater distance demands greater accuracy of throw. The teacher should also stress that the eyes should remain open and fixed on the ball at all times and that a wide base (e.g., one leg forward, one leg back) increases stability and therefore steadies the child in the act of catching.

Activities As for throwing – first of all individually (against a wall/in the air/against the floor), then in pairs (two hands, then one hand; large balls, then smaller balls).

Games Juggling (two balls, then three balls), jacks (various versions, e.g., scatter jacks or stones on the floor, then throwing a small ball into the air try to pick up a jack before catching the ball).

Bouncing

This is a combination of throwing and catching (or patting) and is a useful introduction to both these skills as well as providing the basis for a variety of minor games leading up to basketball.

Activities Static – count the number of bounces (one hand or two, against wall or floor), bounce ball hard and clap hands/spin around/etc. before catching;
    Moving – walk or run in a straight line or around skittles, bouncing the ball with two hands or one; push wheelchair with one hand, bouncing the ball on the floor with the other.

Games Various minor games exist each of which can be adapted to stress throwing, catching or bouncing. Typical of these are Captain ball and Skittle ball:

Captain ball – two teams play on hardcourt or grass with a bench at either end of the playing area. Each team sends one player to stand or sit on the bench at the opposite end of the court. The ball is then introduced and each team has to try to get the ball to its captain on the bench.

Skittle ball – two teams play on hardcourt or grass with a skittle standing at either end of the playing area. Play is usually allowed to extend a little way beyond the skittles so that they can be attacked from all sides, the object of the game being to knock over the opposing team's skittle with the ball.

Kicking

Soccer is one of the most popular of English sports and very few children, boys in particular, go through life without at some stage wanting to kick a ball. Although contact with the ball can be made with the toe, the instep, the top of the foot or the heel, the mechanical act of kicking is much the same. However, as with catching activities, the teacher should stress the importance of 'keeping the eyes on the ball'.

Activities Kicking a stationary ball (standing still/with a run up), kicking a rolling ball (standing still/on the move), kicking a ball held in the hand(s), kicking for accuracy/distance/height (with the instep/toe/top of the foot), kicking with either foot, dribbling the ball with the feet (in a straight line/around skittles), trapping the ball with the foot.

Games Any form of football.

Striking

Most activities which involve striking the ball with the hand (as in fives) or an extension of the hand (as in badminton, table tennis, cricket, rounders, and golf) have become so specific in the manner with which the hand, racquet, bat or club is used, that the teacher has to offer a very wide range of striking activities from very early on, if at a later age the child is to be given any real choice. Fortunately, despite the diversity of styles, there are certain features which are common to them all:

(i) the child should be encouraged to adopt a stable posture (feet apart);

(ii) the child should keep his gaze fixed on the ball right up to the moment of contact;

(iii) the stroke should continue to be played right through the point at which contact is made with the ball;

(iv) in most batting activities the stroke is played sideways on to the intended direction of play (i.e., the right-handed child leads with his left shoulder).

Activities Striking a stationary ball (on the floor/on a tee) standing still/on the move, striking a rolling ball (standing still/on the move), striking a ball whilst it is in flight (standing still/on the move).

N.B. Children generally find striking activities easier in the early stages of learning if consideration is given to the following:
   (i) the size and weight of the bat and ball;
   (ii) the speed at which the ball is delivered (this can be reduced considerably by using shuttlecocks or balloons);
   (iii) whether it is appropriate to use one hand or two.

Games For the hands – fives, volleyball, prällball (a fist variation of tennis developed by amputees in West Germany in which the ball has to bounce *before* it crosses the net).

For playing with a solid bat – table tennis, cricket, rounders, baseball, golf.

For playing with a racquet – badminton, tennis, squash.

Management of daily motor activities

Through the provision of activities of this kind the physical education programme can make an invaluable contribution to the handicapped child's quest for independence. What is more, because of the recreative element inherent in most physical education activities, this can be achieved in ways children find interesting and enjoyable.

The diversity of skills desirable in this context, e.g., dressing and un-dressing, tying up of shoelaces, ability to transfer from bed to wheelchair, etc., means that a large number of the activities which have already been outlined under those sections relating to locomotion, flexibility, strength, etc. can be usefully incorporated into this area as well. But the area which probably deserves most attention in respect of daily living skills is that which embraces fine motor control and hand-eye co-ordination – especially in so far as they affect manual dexterity.

Activities Bead stringing, brick building, rope tying, sorting activities (colours, shapes, textures, etc.), pegboard activities, basketwork, sewing, embroidery, drawing, tracing, cutting out, painting, blackboard activities, etc.

Games Dressing up competitions (against the clock), basic constructional activities (making dens, camp utensils, etc., with wooden poles lashed together with ropes), tent pitching competitions.

Selected play skills

These are particularly important for the physically handicapped child who lives at home (i.e., who does not attend a residential school). On a housing

For the child with impaired balance the tricycle combines speed and manoeuvrability with safety.

estate the sort of body image a child acquires is in large measure a reflection of the status he enjoys among his peers. For the physically handicapped child, therefore, who is unable to join in the usual round of neighbourhood games, the body image inevitably suffers. And far worse than that, it reinforces in able-bodied children the conviction that physically handicapped youngsters are somehow 'different'. If, on the other hand, the child can be taught such activities in school, much can be done to remedy both these situations.

Cycling

Riding a bicycle is usually only introduced after a child has mastered the skills of steering and pedalling on a tricycle. Although some children experience difficulty in maintaining the cross-pattern leg movements required for cycling, this can be overcome by strapping the feet to the pedals and using a cycle with a 'fixed wheel'. It has to be accepted that some children with particular balance disorders may never proceed beyond the tricycle. This is nonetheless a most useful aid to motor fitness and a considerable extension to an otherwise restricted range of mobility.

Skating

Roller skating and ice skating are extensions of walking and running with a greater emphasis placed upon dynamic balance. Progressive practices might include

(i) walking exercises on the balance beam;

(ii) sliding on a slippery floor in socked feet;

(iii) walking on grass wearing roller skates;

(iv) riding a child's scooter;

(v) wearing just one skate and practising gliding;

(vi) receiving a tow wearing both skates;

(vii) skating properly.

Rope skipping

Probably the most popular of all playground activities at the primary school level, rope skipping can be done individually and in groups. Progressive practices might include

(i) jumping or hopping (forwards and backwards) over a rope stretched out on the ground;

(ii) jumping or hopping zigzag fashion along a rope stretched out on the ground;

(iii) running under or over a long rope being swung round by two people (one at each end);

(iv) skipping on both feet with two assistants holding the rope ends;

(v) skipping on each foot alternately with two assistants holding the rope ends;

(vi) skipping holding the rope oneself.

N.B. For older children an introduction to billiards, snooker, table tennis or popular dance forms (of the discotheque variety) might be similarly useful.

Aggression management

This is a two-edged problem particularly common among children with restricted movement potential (see Chapter 4 – 'Maladjustment'). On the one hand, such a life-style can bring about a passivity and weakness of character that affects not only a child's relationship with others, but also his preparedness to tackle novel or difficult situations, and on the other hand, it can create in a child all sorts of pent-up frustrations and an uncontrollable hostility towards others less handicapped.

Highly structured opportunities for such children to 'let off steam' can do a great deal both to instil confidence in the timid child and to reduce the tension within the more choleric child.

Activities Coconut shies – soft balls (or small bundles of rags) are thrown at a pyramid of tin cans/wooden blocks/etc. in an effort to knock them all over.

King of the castle – two children stand opposite each other on a balance beam (or bench) armed with a pillow/sponge roll/etc., and attempt to knock each other off the beam. The winner becomes 'king' and stays on the beam until deposed.

Pick-a-back contests – in a contest between two teams (each of two children) the 'rider' in each team has to try and unseat his opponent. This can be done quite safely on mats or in the shallow end (3-foot deep approx.) of a swimming pool.

Tug-of-war – each of two teams at opposite ends of a long rope attempts to pull the other team across a central 'no-man's-land'.

Tension release

Although Arnheim and Sinclair list tension release first in their taxonomy of task categories (Chapter 5), I have chosen to put it at the end because that is where I have found it most usefully placed in the physical education lesson. A common complaint amongst classroom teachers is that, whenever they teach children immediately after a physical education lesson, the children are either exhausted or over-boisterous; neither condition being conducive to a successful lesson. By finishing the physical education lesson with three or four minutes' silent concentration upon relaxation, controlled respiration and tension release, children should return to their classrooms in a more or less normal state of mind and body.

Activities Imagery – e.g. 'imagine you are a free-fall parachutist, you are floating on air, your arms and legs are weightless'.

Concentration upon muscle tension and relaxation (taking one body part at a time until the whole body is relaxed). Concentration on breathing (not too fast, not too deep).

N.B. Engaging the children in purposeful, preferably topical conversation is also a useful method of bringing excitable children 'down to earth' before sending them off to their next lesson.

Summary

The activities outlined in this chapter and the teaching hints offered as being applicable to those activities are but a small drop in the ocean of activities and teaching techniques that can be employed, with or without modification, in the physical education of physically handicapped children.

Through such activities an attempt can be made to extend the 'limited vocabulary of motor skills and the correspondingly limited range of relevant experience' which the young physically handicapped child brings with him when he first comes to school (Morris and Whiting 1971). If the physical education programme he receives in school is comprehensive, balanced and

appropriately tailored to his own special needs, he should find in time that he has the confidence and the ability to look for and to find appropriate forms of recreational activity, whether this be archery or riding, basketball or swimming.

It is with these major forms of activity that the next three chapters are concerned.

REFERENCES

Arnheim, D. D. & Sinclair, W. A. (1975) *The clumsy child: a programme of motor therapy.* C. V. Mosby: St. Louis.

Barrow, H. M. & McGee, R. (1971) *A practical approach to measurement in physical education.* Lea & Febiger: Philadelphia.

Cooper, K. H. (1970) *The new aerobics.* Evans: New York.

Cratty, B. J. (1975) *Remedial motor activity for children.* Lea & Febiger: Philadelphia.

Geddes, D. (1974) *Physical activities for individuals with handicapping conditions.* C. V. Mosby: St. Louis.

Harvat, R. W. (1971) *Physical education for children with perceptual-motor learning disabilities.* Charles E. Merrill: Ohio.

Morgan, R. E. & Adamson, G. T. (1961) *Circuit training.* 2nd Edition. Bell: London.

Morris, P. R. & Whiting, H. T. A. (1971) *Motor impairment and compensatory education.* Bell: London.

7

The major games component of physical education

The number of games and sports that can be introduced to the child in the special school through the medium of the physical education programme is as immense as the benefit that can be derived from such participation.

The difference between a game and a sport, or a minor game and a major game, is a slender one, although in general terms it would appear to be a distinction of quality rather than kind. If all such activities were to be placed on a continuum measuring a high/low organisation factor, this difference would probably become more obvious: the low-organisation activities such as darts and draughts being commonly identified as games, and those with a high-organisation component, i.e., a more complex structure, such as basketball and fencing, being given the 'elevated' status of sports.

It is with this latter category, the sporting activities, that this chapter is concerned. In particular, for reasons of conciseness, it focuses upon

(i) those sports already popular in disabled circles and

(ii) those sports which, whilst to date they have no great following, are seen to hold great potential, whether for physical, psychological, sociological or other reasons.

In most of these activities competition is an intrinsic part of their character. But it need not dominate every situation. Competition can be made to feature as much or as little as befits the situation in hand. By emphasising particular skills, tactical ploys or simply 'playing for fun', the competitive element can be played down. This is often desirable for children who have only recently become disabled and also for those in whom, by virtue of their condition, a highly competitive situation produces either muscular spasms or emotional instability. For others, competition can be extremely useful in arousing interest and stimulating effort. Games which are inherently repetitive, e.g., table tennis, can become monotonous even to the most enthusiastic child. In cases such as this, competition, either against other individuals, on a league basis, or even against one's own personal performance, can add a new dimension to an otherwise tiresome experience.

The activities outlined below are described, where appropriate, from several points of view, namely, (i) the history and character of the activity, (ii) variations in form, (iii) progressive practices/lead-up activities, and (iv) special considerations for the teacher in the special school. The status of any activity within a school programme varies according to each situation.

116

For the child with spina bifida, archery is more than an enjoyable pastime, fostering upright posture, balance and coordination.

Dartchery: variations in play are as numerous as there are dart games.

Archery

The origins of archery are in its use as a means of hunting and thence as a means of personal defence and attack. The progression from this stage, some 5,000 years ago, to the use of the bow and arrow as a sophisticated martial art was presumably quite rapid. The sporting element, in England at least, was introduced in the Middle Ages as a testament to hunting prowess and encouraged by kings and feudal overlords, as an insurance against invasion.

Archery for the disabled has been practised since the 1940's when it was introduced at Stoke Mandeville Hospital. Nowadays it commands a place of respect in the rehabilitation of paraplegics, and is practised worldwide by young and old alike with all manner of disabilities.

Basically there are two forms of archery, long bow archery using the conventional bow and arrow, and cross bow archery incorporating a trigger release mechanism on a central stock and using a short bolt or dart instead of the arrow (Fig. 15). The sporting activities which are commonly pursued by both types of archer are field archery and dartchery.

Field archery

This is practised with a circular straw target (80cm or 122cm in diameter) at distances of 30m and 50m using the smaller target and 60m, 70m and 90m using the larger target. The face of the target is marked with five concentric colour zones, each of which is further divided into two zones, an inner and an outer, by a thin line. Scores are recorded according to the position of the arrow relative to the centre of the target (Table 18).

Table 18. Field archery scoring values

Colour	Zone	Score
Gold	Inner	10
	Outer	9
Red	Inner	8
	Outer	7
Blue	Inner	6
	Outer	5
Black	Inner	4
	Outer	3
White	Inner	2
	Outer	1

Dartchery

This is generally practised over a much shorter distance, usually 15 metres, and involves the same sort of target as in field archery but with a dartboard face. The variations in play are therefore as numerous as in dart games.

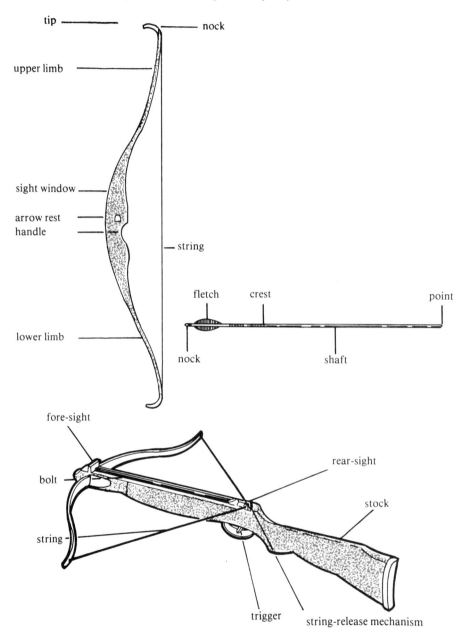

Figure 15 Anatomy of the bow and arrow

Long bow

The same basic routine is adopted for all activities.

(i) Position – the same principles apply to the stance whether the archer is seated or standing. The right-handed child holds the bow in the left hand and faces at right angles to the direction of flight with the left shoulder leading. In the wheelchair case, the chair itself is at right angles to the direction of flight. In the standing position, the feet are comfortably apart to increase stability. The bow is held in the left hand (all instructions from here on relating to the right-handed performer) in such a way that when the bow is held at rest, i.e., by the side, the string naturally assumes a position directly above the bow.

(ii) Nocking – this is the technique of placing the arrow in the bow. The arrow is taken in the right hand and laid across the bow in such a way that the shaft of the arrow rests on the ledge and the nock fits around the string. Most arrows have three flights or fletches, in which case care must be taken to ensure that the cock feather (i.e., the fletch at right angles to the nock and usually of a different colour) is always on the outside.

(iii) The Draw – this is achieved by extending the bow arm and drawing back the string with the other. The string is held by three fingers, the forefinger above the arrow and the next two below, *none* of which grasps the arrow itself, as this would cause a deflection of the arrow on release. In the full-draw position, the extended bow arm points at the target, the string immediately above the arrow creases the midpoint of the chin, and the right arm flexed at the elbow forms an extension of the arrow shaft.

(iv) The Hold – at the full-draw position a brief pause should be made to check that everything is properly aligned. Too much delay causes trembling. Sighting of the target can be done 'free' or using a fixed sight, the proper use of which needs personal instruction.

(v) The Loose – this must be done as smoothly as possible and, in effect, is a straightening of the fingers around the string. Having 'loosed' the arrow, the position should be maintained until the arrow (hopefully) hits the target.

Cross bow

The cross bow is normally only used in schools by those children who are unable to manage a long bow. As the bow can be set in the full-draw position by the teacher and as the whole apparatus can be mounted on a tripod via a ball-and-socket joint, all the child has to do is take aim and shoot. In this way, even advanced muscular dystrophies can be actively involved in competitions to the same extent as their less handicapped peers.

SPECIAL CONSIDERATIONS FOR THE TEACHER

Apart from the numerous aids available for the able-bodied archer, finger-tabs, arm-guards, arrow quivers, etc., there are also some which have been developed specially for the physically handicapped including a wide range of attachments to facilitate the drawing/releasing process. Additionally, the

teacher must never forget that the bow and arrow were created as a lethal weapon. At all times, therefore, in the teaching of archery certain safety precautions must be observed.

(i) The archery range should not cross any thoroughfare and wherever possible a safety net should be erected behind the target.

(ii) A bow should never be drawn and released without an arrow in it.

(iii) All children, participating or otherwise, should be kept behind the shooting line at all times unless otherwise instructed.

(iv) Children should not be sent to retrieve arrows until *all* have finished shooting.

(v) Arrows should never be shot straight up in the air.

(vi) Children should only be allowed to bring bow and arrow to the full-draw position when they are at the shooting line and facing in the right direction. Games of pretence can be fatal.

(vii) It is not recommended that more than four or five children be allowed to shoot at any one time. A group of eight to ten children would therefore seem to be appropriate for this type of activity.

Athletics

Track and field athletics as they are known today have remained virtually unchanged since their inception at the Ancient Olympics of Greece some two thousand years ago.

One of the advantages of this form of activity for the physically handicapped child is that one or two very specific activities can be selected from within a wide range (i.e., one doesn't have to be an all-rounder). Another is that very little is required in the way of modification. One of the disadvantages, especially in the field events, is the degree of precision that is required for the satisfactory execution of any given skill. Nonetheless, athletic training is quite common in schools, which presumably reflects the usefulness of this activity in respect of improved locomotor skill, motor fitness and gross motor co-ordination.

Although it is customary to group athletic events into just track and field, it is more convenient in this instance if they are categorised track, throwing and jumping events.

Track events

These can be further subdivided into sprints, long distance events and wheelchair slalom.

In Chapter 6 reference was made to research evidence which suggests that an individual has an inherent physical preference for activities involving either strength or endurance (Cratty 1975). Such an inclination is particularly relevant to a child's suitability for sprinting or long distance events; the sprinter requiring explosive power (i.e., strength) and the long distance

performer requiring efficiency of movement and stamina (i.e., endurance). Training procedures for each, whether they are to be performed running or in a wheelchair, must therefore differ accordingly.

The only special technique that has to be introduced is the sprint start for the ambulant children. Although a standing start, i.e., legs slightly bent, one forward, one back, has widespread application until such time as competition becomes intense, the basic procedure for the crouch start is worth noting.

(i) 'On your marks' – feet and knees should point straight down the track; the rear knee should rest on the ground beside the front foot; the fore-finger and thumb of both hands should be behind and in line with the start line and a 'bridge' made with the other fingers; hands should be shoulder-width apart.

(ii) 'Set' – the rear knee is lifted from the ground, thus tilting the body forwards; with the weight being taken by the arms and forward leg, the body hovers in balance.

(iii) 'Go!' – the sprinter drives forwards and upwards, each stride increasing in length until a normal running pattern is established.

The introduction of hurdling for the ambulant child will necessitate both sprinting practices and the 'grooving in' of a hurdling technique. This varies considerably according to the condition of the individual i.e., whether spastic, amputee, or whatever, although most children respond favourably to the following progression:

(i) Sprinting without obstacles with an emphasis on regularity of stride – this can be achieved even if the pattern is somewhat unusual; (Activities designed to promote rhythmic movements are to be found in Chapter 6.)

(ii) Sprinting over canes laid out on the floor at regular intervals appropriate to the stride-length/age/size of the children;

(iii) Gradually increasing the height of the canes until a standard hurdle height is reached.

One other track activity which is very popular amongst children who have to use wheelchairs is the slalom. This was described in some detail in Chapter 6.

Throwing events

These include shot, discus, javelin and club throwing, all of which are power events. As a result, most enthusiasts derive considerable benefit from incorporating strength exercises into their training schedules. To a lesser extent, exercises designed to increase shoulder mobility are beneficial.

Putting the shot can be performed on the move, standing still or from a chair, provided the complete action takes place within a circle 2.13 m in diameter. The only other major impositions are that the put must be made from the shoulder using just one hand and that the shot must land within a designated area (the latter being a safety precaution). The weight of the shot varies according to age and disability within a range of 2 to 4kg.

The same sort of procedure exists for throwing the discus and, for the wheelchair athlete, club throwing as well. In both cases, the missile (discus or

club) has to be held in one hand; the difference being in the style of throw. By convention, the discus is thrown after a series of swinging movements of the arms and trunk, supplemented in the case of the ambulant performer (at his own discretion) by rotation of the whole body. The club, 39cm long and weighing approximately 10g, is normally thrown over-arm.

The javelin used by handicapped athletes is the standard women's javelin (2.20 m long and weighing 600g). Competitions exist at various levels, for adults and children, in distance javelin throwing and precision javelin throwing. The former is a straightforward measure of the distance thrown (from either a sitting, standing or running start). The latter, as its name suggests, is a test of accuracy. The target is a series of concentric circles painted on to grass and throwing is normally done from a distance of 10 m (or less).

Jumping events

Long jump, high jump and triple jump (hop, step and jump) are all activities which require strength of legs and, in two of the three, sprinting ability as well. The finer points of jumping technique are only likely to be of significance to the more able performer and so in this instance the training procedures outlined in Chapter 6 (see 'locomotion') are considered sufficient.

SPECIAL CONSIDERATIONS FOR THE TEACHER

The teacher's biggest area of concern in the teaching of athletics is the supervision of throwing activities. In competition it is necessary to have measuring officials forward of the throwing line or circle, but even so their numbers should be restricted. However, the very fact that such officials are necessary provides the less able child or the child with other interests to play a most useful role without actually competing. In group training sessions, it is recommended that the same sort of precautions as were outlined for archery be adopted. Secondly, although artificial aids are not often necessary for athletics, one or two such aids do exist e.g., the arm-amputee's cup attachment for shot putting.

Badminton

The game of badminton was originally played by the British Army in India in the late 19th century. At the time it was called 'Poona' and it only took its present name after it had been popularised back in England by returning Army officers who played it on the Duke of Beaufort's estate at Badminton in Gloucestershire.

In the regular version the game is played with racquets and a shuttlecock by two or four players (singles and doubles). Opposing players or teams stand on either side of a net 5 feet high and the shuttlecock is volleyed from one side to the other, each team being allowed only one hit each time the shuttlecock is its

side of the net. Points can only be scored by the serving team and they are made either by forcing an error on the part of the opposition (so that they either hit the shuttlecock into the net or out of court) or by hitting the shuttlecock in court in such a way that the opposition cannot play it before it touches the floor. Each game is won by the first side to score fifteen points.

Variations which have been devised either for young children or for the physically handicapped include batinton and balloon badminton. The former differs from badminton in that a solid bat is used and the shuttlecock is more heavily weighted, and the latter differs in that the shuttlecock is replaced by a balloon. The advantage of batinton to the learner is said to be that a weighted shuttlecock follows a more natural flight path, whilst the advantage of the balloon is that it takes an unnaturally long time to descend, thus giving the slow or poorly co-ordinated child more time to position himself and prepare for his next shot. In addition, modifications to this and any other court game can always be achieved through either reducing the court size or increasing the number of players in a team.

SPECIAL CONSIDERATIONS FOR THE TEACHER

Badminton, batinton, balloon badminton and any other such variation of the parent game are all similarly useful aids to the training of gross motor control and hand-eye co-ordination. At a more advanced level, such activities also have a positive effect on motor fitness, in particular on flexibility, agility and endurance.

When introducing the game to children, it sometimes proves helpful to have them 'shake hands' with the racquet. This should ensure a more or less proper grasp of the racquet handle. In the early stages, too, it is more beneficial for children to play in co-operation with each other than in competition with each other. 'See how many times you can hit the shuttlecock to each other' is far more likely to be successful as a training procedure than to have children continually hit the shuttlecock out of reach of their partner. In this way also, the various strokes can be introduced and rehearsed (e.g., the drop shot, the smash and the high clearance shot) without having to cope with the pressures of the game situation.

Amongst the various artificial aids which have been devised, probably the most useful are the arm-amputees serving tray (an attachment to the forearm prosthesis) and the use of Velcro around the head of the racquet and shuttlecock to enable the child in the wheelchair to pick up the shuttlecock from the floor.

Basketball

The game of basketball did not have the natural evolution of most other sports. It was invented in the late nineteenth century by a group of American businessmen at a YMCA gymnasium as a less demanding, indoor alternative to football or baseball.

Wheelchair basketball: popular with both boys and girls.

The game is played on a court of indeterminate size with a basket suspended 10ft above the ground at each end. It is played by two teams of five players, although the rules provide opportunity for numerous and frequent substitutions. The following is an extract from Rule One: 'The Definition' as adopted by the International Amateur Basketball Federation:

> The purpose of each team is to throw the ball into the opponent's basket and to prevent the other team from securing the ball or scoring. The ball may be passed, thrown, batted, rolled or dribbled in any direction, subject to the restrictions laid down in the rules.

Basically, these rules determine the manner of dribbling (i.e., with either hand but not both) and the permissible forms of screening and blocking (it is essentially a non-contact sport). The rules for wheelchair basketball only differ where this is unavoidable, e.g., with regard to dribbling, jump ball, etc.

Both ambulant and wheelchair versions are excellent aids to the development of locomotor skills, gross motor co-ordination and motor fitness as well as providing a very good introduction to the intricacies of team play, co-operative endeavour and tactical expertise. In training for either version, the same five aspects of play need to be mastered before consideration is given to any of the finer points.

(i) Movement about the court – the accent should be on speed of movement and control in stopping. An ability to move forwards and backwards is necessary as well as to turn quickly in either direction. A simple game of tig is very useful in this respect. In the game situation the two most common modes

of play are man-to-man and zone play, and the selection of one as opposed to the other in some measure dictates how much movement about the court is necessary.

(ii) Passing – both two-hand and one-hand passes are permitted, the most common forms of which are the overhead pass, the javelin pass, the chest pass and the bounce pass. Each of these should be practised in a number of different situations, beginning with passing the ball in pairs or against a wall and progressing, via such activities as Captain Ball and Skittle Ball (Chapter 6: 'Projectile Management'), to a restricted full-game situation where emphasis can be placed on passing by the prohibition of dribbling for example.

(iii) Catching – this is the complementary activity to passing and is best practised via the same sort of progression, i.e., two-hand catching in the first instance, then one-hand; standing or sitting still, then on the move. A particularly useful skill for the wheelchair performer to master is the ability to gather the ball up from the floor by rolling it up the rim of the wheel as he drives past it.

(iv) Dribbling – in the ambulant and wheelchair versions of the game either hand can be used and so dribbling practices should cater for both left and right hand, either alternately or in sequence. The wheelchair dribble constitutes two bounces with one hand followed by two consecutive pushes of the wheelchair. Practices should be unopposed in the early stages, with opposition (passive at first) being introduced only gradually.

(v) Shooting – this can be done with one hand or two and should be practised both standing or sitting still and on the move, i.e., the lay-up shot. Numerous mini-competitions can be devised to make this most important (yet frequently neglected) aspect of training interesting and enjoyable.

SPECIAL CONSIDERATIONS FOR THE TEACHER

Apart from the many minor games which can be used as lead-up activities to basketball, variations on the full game can be achieved by using a lighter ball, lowering the basket or introducing new rules such as a one-yard encroachment prohibition rule to give the player with the ball more space and more time to assess the field and decide upon an appropriate course of action, i.e., whether to dribble, pass or shoot. The game is also of interest to the teacher of mixed ability groups because of the number of officials which need to be (or can be) employed (Chapter 5: 'Games').

Bowling

Bowling in its more traditional forms appears to be of European descent, having been played in its skittles variety in Germany and Holland as far back as the fourteenth century. One version, nine-pin skittles, is still very common in certain parts of England, e.g. Gloucestershire, although in many other regions it has been superseded by crown bowls, an equally long standing

tradition, or more recently by ten-pin bowling.

Although all three versions can be played by ambulant and wheelchair disabled alike, the most commonly played in schools is probably nine-pin skittles, presumably reflecting its simplicity of form; whilst in adult circles the most popular is probably crown bowls.

Nine-pin skittles
This is normally played on a wooden or concrete 'alley' (although any hall or corridor floor will suffice) with the nine pins or skittles arranged in diamond formation (Fig. 16). Each player bowls three balls underarm in an attempt to knock over all nine skittles. Should he do so with one or two balls, the skittles are re-erected and he throws the remainder, adding his tally to the original nine points scored. The theoretical maximum therefore for a three-ball 'hand' is twenty-seven points. Normally the winner is the player with the highest number of points after six hands, although this is variable.

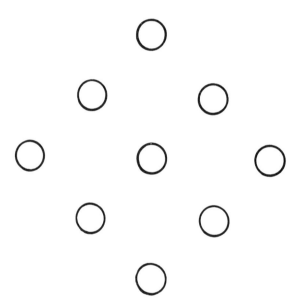

Figure 16 Nine-pin skittle formation

Ten-pin bowling
This is a younger, usually mechanical variation of the nine-pin game, in which the skittle formation is slightly different and the ball is considerably larger with three holes inset for fingers and thumb. Whereas the nine-pin skittle player has three balls, the ten-pin bowler has only two attempts per hand or 'frame'. Otherwise the rules are much the same, although the ten-pin game is normally extended to consist of ten frames rather than six.

Crown bowls

This is generally considered to be the most difficult to perform well as it combines accuracy of delivery with a precise control over force applied. It is played both on grass and indoor rinks and involves each player in an attempt to place his three biased 'woods' as close as possible (i.e., closer than those of his opponent), to a smaller round 'jack' which is previously rolled to the other end of the green. Each game is played over an agreed number of 'ends'.

SPECIAL CONSIDERATIONS FOR THE TEACHER

In all three activities the basic delivery is the same (with the exception of the finger position in ten-pin bowling), i.e., the ball is bowled underarm using one hand swung in a pendular movement. Through the use of specially constructed chutes all three versions are theoretically possible even for those children with little or no mobility of arm and shoulder.

Cricket

According to tradition, the game of cricket is derived from the mediaeval English game of stool ball, in which the batsman stood in front of a three-legged milking stool. Within the last century however, it has become almost indescribably complex and so only the basic structure is outlined here.

The central arena is a twenty-two yard strip of grass between two sets of three stumps or wickets, 28 inches high and 4 inches apart, each of which is defended by a member of the batting side. In its standard form, each team has eleven players and, whilst all eleven of the fielding side play together, only two members of the batting side take the field at any one time, remaining at the wicket until bowled, caught or stumped out. Scores are made by the batsman who faces the bowler hitting the ball far enough for himself and his partner to have time to change ends before the ball is retrieved; this constituting one run. Although technically any number of runs can be scored in this way, the number of runs taken rarely exceeds three. If the batsman hits the ball to the boundary, and providing the ball touches the ground on its way to the boundary, four runs are given. If the ball goes beyond the boundary without bouncing, six runs are awarded. Each bowler delivers an 'over' of six balls from the same end; the direction of play and the bowler being changed with every over. The winning team is normally that which can amass the highest number of runs before ten of its number have been played out.

SPECIAL CONSIDERATIONS FOR THE TEACHER

Variations in play to suit the needs of children in school, ambulant and chair-bound, are numerous.

(i) For children who have movement problems, the game can be simplified by having the bowlers bowl always from the same end to avoid the need to reposition the fielding side after every over, and the batsman provided with a runner.

Cricket: numerous modifications exist for children with movement problems or reduced arm strength.

(ii) For children with reduced arm strength, lighter bat and ball can be used and although by convention the batsman uses two hands, this rule can be relaxed to allow for participation by amputees, hemiplegics and the like.

(iii) To reduce the length of the game, either the size of each team can be reduced or each batsman can be allowed to face only a certain number of overs. In the latter case, the result would therefore depend upon the number of runs scored, the number of wickets taken and the number of declarations made (i.e., the number of players who were 'not out').

(iv) To make the batting more exciting, variations of 'non-stop' cricket can be played, whereby the batsman is forced to run every time he hits the ball and the bowler is allowed to make his next delivery even if the batsman has not yet returned to his crease.

(v) Another popular modification is the 'round robin' which can be played equally successfully indoors. In this version, there are no teams; instead, every player is given a number. Having set his field (one batsman, one bowler, one wicket-keeper, etc.) the teacher commences play in the normal way. After an agreed period (a set number of deliveries, until the batsman is out, or whatever) each player moves on to a new position (again in a predetermined order).

Fencing

Like archery, the sport of fencing has developed out of a martial art, deriving its basic form from the ancient art of offence and defence with the sword. Currently three forms of fencing are pursued competitively, each of which in

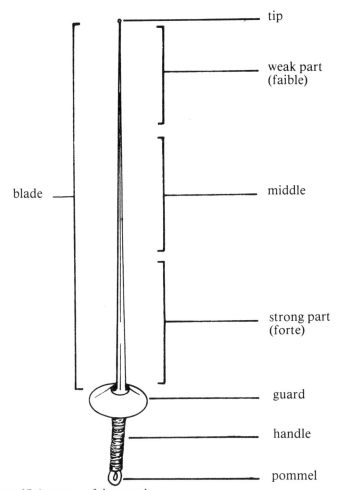

Figure 17 Anatomy of the sword

its own way reflects the sport's military history. The foil is derived from the traditional training weapon, the epée is a derivation of the duelling rapier, and the sabre was developed for use on horseback. Although the details of the three types of sword vary according to their function, the basic anatomy is the same in each case (Fig. 17).

In wheelchair as in ambulant competition, fencing with the foil is practised by men and women, whereas epée and sabre are reserved for the male competitor. Whilst ambulant competitors are allowed to move forwards and backwards along a 'piste' (12 metres long for foil, 14 metres long for epée and sabre), the wheelchair competition is conducted in static form with the chairs anchored to a frame on the floor. The position of each chair relative to the other depends upon whether the fencers are of the same hand or of opposite hands (Fig. 18).

For fencers of the same hand

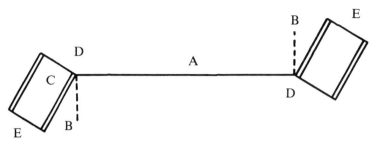

For fencers of opposite hands

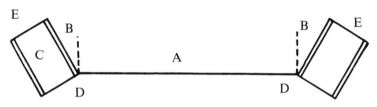

left-hander   right-hander

A — Adjustable central bar
B — Equal angles of between 15° and 20°
C — Whole section adjustable for left-handed fencers
D — Rail allows front wheels to touch the central bar
E — System of rails to allow chairs to be wheeled on, secured and
     aligned correctly.

Figure 18 Layout of the fencing frame (Guttmann 1976)

Foil

In fencing with the foil all scoring is done with the tip of the weapon and must involve a positive contact established on a valid part of the target, i.e., the body, front and back, excluding the head, arms, legs and buttocks.

Epée

In epée competition, as with foil, all scoring has to be done with the tip of the sword, but in this case the target area is extended to include the whole body.

Sabre

As this was initially a cavalry weapon, it is, even in competition today, primarily a slashing instrument. Hits can be made not only with the tip, as in the other weapons, but also with the whole of the front edge of the blade and the upper third of the back edge. The target area is the trunk, the arms and the head.

SPECIAL CONSIDERATIONS FOR THE TEACHER

Fencing is a dynamic sport whether performed standing or from a wheelchair, promoting balance and flexibility, precision of movement and concentration. It is also, in untrained hands, an extremely dangerous sport and the following precautions should be taken at all times:

(i) No-one should ever be allowed to engage in sword play unless properly clad in mask, jacket or 'plaestron', and, preferably, gloves;

(ii) The condition of all weapons, particularly their tips, should be checked before each contest.

(iii) Even in practice, sword thrusts should be confined to the valid target areas.

Because of the complexity of this sport, not only from the point of view of performance and coaching, but also of judging and presiding over competitions, unless the teacher is suitably proficient himself, the services of a professional should be employed.

Hockey

Depending on the country of one's birth, the word 'hockey' is associated either with grass or with ice. In its original form, however, it was played on grass or dirt, and, like many other activities, it was the British Army of the nineteenth century which was responsible for its world-wide dissemination and diversification. Then, as now, field hockey was played at a very high level in Europe and in India. But it was when faced with the harsh winters of Canada that the British Army first found a need to find an alternative surface on which to play. Today ice hockey is Canada's national sport.

Although there is inevitably some variation in the rules, basically both forms of the game have the same objects. Both games are played on a rectangular pitch with a netted goal at each end. Two teams are involved in the contest, each attempting to make the ball or puck enter the opponent's goal. The hooked stick carried by each player is generally the only means of propelling the ball or puck allowed. The goalkeepers however are also allowed to use their feet and in field hockey the hands can be used, but only to stop the ball in flight, not to throw, push or bat the ball.

SPECIAL CONSIDERATIONS FOR THE TEACHER

Whether played in wheelchairs, on the feet or on skates, hockey can be a most enjoyable activity, combining gross motor skills with precise control of the hands. It is an excellent aid to motor fitness and provides a good introduction to team play. For those children who have movement problems or who experience difficulty in the control of a stick, the game can be played indoors or on a smaller outdoor pitch, and a lighter, larger ball can be used. Additionally, in activities modelled on field hockey, it is also worth considering the use of back sticks (i.e., permitting the use of both sides of the stick) even if only in the

early stages of play. Other variations in play include the following:

(i) Roller hockey – for ambulant children who do not have access to an ice rink, hockey played on roller skates is an interesting alternative which can be as demanding as it is enjoyable. An ability to roller skate is an obvious prerequisite, and basic skills should be mastered *before* a child is allowed to participate in any activity as fast as roller hockey;

(ii) Wheelchair hockey – indoor hockey played in wheelchairs can be very taxing and very skilful. If shortened hockey sticks can be used – short enough to be managed in one hand – then impairment to chair control is only minimal. A small, deflated plastic football makes a useful puck-substitute;

(iii) Scooter board hockey – For ambulant children and those normally confined to a wheelchair, scooter board hockey provides an opportunity to compete together on equal terms. The scooterboard is rather like a large tray on castor wheels and is propelled by pushing against the floor with the hands. Because play is so close to the ground it is advisable to use sticks with short handles as in wheelchair hockey.

N.B. The only dangers inherent in the playing of hockey (other than those associated with any form of locomotor activity) are those arising from over-enthusiastic use of the stick. If the emphasis is placed on keeping the stick low at all times, and on hitting the ball or puck accurately rather than hard, then hopefully such accidents can be avoided.

Rounders

The game of rounders is probably as old as the game of cricket if not older, and being similar in form, it requires the same sort of skills of each participant. Strangely, rounders is now almost universally considered a girls' game, though it is difficult to imagine why this should be so; particularly as in America it has given rise to one of the most popular bastions of male athleticism, the game of baseball.

Rounders, baseball and softball are so similar in fact that there is need only to outline one of them. The teacher interested in promoting either of the other two should find little difficulty in adapting what is written here to his own particular needs.

Rounders, like cricket, is a bat and ball activity. But whereas in cricket the batsman runs a straight-line course, in rounders the batsman has four bases to run around, the infield area being vaguely diamond-shaped (Fig. 19). With the fielding team in position, one member of the batting team goes to the batting square to face the bowler. With the bowler bowling underarm, the batsman must attempt to hit the first good delivery and then run for the first base. Should he be unable to run all the way round, he can stop at any of the other bases en route, provided one of his teammates is not already occupying that base. A rounder is scored for every person who manages to run all the way round *without* stopping on the way. A player is declared out either if the ball

he has just hit is caught before it touches the ground, or if one of the fielding team manages to place the ball on the base to which he is running before he can reach it. Each team carries on scoring until all its players are declared out.

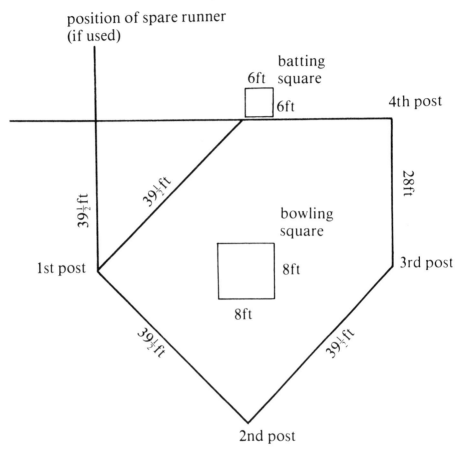

position of spare runner
(if used)

batting
6ft square
6ft

4th post

bowling
square
8ft

1st post

3rd post

28ft

$39\frac{1}{2}$ft

$39\frac{1}{2}$ft

$39\frac{1}{2}$ft

$39\frac{1}{2}$ft

8ft

2nd post

Figure 19 Layout of a rounders pitch

SPECIAL CONSIDERATIONS FOR THE TEACHER

In the special school, rounders is often taught in preference to cricket. In part this is because it is more acceptable to both sexes, and in part it is because of the provision for resting en route whilst batting. Additionally, because of its compactness it is more suitable for play indoors, and as the bat and ball used are smaller and lighter, it only requires the batsman to use one hand.

Variations in play tending to make the game more attractive to the novice include

(i) Allowing each batsman three attempts at hitting the ball. If he hits either of the first two well enough, he can elect to run then; after the third attempt he must run regardless;

(ii) Speeding up the game by declaring a whole team out on a single catch.

N.B. Whilst the game is wholly appropriate for chairbound and ambulant children, care needs to be taken to ensure that children waiting to bat or children already out sit well back behind the batting square so as not to obstruct play.

Soccer

The game of soccer, or Association Football as it is properly called, is descended from a game called 'harpastum' which was popular in Ancient Rome. Even in its present form, its history goes back as far as mediaeval England when games of football are said to have been played between whole villages over miles of open countryside with very few rules!

The modern game, played on a rectangular pitch 100–130 yards in length, is more civilised and, like field hockey, involves just eleven people in each team in an attempt to make the ball enter the opponent's goal. But whereas in hockey the ball is propelled with a stick, in soccer just the feet are used; or more accurately the feet, knees, chest and head. In fact the only body parts which cannot be used (except by the goalkeepers) are the hands and arms. As a result, the effective training schedule includes not just kicking (which should aim at accuracy rather than distance), but also heading and more general ball skills such as trapping the ball on the thigh or the chest, dribbling, tackling and shielding the ball from an opponent.

Kicking
Practices should not only be performed with the dominant foot. Various types of kick should be practised, e.g. high/low, short/long; with instep/top of foot; etc. Passing drills should stress accuracy and can be practised unopposed in pairs first of all and then in two versus two and three versus three situations.

Heading
Emphasis should be placed upon 'keeping the eyes on the ball'. This encourages a correct position i.e., the ball being met by the forehead. Drills should begin at close range with one child throwing the ball up to another to be headed back.

Trapping
Traditionally, the ball is 'trapped' between the underside of the foot and the ground, although a more fashionable alternative involves controlling the ball on the chest, the thigh or the top of the foot. As both skills are primarily a question of timing, they can only be improved by practice.

Dribbling

Emphasis should be placed on close control of the ball using both feet. Progressive practices should include slow dribbling unobstructed, faster dribbling and dribbling around obstacles.

Tackling and shielding the ball

These are best practised in controlled situations in the first instance and only gradually incorporated into complex game situations.

A popular variation on the full game is five-a-side soccer which is usually played indoors. For this reason the ball is not normally allowed above shoulder height. This tends to be a much faster, more fluent game as the ball is kept in play by the surrounding walls. For this reason too it is particularly attractive to the child with movement difficulties or poor ball control.

SPECIAL CONSIDERATIONS FOR THE TEACHER

To play soccer one obviously needs to be able to use the feet. However, because of the enormous following which soccer enjoys by handicapped and able-bodied boys alike, numerous modifications exist, most of which are in fact a combination of soccer, hockey and handball.

The game of handball is extremely popular on the Continent although it has yet to establish itself on a large scale in Britain. Nonetheless, it would appear to be the ideal complementary activity to soccer for those children who are unable to use their feet.

Table Tennis

Table tennis was first introduced as an indoor alternative to lawn tennis in London in the late nineteenth century. Since that time it has achieved world-wide popularity.

In the standard version, the table is 9 feet long by 5 feet wide and set at a height of 2 feet 6 inches above the floor. The top surface of the table is divided into two by a net 6 inches high across the middle.

The object of the game as in all the racquet games, is to hit the ball 'in court' and yet in such a way that the opponent is unable to return it. In table tennis 'in court', in all situations other than the service, implies that the ball has crossed the net without bouncing and then bounced on the opponent's half of the table. In the service, the ball must bounce on both sides of the net.

The game can be played singles or doubles and the winning team is the first to reach twenty-one points, provided the winner is at least two points clear. Otherwise play continues until either team establishes a two-point lead. In both singles and doubles, each team serves for only five points at a time. In rallying too, doubles players must alternate, being allowed no more than one shot each in sequence.

The only strokes that need teaching to the novice are the service and the

Wheelchair handball.
The ideal complement to soccer for those children unable to use their feet.

basic forehand and backhand drive, although after a time top-spin and back-spin can be introduced.

SPECIAL CONSIDERATIONS FOR THE TEACHER

Table tennis is extremely popular in the special school and not without good reason. It requires neither great strength nor mobility, yet it can be very competitive and thoroughly enjoyable for expert and novice alike. Similarly the equipment required is minimal and this needs little if any modification. The only other considerations I would recommend to the teacher are as follows:

(i) Although there is no reason why children in wheelchairs should not play table tennis – there are after all international competitions for adult paraplegics – when playing against ambulant children in competition, the ambulant child should be seated as well. Apart from the disadvantage the chairbound child has in terms of mobility about the table, the player accustomed to wheelchair table tennis is used to receiving the ball at a totally different angle from that delivered by a player in the standing position.

(ii) The grip most commonly used for table tennis is that whereby the thumb and forefinger lie flat on opposite faces of the bat whilst the three remaining fingers are wrapped around the handle. For high level quadriplegics and others unable to hold the bat, the hand should be bandaged to the bat in this position. For the more able wheelchair player, however, it is sometimes helpful to teach the 'pen-hold' grip because of the angle to the table which the wheelchair player is forced to adopt. In this grip, as the name suggests, the handle is held as if holding a pen with the head of the bat pointing down.

Volleyball

Volleyball like basketball owes its beginning to an American and to the YMCA. It was created in 1895 and, just as badminton and hockey had been internationalised by the British Army, it too was first introduced to the world by the U.S. Army. By 1918 it had reached Britain and by the end of the Second World War it was being played extensively throughout Europe and the Far East.

In its usual form, volleyball is played on an indoor court approximately 60 feet long by 30 feet wide across the centre of which is a net 3 feet 3 inches deep so positioned that at its edge it is 8 feet above the floor. The game itself is played by two teams of six people using bare hands and a ball which, although it is almost as large as a football (26 inches in circumference as opposed to 27), is considerably lighter in weight (9–10 ounces as opposed to 14–16 ounces).

Like badminton, the game is played on the volley (hence its name), but in volleyball each team is allowed to play the ball three times before it has to cross the net. Points are awarded in exactly the same way as in badminton, i.e., they can only be scored by the serving team and are made either by forcing an error on the part of the opposition (e.g., by their hitting the ball into the net or out of court), or by hitting the ball in such a way that the opposition cannot play it before it touches the floor. Each game is won by the first side to score fifteen points.

The basic shots in volleyball, which really need to be practised in isolation before they are introduced to the game situation, are the serve, the dig, the set, the spike and the block.

The serve

This is taken from the back right-hand corner of the court and can be played overarm (as in the tennis serve) or underarm. Like all other shots in volleyball the serve has to clear the net without bouncing.

The dig

This is the basic defensive shot. Although it is usually played with two hands, it is particularly useful for wheelchair players to be able to return the ball with one hand.

The set

This is a high shot played to or along the net with the intention that the ball will be hit across the net with greater effect by another player on the same side.

The spike

This is the complement to the 'set' and is usually played by a player at the net who hits the ball across the net hard and in a downward direction.

The block

This is the defensive position adopted to oppose the 'spike'. It is played by jumping with both arms extended at the place where the spike is to be made.

SPECIAL CONSIDERATIONS FOR THE TEACHER

Variations on volleyball are becoming very popular with handicapped children because of the extent to which the game can be slowed down or otherwise modified. Even for teams composed entirely of wheelchair players the only shots which cannot be played are the spike and the block, although with some adjustment to the height of the net even these are possible. Other adjustments to the normal game which can prove helpful in the special school are the following:

(i) Although the conventional service should be used whenever possible, (and for wheelchair players the underarm serve played at the side of the chair is usually easiest), it makes no real difference to the rest of the game if the server is allowed to throw the ball into play.

(ii) For children who find they cannot cope with the volleying game, a catch-and-throw version can be quite effective, particularly if the net is raised a little to give the other side more time to prepare for the catch.

(iii) For severely handicapped children who for various reasons are too slow and/or weak to cope with the speed and weight of the ball, a balloon can be substituted to great effect. With the net lowered slightly this version can be played in the standing position, from the wheelchair or sitting on the floor.

Summary

Twelve major sporting activities have been reviewed in this chapter, archery, athletics, badminton, basketball, bowling, cricket, fencing, hockey, rounders, soccer, table tennis and volleyball. The treatment each has received, whether from the point of view of its history, character, system of rules or teaching, has been unavoidably scant. Inevitably, there are other major activities, such as tennis, golf, croquet and snooker, that have not been mentioned at all.

But the intention was never to offer detailed coaching schedules in the first place. Whole volumes have been written with this in mind for *each* of these sports. The interested reader has only to consult his library. What has been attempted through this chapter is the presentation of a representative cross-section of activities to demonstrate the scope that exists in the recreation field even for severely physically handicapped children.

Obviously not all children are able or even want to play in all of these activities. Some, presumably, will want to play others. In either case, using the information contained in this chapter as a model (in particular the sections on modifications and other considerations for the teacher), it should be quite possible for the teacher to devise similar routines appropriate to the situation in hand.

In the case of the child not interested in any competitive sports, there are alternatives which are equally valuable, such as recreative swimming and outdoor pursuits. It is with these activities that the next two chapters are concerned.

REFERENCES

Adams, R. C., Daniel, A. N. & Rullman, L. (1975) *Games, sports and exercises for the physically handicapped*. Lea & Febiger: Philadelphia.
Guttmann, Sir L. (1976) *Textbook of sport for the disabled*. HM & M Publishers: Aylesbury.
Shivers, J. S. & Fait, H. F. (1975) *Therapeutic and adapted recreational services*. Lea & Febiger: Philadelphia.
N.B. Reference was also made to the Official Handbooks of certain of the National Governing Bodies of Sport in the United Kingdom.

8

Swimming

People have probably known about the values of exercising and even resting in warm water since time immemorial. Certainly the Romans had it down to a fine art some 2000 years ago. But the marriage of these restorative and curative aspects of water immersion with the use of swimming as a form of recreation is considerably younger. And the application of these techniques to the rehabilitation of the physically handicapped is younger still.

> Although the use of water as a therapeutic agent has been used for many years, the utilization of definite swimming strokes and swim play adapted and modified for the physically handicapped is a comparatively recent development (Newman 1976).

One of the most significant factors in this recent popularisation of swimming for the handicapped has been the growing awareness of the values of a comprehensive programme of physical education in special schools.

As was indicated in Chapter 2, of the ninety schools which proffered information on their programmes and facilities, only four do not teach swimming. What is more, fifty-seven of the ninety (63%) have their own pool; a requirement which more and more nowadays is featured as a priority when new schools are being planned. And despite the expense this incurs, one does not have to look far to find reasons to justify this provision.

Once they are in the water, even children who spend most of their lives being supported by calipers, crutches, wheelchairs or artificial limbs find, to their amazement and disbelief in the first instance, that they are able to support their weight totally unassisted (Froude's Law, Chapter 5, p. 87). For many, swimming provides the only opportunity in their whole lives where such independence of movement is possible. There can surely be no greater motivation towards further participation in an activity nor greater justification for the provision of facilities.

But even for children whose handicap is not so severe, the benefits which can be derived from swimming are numerous.

(i) Swimming stimulates the blood circulation, improves muscle tone and is universally recognised as one of the best ways to increase or to maintain motor fitness.

(ii) Because of the supportive qualities of water, the psychological boost which accompanies the experience of independence of movement is immensely

valuable, carrying over its effect into many other aspects of life.

(iii) Swimming is possibly the only activity in which almost all children can participate, irrespective of handicap. As such, it is the ideal medium through which to foster social and recreational integration. For such integration to be possible special consideration needs to be given to one thing only, water temperature.

For most normal purposes, swimming pools are maintained at approximately 76°F (24.5°C), although by some teachers this is believed to be a little on the cool side not just for teaching beginners, but for any activities which do not entail constant movement. For hydrotherapy purposes on the other hand, a temperature of 94°F (34.5°C) is required; this being an optimum for the stimulation of blood circulation and, in consequence, for the loosening of stiff joints. For teaching purposes in the special school therefore, a compromise is recommended. For most situations a water temperature of 86°F (30°C) is appropriate, although for more active children, particularly when involved in competition, this can be safely reduced to 82°F (28°C).

Having gained access to a pool and having established a suitable water temperature, the teacher's thoughts must return to pedagogy. And in the early stages of teaching, i.e., with beginners, the biggest question is not so much what should be taught as by what method(s) it should be taught.

The former is quite straightforward. Most teachers would agree that the first priority is survival, this being assured through the acquisition of confidence in water, an ability to maintain a stable position, i.e., wherein breathing is not obstructed, and ultimately through an ability to swim. Recreational pursuits and the ability to swim using a variety of strokes are of secondary significance.

But an answer to the question of teaching method is more difficult to achieve; this being the product of deliberations concerning individual differences (both in those under instruction and in those teaching), the type and extent of facilities, the number of staff available, the size of group under instruction and the objects of any one lesson. Although it is not recommended that teachers opt for any one method to the exclusion of all others, there are a variety of techniques which can be employed, (e.g., the shallow-water method, the single-stroke method, the multi-stroke method). Basically, however, these all fall into two groups, those which permit the use of artificial aids and those which do not. It is with this distinction that the next section is principally concerned.

Aids v. no aids

As the defence of either case depends to some extent on the size of the group under instruction and the number of instructors available at any one time, reference is made once again to the research findings outlined in Chapter 2.

Despite the fact that the size of group considered appropriate in the special school is very much smaller than that which is common in ordinary schools, there is still considerable variation in actual group size; some groups being

smaller than five in number, whilst others total more than fifteen (Table 9, Chapter 2).

By far the most important implication from this is that what is necessary and/or appropriate for one child is not necessarily so for another. As a result, there can be no hard and fast rules as to which is the most acceptable form of instruction. The question of the method by which children are taught to swim must depend on the specific needs of the individual, whether instruction be in a group or on a one-to-one basis. There are of course advantages and disadvantages to both methods. The teachers should be aware of these and assess their relevance to each child separately. In the final analysis, it should be this process which determines how many children are able to cope with group instruction and how many need teaching on a one-to-one basis.

Basically, the main advantage of allowing a child to use an artificial aid, an inflatable tyre, a buoyancy jacket, water wings or whatever, is that he is immediately able to 'swim' independent of adult assistance. This means that from very early on one instructor in the water can cope with several non-swimmers, even though they might be quite unable to stand on the bottom. Obviously this sort of economy is not possible for the teacher who insists on teaching without the use of artificial aids. In the early stages at least, i.e., until each child can swim properly, all such teaching has to be on a one-to-one basis.

But there are disadvantages too in the use of aids. Many children tend to develop a dependence on their tyre as they do upon their sticks or wheelchair, and they are often reluctant to relinquish it, even when it is no longer necessary. Additionally, for children who have defective balance mechanisms, the tyre represents a form of buoyancy and stability which is unnatural and therefore confusing.

However, because of the 'short-circuiting' effect of using aids, given a suitably disposed group of children of manageable size (preferably five to ten in number), the teacher can very quickly reach the stage where proper swimming strokes are taught, by methods which vary very little from the conventional. (See 'Swimming Strokes' p. 146.)

But in most schools there are inevitably some children who, for reasons physical or psychological, are not likely to respond to this sort of programmed instruction. For these, provision should be made for individual teaching on a one-to-one basis. This can be done quite successfully using aids if the teacher deems it appropriate, but should he not, there is one technique in particular which has the distinction not only of denying *all* use of aids, but also of having been devised specially for use with physically handicapped children. This method begins, not with any of the four standard swimming strokes, but with the pattern of movement peculiar to the individual under instruction. From this a tailor-made, often unique 'stroke' is fashioned. Because of the success this technique has enjoyed since its creation in 1949, the Halliwick method is therefore worthy of special mention.

The Halliwick method

This method of swimming instruction was developed by an engineer and, not surprisingly, was based upon sound scientific principles (McMillan, 1970 & 73). The starting point in the creation of this technique was the recognition of the fact that no human being willingly makes a movement other than from a position of stability. Consequently, even for the handicapped child, whose balance is likely to be defective, an essential prerequisite to swimming has to be the (learned) ability to stabilise the body in water. This indicated to McMillan the need to study the problems relating to the shape and density of the handicapped in water and thence to develop techniques to compensate for these problems, applying to this task an engineer's knowledge of the characteristics, properties and principles associated with water. It was as a direct result of these investigations, based on sound physiological and hydrodynamic principles, that the teaching progression known as the Halliwick Method was created. Basically, the complete programme is divisible into ten stages.

(i) Mental adjustment The teacher's first task is the familiarisation of the child with the strange, new environment in which he finds himself. This can be achieved through any number of play situations, depending on the age of the child, each of which should be designed to enable the child to compare and contrast the properties of air and water.

(ii) Disengagement Through head control and the ability to balance in the water, the child is encouraged to accept independent status in the water, standing and/or floating without support from the teacher.

(iii) Vertical rotation control The child learns to originate and control all movements in a vertical plane, i.e., in rotation around the pelvic axis. This enables the child to move from an upright position to a prone or supine floating position.

(iv) Lateral rotation control The child learns to originate and control all movements in a lateral plane, i.e., in rotation around the spine. This enables the child to move from a supine floating position through the prone position and on or back to the supine position.

(v) Combined rotation The child learns to originate and control movements occurring in both vertical and lateral planes simultaneously. This enables the child who is unsteady on his feet to control a fall forwards (vertical rotation) by turning sideways (lateral rotation) thus ending up on his back.

(vi) Use of upthrust This is an extension of the mental adjustment process and might alternatively be called 'a period of mental inversion', as it involves demonstration of the fact that the force of water acts upwards and *not* downwards as most people fear. It is at this stage that the 'swimmer' is taught to use his patterns of rotational control to return to a safe breathing position.

(vii) Balance is stillness The child is taught to control his position in the water by resisting the effects of turbulence applied at specific points about the body. To do this successfully, the child is forced to use contra-rotational patterns in his efforts to maintain a balanced position.

(viii) Turbulent gliding Having learnt to control his body in a static position, the child is next taught to maintain his balance whilst the body is being moved through the water in a swimming position. This is done without touching the child by the use of turbulence, or more specifically, by the exploitation of the Transom Effect, i.e. by a rapid paddling action with the hands just below the surface of the water, a negative pressure area is created towards which the floating child is drawn. If the teacher moves about the pool whilst continuing this action, the child follows even though at this stage he is required to make no positive contribution himself.

(ix) Simple progression The swimmer makes small and very controlled movements in an effort to create independent propulsion. At this stage he is still assisted by the effects of turbulent gliding created by the teacher, but to an ever decreasing extent.

(x) Basic movement A basic swimming movement is developed, using the arms, legs, or both according to the capabilities of the individual. The child is now swimming totally independently.

It was mentioned earlier, both in this chapter with regard to swimming and in Chapter 5 with regard to gymnastics, that it is sometimes deemed necessary by teachers to opt for one particular method of instruction to the exclusion of all others. Once again, I would suggest that it might be preferable for a teacher to have more than one 'string to his bow'. Within the special school the differences between individuals are so numerous and so extensive that some children will respond best to one method, e.g., a personalised style of teaching such as the Halliwick method, whilst others will respond better to another method, e.g., by more conventional methods of instruction. Both can be successful: it is for the teacher to decide which is appropriate for each child. But, whichever is used, it should be remembered that neither has any magical properties. Used sensibly, either can enable even a severely handicapped child to move independently in water. But neither can transform the movement potential of a particular handicap. So, whilst a spina bifida child might reasonably be expected to develop efficient front and back crawl and breast-stroke as well (in each case using arms only), and a spastic hemiplegic might develop his own unique one-sided stroke until he can swim both fast and far, the advanced muscular dystrophy sufferer, and probably the severe spastic quadriplegic as well, is never likely to proceed beyond a slow laborious back-sculling action. In each case, however, for the individual concerned, any progress is immeasurably worthwhile.

Swimming strokes

Whether a child has been taught the rudiments of watermanship via the spontaneous 'independence' of the inflated tyre or the more circuitous route of the Halliwick method, at some stage for most children the time comes when they are ready to receive instruction in orthodox swimming strokes – even if the end result is likely to be somewhat unusual.

It is for this reason that the following brief description of each of the conventional swimming strokes is offered. The order in which they are presented is that in which they are most commonly taught, although the decision as to whether a child starts on his back or on his front is a matter of personal preference. No child should be forced to learn back-sculling, breaststroke, or any other stroke as his first introduction to swimming simply because everyone else in his class is doing so.

Each stroke is described as it is performed by the able-bodied swimmer and it should be remembered that many handicapped children will only approximate to these patterns. In each case the teacher should recognise that confidence in the water, independence of movement (by whatever means) and regular respiration are far more important than 'good style'.

Whichever stroke is being introduced, however, for children with a minimal degree of motor impairment the teacher might find the technique of 'swim patterning' useful.

Swim patterning is a method whereby the development of the child can be aided through the use of a series of co-ordinated patterns (Newman 1976).

More specifically, it is a means of 'grooving in' those parts of a swimming stroke which a child finds difficult to perform. It is the application to swimming of the standard therapeutic technique of movement patterning, whereby each required movement is rehearsed many times over. (Such rehearsal can therefore be practised on land as well as in water.) In the early stages the teacher or therapist holds the limbs being exercised and actually moves them through the appropriate range of movements with the child playing a totally passive role. Gradually the child applies force to the movement as well, thus reinforcing the efforts of the teacher with valuable internal feedback, until ultimately he is capable of performing the movement without any physical guidance from the teacher at all. It should be emphasised, however, that this method of patterning is only likely to be successful with children whose movement impairment is largely experiential (e.g., the asthmatic child whose shoulder immobility is such that his back stroke is severely restricted). No amount of exercise is going to restore function to completely paralysed limbs.

There now follows a description of those strokes which can reasonably be expected to be acquired by children with various forms of physical handicap.

Back-sculling

This is generally the first stroke to be introduced as it does not require any special training in breathing. It has the added advantage of being equally possible for children who have either no use of their legs or no use of their arms.

Basically it requires the swimmer to lie on his back (Fig. 20) and perform symmetrical and simultaneous adductor thrusts of the legs or the arms or both. After each stroke, there should be a pause to enable the body to glide, but this is variable in its importance depending on the extent to which arms, legs, or both can be used to full effect. The less power that is created with each stroke, the less successful the glide is likely to be.

Old English back stroke

This is a natural extension of the back-sculling pattern of movement for those with good use of arms and shoulders (Fig. 21). It combines the same leg movement with a much fuller sweep of the arms, bringing them both out of the water as far above the head as possible. This extended arm action almost inevitably means that the face is splashed quite a lot with each stroke. As such it should not be introduced until the child is totally water-confident.

Back crawl

Although the transition from the symmetrical pattern of the Old English back stroke to the asymmetrical action of the back crawl (Fig. 22) is sometimes a problem – arm circling in the gymnasium can be useful in this respect – the latter is a far more efficient stroke in that the 'windmill' arm action causes continuous pressure to be applied to the water (i.e., by one arm then the other). This avoids the tendency for the head to sink during performance of the Old English back stroke by eliminating the glide phase. The leg action for both front and back crawl is a fast, short, alternating kick.

Breast stroke

This is a particularly useful stroke for paraplegics as it can be performed quite satisfactorily using just the arms. The actual stroke pattern (Fig. 23) is much like the back-scull, incorporating a symmetrical 'frog-kick' and an abduction-adduction pull with the arms. As with the other symmetrical patterns, when performed well there is an extended glide between each stroke.

Front crawl

This is generally the fastest and most efficient stroke of all (Fig. 24) combining a rapid, alternating leg kick with a continuous, streamlined windmill arm-action. It is also commonly the last stroke to be mastered as it involves prone lying and facial immersion, the two aspects of watermanship most frequently resisted.

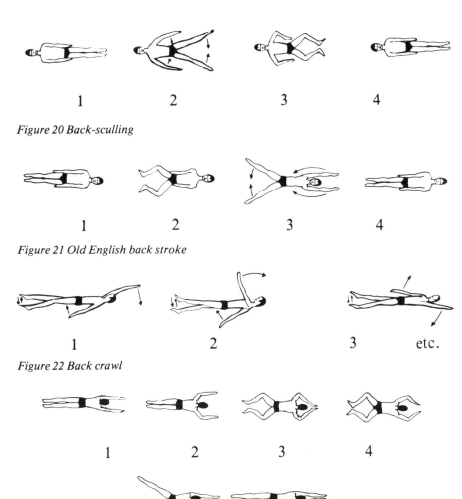

Figure 20 Back-sculling

Figure 21 Old English back stroke

Figure 22 Back crawl

Figure 23 Breast stroke

Figure 24 Front crawl

Other aspects of the swimming programme

Apart from basic watermanship and the teaching of swimming strokes, there are various other activities which might usefully contribute to the overall swimming programme. These include personal survival/drown-proofing techniques, life saving, sub-aqua, synchronised swimming and water polo.

Personal survival

This part of the swimming programme provides a practical application of swimming ability in situations which simulate real-life emergencies in water. The techniques that need to be mastered include treading water, floating, surface diving, swimming underwater, swimming in clothes and the use of clothing as floats.

Life saving

Although with severely physically handicapped children this aspect of water safety is likely to have little practical application, to the minimally impaired child it can mark a very real achievement on a scale which permits direct comparison with their able-bodied peers. Techniques include various forms of towing and controlling a struggling swimmer, artificial respiration and distance swimming, all of which have to be supported by an understanding of basic anatomy and physiology.

Sub-aqua

The sport of underwater swimming, whether using snorkel or aqualung, is well within the realm of possibility for many physically handicapped children once they have demonstrated competency at surface swimming. It is, however, an obviously dangerous pastime without expert supervision and should only be taught by persons qualified to do so.

Synchronised swimming

This can be a most useful adjunct to the teaching of surface swimming strokes as well as an opportunity to introduce children to 'aquabatics'. In general terms, synchronised swimming involves the simultaneous performance by a group of swimmers of a prescribed sequence of movements, usually combining controlled swimming with various twists, turns and somersaults. However, it can be as interesting, enjoyable and useful to the relative novice (through the rehearsal and rhythmic performance to music of even basic swimming strokes) as to the more advanced swimmer.

Water polo

This is a most popular ball game, rather like handball, only played in water. It combines the gross motor control and motor fitness achieved through swimming with the hand-eye co-ordination, tactical skill and sheer enjoyment of a ball game. Not surprisingly, therefore, it is very popular as an end-of-lesson 'perk'.

Special considerations for the teacher

Obviously, neither all of these activities nor all of the swimming strokes which preceded them are possible for all the children in the special school. But many develop sufficient expertise in water to be able to tackle most of them. Nonetheless, particular handicaps do bring with them particular problems, and where such exist, the teacher should be aware of them.

Spina bifida

Spina bifida children share a common difficulty or embarassment with all other flaccid paraplegics, namely, because their legs contain no tonic muscle there is a tendency for them to float. Unfortunately they do not all float to the same extent and for some children who swim an upright sort of breast stroke, unless they are swimming at speed (which lifts the legs to the surface), the legs are often in danger of dragging along the bottom of the pool. Apart from the obviously detrimental effect this has on the progress of the swimmer (even though the cause of his slow progress cannot be felt), such a child runs the risk of sustaining quite extensive damage to the feet, sufficient to keep him out of the pool for several weeks. This unfortunate situation can be avoided if children at risk wear nylon socks or some other such protective covering.

Cerebral palsy

It has already been said that no two cases of cerebral palsy are the same. Each child presents a completely new challenge and, perhaps more than with any other condition, individual teaching is essential. There is, however, one problem particularly associated with cerebral palsy sufferers, namely, a difficulty in trying to cough or to exhale forcibly through the mouth. This can be taught by using pop-out paper whistles in a pool-side situation or by playing with plastic 'poached eggs' in the water. These can be made to flip over if they are blown forcefully enough.

Epilepsy

Although it would be overcautious to suggest that epileptic children should not be allowed to go swimming at all, one cannot stress too strongly the need to maintain a constant vigil – preferably by a pool attendant set aside just to keep an eye on them – whenever such children are in the pool – even if there are only one or two. Although it is uncommon for epileptics to go into spasm when they are actively involved in something, I have personally known an epileptic boy have a fit whilst swimming under water. In such a case, prompt action is imperative. The child should be brought to the surface and, depending upon the severity of the attack, it should be allowed to run its course either with the child being supported in the water, or, in the less severe case, after the child has been put on the pool surround.

Children who are unsteady on their feet or who normally use calipers, sticks or wheelchair need to be escorted to the poolside until an alternative, independent mode of transfer can be devised.

Among other considerations which the teacher might find useful are the following:

Methods of entry and exit

ENTRY

Children who walk quite normally should have no problems entering or leaving the pool although they should be reminded that pool surrounds inevitably become wet and are therefore dangerous. Running on the poolside should be prohibited at all times.

Even though some children walk quite well in orthopaedic shoes, in calipers or on sticks, walking bare-foot is quite a different matter. Unless they can reach the poolside by some other method, e.g., crawling or shuffling without risk of abrasions to feet, knees or other body parts, they should use a chair. Children who are unable to stand at all have to use a chair.

For these purposes the ideal means of conveyance is the shower chair as these are rust-resistant. Particularly with children with paralysed legs one should always pull the chair backwards as this avoids the possibility of catching the feet on the floor or trapping them under the wheels.

Once at the poolside, the easiest method of entry for such children is a rolling action, whereby the child sits with his feet in the water, turns or is turned onto his front, and lowers himself or is lowered into the pool, where, in the case of the severely handicapped child, someone should be waiting to receive him. Alternatively, where the design of the pool permits, children may shuffle down a ramp into the water in a sitting position, or else use a mechanical hoist.

EXIT

Most ambulant children manage to find their own way of getting out of the pool quite successfully. The only children likely to need special help in this respect are arm-amputees and hemiplegics, both of whom usually devise methods adapted to their own special needs.

More severely handicapped children need assistance of a more positive kind, usually involving able-bodied aides both in the water and on the poolside. Perhaps the most common technique is that which uses the buoyancy of the water to help 'bounce' the child onto the poolside. But whichever method is used, one should never pull children out of the pool by their forearms. If there is no weakness of the shoulders and arms, lifting under the armpits is permissible; otherwise such children should be lifted bodily. In these cases a ramped entry or a mechanical hoist can be very useful.

Safety

As one of the main objectives in teaching swimming is to preserve life in the event of an accident, it should never be forgotten that man in water is out of his natural element. Wherever possible the following guidelines should be observed:

(i) No child should enter the water until the teacher gives permission;

(ii) In teaching a child to swim without the use of aids, a one-to-one relationship must be maintained at all times;

(iii) No non-swimmer, however well supported by aids, should be allowed out of his depth unless accompanied by a competent swimmer;

(iv) All swimming aids, particularly the inflatable variety, should be regularly inspected;

(v) No child learning to swim using an artificial aid should be allowed to remove this aid without permission. Where such permission is given, the child should be supervised on a one-to-one basis;

(vi) Teaching physically handicapped children to swim usually requires the teacher to be in the water with the children. Whenever this is the case, an assistant should always be available on the poolside so that, in the event of an emergency, the teacher does not have to leave the rest of his group unattended;

(vii) At least one member of the staff present on the poolside should be qualified in life-saving.

Recognition of achievement

For a child in any learning situation, it is a tremendous incentive to know that there is a recognisable and tangible goal at the end of his endeavours, and a source of great satisfaction when such a goal is achieved.

The example which is cited in Fig. 25 has been used quite successfully with children of all ages and of many different disabilities. It is not perfect in its design, nor does it have any magical properties. Even at this level, there are some children who cannot progress through the whole range. But at least through this scheme they can all get beyond the starting line.

YELLOW	GREEN	BLUE	RED
One Length Front or Back Float or Ring	One Length Front Aids Allowed	Two Lengths Front or Back Unaided	Five Lengths Front — Unaided
		One Length Not as Above Unaided	Five Lengths Back — Unaided
	One Length Back Aids Allowed		One Length Underwater
Total Head Immersion		10 feet Underwater	One Length Clothed
	Log Roll	Tread Water For One Minute	Tread Water For Three Minutes
Manoeuvrability	Push and Glide Legs or Arms	*Forward Roll	Surface Dive
		*Sink to Sit	*Backward Roll
One Lap of Pool Holding the Rail	Touch Bottom or Lift Brick	*Exit Unaided	*Entry Unaided
			*Exit Steepside

*Select two out of three.

Figure 25 A preliminary swimming award scheme for physically handicapped children

In swimming there are several award schemes in existence, each of which provides a most popular 'carrot' for the teacher to wave before his pupils. With many of these awards (and they include distance swimming, diving, synchronised swimming, personal survival and life saving awards) cloth badges are available which can be sewn onto a child's swimming costume as a testament to his prowess in the water. By any child these are worn with great pride; by the physically handicapped child, who is quite unused to success of

any sort, the effect can be dramatic, even bringing forward extra effort in other school activities.

Unfortunately, these schemes are not always as accessible to the severely handicapped child as they might be. Although distance awards which make no stipulation as to the type of stroke which is employed are possible, many of the other awards are so complex in their requirements that, for many disabled children, they are quite unrealistic. Additionally, because of the high standards which have to be achieved in order to qualify for these awards (even at the lowest level), to the handicapped beginner they are about as remote as the possibility of climbing Everest.

For both of these reasons, it can prove extremely useful to the teacher in the special school if he can create his own award scheme. This can serve both to bridge the gap between the novice and the conventional award schemes and also to bring some measure of recognition to the achievements of even the most handicapped swimmer.

Other recreational outlets

Having achieved even a basic mastery of swimming, there are many other activities which can be introduced to the child, through which he can extend his physical, psychological and social horizons. Some of the more common of these, canoeing, sailing, water skiing, etc., are outlined in the next chapter.

REFERENCES

Amateur Swimming Association (1963) *Swimming Instruction.* Educational Publications: London.
Anderson, W. (1968) *Teaching the physically handicapped to swim.* Faber & Faber: London.
Guttmann, Sir L. (1976) *Textbook of sport for the disabled.* HM & M Publishers: Aylesbury.
McMillan, A. (1970) *The Halliwick Method.* Unpublished paper presented to a seminar on physical education for the physically handicapped at Castle Priory College, Wallingford, England.
McMillan, A. (1973) *The Halliwick Method.* Unpublished paper presented to an International Sport and Leisure Conference at Linköping, Sweden.
Newman, J. (1976) *Swimming for children with physical and sensory impairments.* Charles C. Thomas: Illinois.
Trussell, E. (1971) *Guidelines for teaching the disabled to swim.* Swimming Teachers' Association/Netherton Printers: Dudley.

9

Outdoor pursuits

For the child in the special school who is either not motivated towards participation in highly structured or competitive sports, or who wishes to put his swimming ability to some practical application, an introduction to one of the outdoor pursuits could mean the difference between a totally inactive adulthood and one enriched by a variety of experiences, each of which in one way or another can make a significant contribution to a person's physical and mental wellbeing.

Broadly defined, outdoor pursuits are those activities which are undertaken in the country or on open water. As such, they include hill walking, riding, orienteering, canoeing and other such activities.

But as with all the other aspects of the physical education programme, it has to be recognised that not all of these activities are appropriate for all handicapped children. Even if they were, there would still be some children who are more interested in some activities than in others. Where interest does exist, however, it is amazing what can be achieved. Although they are not all known to me personally, I know of at least one cerebral palsied glider pilot, a quadriplegic sub-aqua instructor, a paraplegic sailing instructor and both blind and leg-amputee mountaineers.

The important thing for the teacher in school to remember is that, although the learning of any new skill and the exploration of any new environment is inevitably and invaluably an educative process, outdoor pursuits are primarily recreational activities; the sort of activities which hopefully children will continue to pursue after school and into adulthood.

The emphasis placed upon any particular aspect of an outdoor pursuits programme, therefore, must reflect a number of considerations, namely

(i) The age of the children under instruction and their level of competence at the activity being taught;

(ii) The extent to which a thorough understanding of basic principles is essential to the *safe* performance of an activity;

(iii) The extent to which an activity is going to be a realistic proposition for a child once he has left school.

The last question can usually be disregarded: if hills, lakes, reservoirs or whatever are available for use by the school, then it is highly probable that similar provision will exist for participation by adults, either on their own or through membership of a club. Only where this is not the case should the

teacher analyse more closely the relative advantages and disadvantages of devoting a significant portion of his timetable to an activity which his pupils will be unable to pursue once they have left school.

The former considerations, on the other hand, merit closer attention. Most activities which involve interaction with a natural environment, whether this be a mountain or a lake, carry with them a significant risk-factor. As such, in the teaching of most of these activities it is important that all children are taught basic skills, safety precautions, etc. in a thorough and proper manner. Only when this has been done can it be considered safe for children to look upon these activities as recreational. In any event, before any child takes part in these or any other out-of-school activities, both medical and parental consent should be obtained in writing.

Probably the best procedure the teacher can adopt in this respect is that whereby he selects a representative sample of outdoor pursuits (according to the criteria outlined above), gives all children an introductory course in each, and then allows the older children to opt for the activity which most appeals to them—if possible, encouraging them to join a local club at the same time. This element of choice, particularly with the older children, is most important.

Outdoor pursuits should be enjoyed, not suffered, and it is unlikely that anyone will enjoy an activity if he has not freely chosen to take part. The reluctant participant may be more inclined to fail (Croucher 1974).

But deciding that there might be considerable benefit to be derived from a comprehensive introduction to a variety of outdoor pursuits still leaves the most important question unanswered, *how* are these activities to be taught and *by whom*?

Unlike many major games whose structure is such that a person trained in one can easily apply his knowledge to the teaching of another, most outdoor pursuits tend to be rather task-specific. Additionally, given inexperienced leadership they can be extremely hazardous. As a result, it is *not* sufficient for a teacher with a general training to dabble with instruction in an activity of this kind which is completely new to him. In any teaching of outdoor pursuits the teacher in charge *must* be properly trained (and preferably qualified by an approved authority) in each activity that is being taught.

It is for these reasons among others that the activities listed below are described in general terms only. It is *not* intended that this be used as a training manual. Although I have had some experience of several of the activities mentioned, both as an enthusiast myself and as a teacher with physically handicapped children, I do not profess to be an expert in these fields.

The teacher who is encouraged by what is written to consider further the incorporation of these activities into his physical education programme is advised to consult the regional office of the appropriate National Governing Body. Where such offices do not exist or cannot be found, the National

Headquarters should be consulted, the addresses of which are listed in Appendix 4.

As with the major games which were outlined in Chapter 7, the presentation of these various activities is alphabetically determined, as the criteria for ranking them according to the relative contribution each might make to the physical education programme as a whole are entirely situation-specific.

Angling

Angling is the art of fishing with rod and line. In Britain coarse fishing, angling in its inland, freshwater form, is one of the most popular of all recreational pastimes.

The other common forms of angling are fly fishing and sea fishing, and whilst both of these incorporate some variation in technique, in all three the only motor skill required is the mastery of the cast.

As such, angling is a sport which is possible for children with almost any sort of handicap, whether ambulant or chairbound. The only problem the handicapped angler is likely to encounter is one of access to the bank or shore. Many inland water authorities are now alert to this problem, however, and several stretches of river-bank have now been made accessible and are reserved for use by disabled anglers.

In most regions angling clubs are only too willing to help in this integration process and are quite prepared to offer equipment and instruction. The National Anglers' Council too is very active in this respect and has produced an excellent film on angling for the disabled (see Appendix Three).

Special considerations for the teacher

(i) So as to avoid disappointment on reaching the water front, casting practices can be held in the school grounds. When children become proficient, 'target casting' can be introduced.

(ii) With cerebral palsied children whose problems are essentially those of motor co-ordination, a much greater emphasis needs to be placed upon the patterning of an appropriate casting action. But the teacher should not expect too much too soon. Excitement, tension and nervousness only serve to increase the involuntary movements which interfere with the movement pattern the cerebral palsied child tries so hard to achieve.

(iii) The spina bifida child should find the casting action itself no problem, but according to the height of the lesion in the individual case, such a child may well tend to topple over having executed the cast. In such cases, a safety belt or harness should be worn attached to the back of the wheelchair.

(iv) To help the amputee child, the hemiplegic and other children with little or no use of one of their hands, a special harness has been designed which holds the rod firmly against the chest, leaving the good hand free to operate the reel.

Camping

Camping requires 'living in and appreciating the outdoors' (Shivers and Fait 1975). Although it commonly involves children in all sorts of activities which are peculiar to the camping situation, such as constructing kitchen utensils, plate racks, etc., pitching tents and lighting open fires, it can also be used as a direct extension of routine daily living. As such, it is immensely valuable to all children, irrespective of handicap, who spend a greater part of their lives 'institutionalised'. Perhaps for the first time in their lives, through camping such children are placed in a situation where they are not reliant upon the services and amenities of the home or residential· school. The sharing of responsibilities, whether these be cooking, washing up, digging trenches or simply collecting litter, teaches children not only more about how to get along with others but also more about themselves.

Although the lightweight camp, i.e., that which is carried on the backs of the campers and moved to a new site each day, is possible for some minimally handicapped children, it is the standing camp that has the more widespread application. In this situation, particularly if it is erected next to a more permanent structure such as a Scout hut, children of almost any degree of disability can be accommodated. In addition, this sort of camp makes a very useful base for participation in other outdoor pursuits, allowing larger items of equipment to be stored overnight in situ ready for use each day.

Special considerations for the teacher

(i) When camping some distance from school, i.e., several miles away, it is advisable to find the location and telephone number of the nearest hospital and doctor's surgery *before* such information is needed. It might also be helpful if the local doctor could be informed of the visit and given details of all handicaps, drug requirements, etc.

(ii) There are several camp sites and field study centres in existence nowadays which have been specially created for use by the physically handicapped. If the camp site has not been specially designed, however, it is recommended that a member of staff visits the site beforehand.

(iii) With some children, particularly the paraplegics, special care needs to be taken to ensure that sleeping arrangements are satisfactory; e.g., when sleeping out of doors that the legs are well insulated against the cold and that fragile limbs are not going to become tangled (and therefore at risk) in loosely fitting sleeping-bags.

(iv) Whenever children who are incontinent are taken camping, care should also be taken to ensure that toilet facilities are both adequate and hygienic.

(v) If the children are to be involved in the process of erecting the camp, pitching tents, etc., it is usually helpful to have practised such skills in the school grounds beforehand.

Canoeing

There are two main types of canoe, the open Canadian type and the closed Eskimo Kayak, both of which can be used quite successfully by the physically handicapped. Although in able-bodied competition both types are used on white water slalom courses, it is as cruising vessels that they are probably most useful to handicapped schoolchildren. In this way, even children whose mobility is otherwise severely limited, e.g., through confinement to a wheelchair, can cover considerable distances through quite rugged country-side, on equal terms with their able-bodied peers. As such, canoeing provides an excellent opportunity, both in school and through clubs, for handicapped children and able-bodied children to participate in an activity together.

Special considerations for the teacher

(i) All canoeing instruction is normally commenced on an indoor pool where children can be taught capsize drills and use of the paddle(s) in a controlled environment.

(ii) Even though in open-water canoeing, life jackets should be worn at all times, no child should be allowed to participate in this sort of activity until he has demonstrated an ability to swim; the standard test used being a 200-yard swim followed by 5 minutes treading water.

(iii) It should be remembered that paralysed limbs are not only fragile (therefore requiring care and attention in the performance of capsize drills) but also prone to hypothermia (therefore needing ample coverage even when canoeing). In both respects the wearing of a wet-suit can be advantageous.

(iv) In the early stages of canoeing both ambulant and non-ambulant children are likely to need help in getting into and out of the canoe.

Caving

The exploration of underground passages is an exhilarating experience and a dangerous one. For the minimally handicapped, ambulant child however, there is no reason why (given appropriate medical clearance) such an activity should not be undertaken given the following provisos:

(i) The group is led by a qualified and experienced instructor;

(ii) All children are issued with proper equipment, preferably including wet suits.

Special considerations for the teacher

When considering a child's suitability for this sort of activity, the following points might usefully be borne in mind:

(i) Apart from a child's physical disabilities, his psycho-emotional state should also be considered. Even some able-bodied people are 'quite unable to go caving because of the psychological effects of the darkness and the feeling of being closed in' (Croucher 1974);

159

(ii) Caving can be taxing both physically and mentally. Unless children have proved their ability to cope with both sorts of pressure over an extended period of time, they should be discouraged from this sort of activity until such a time as they have done so;

(iii) Caving should not be recommended to any person in whom there is a tendency to spasm, or whose balance mechanisms are at all defective. As a general rule, any child who would be considered unsuitable for climbing would similarly not be suited to caving, as both activities require the same abilities.

Cycling

Cycling, on a bicycle or tricycle, can be a most enjoyable and healthy means of travelling about the country, possible even for some children who have difficulty in walking. When touring, especially with children who have balance problems, it is advisable to keep to the quieter country roads, and, as with any other strenuous activity, long distance cycling should only be attempted after an appropriate course of training. Shorter tours of one or two hours duration are probably quite sufficient in the first instance, but even this will be a considerable extension to a handicapped child's normal range of movement.

Hill walking

Although it might be possible, given enthusiastic pushers, to involve children in wheelchairs in some of the shorter, low-level climbs, in general, this is an activity which is only suitable for ambulant children. It need not be supposed, however, that only those children with a normal gait can walk long distances. Such activity is quite appropriate for hemiplegics, spastic diplegics and others with ambulation problems *provided* they are allowed to walk at their own speed.

This might even be referred to as the golden rule of hill walking: *that everyone, whether handicapped or able-bodied, should proceed according to his own personal limitations, and each group should move at the speed of the slowest person in that group.*

Given experience and ability, some hill-walkers graduate to rock climbing (involving the use of ropes on vertical rock faces) and mountaineering (a combination of hill walking and rock climbing), but each of these requires experienced and qualified leadership and access to proper clothing and equipment.

Special considerations for the teacher

(i) Good route planning and recognition of the right time to turn back are imperative, especially for groups which cannot move quickly or over long distances.

(ii) Anyone leading a group in an unfamiliar area, even if only on a short

walk, should consult local police or mountain rescue personnel beforehand.

(iii) Generally speaking, handicapped walkers have to work harder than able-bodied walkers. As a result, at any one time their resistance to the effects of exposure or dehydration is likely to be lower.

(iv) Whenever compass work is involved, care should be taken to ensure that the metal in calipers or artificial limbs is not allowed to cause the compass needle to deviate.

(v) In all walking or climbing activities a comprehensive First Aid kit should be taken along. This is particularly important with children who wear calipers or prostheses as there is always the possibility of these chafing and causing blisters. Care should also be taken to ensure that boots or shoes are well-fitting.

Orienteering

In a school situation this activity, which combines map reading ability with cross-country running or walking, can provide a very useful preparation for the skills of hill walking – at a level which can involve ambulant children and those in wheelchairs to the same extent. At a more advanced level, competitions exist nationally and internationally for those who are able to run, or at least walk quickly, over very long distances. As the only equipment which is required is a Silva compass and a map, this is just as possible for the one-arm amputee, and to a lesser degree the hemiplegic, as it is for anyone else.

Special considerations for the teacher

(i) Short-course orienteering in the school situation can be successful as a partner activity, teaming up one ambulant child with one in a wheelchair.

(ii) It is not recommended that children with certain handicaps be sent out on orienteering courses on their own; these include the hemiplegic child who when he falls over is unable to pick himself up and the grand-mal epileptic.

(iii) As was mentioned above under 'hill walking', calipers, artificial limbs and other metal objects can cause a compass needle to deviate from its true position. In both hill walking and orienteering this can have dramatic effects!

Riding

Riding and pony trekking have been organised on a large scale in England for many years. According to the Riding for the Disabled Association's census of 1974 there were at that time 4399 handicapped children riding regularly in some 222 different groups (Croucher 1974).

The object of this Association is

the relief of disabled persons by the provision or assistance in the provision of facilities for riding so that all disabled persons who would benefit in their

mental or physical health from riding shall be given the opportunity to do so. (Riding for the Disabled Association 1971)

Through this Association, fifty-six (62%) of the ninety schools to which reference was made in Chapter 2 are able to include riding in their school physical education programme. The advantages of so doing have been summarised as follows:

Horseback riding requires the involvement of the whole body and utilizes every muscle and joint. The building of muscle strength, as well as body image and whole body awareness, is a significant therapeutic contribution. Moreover, the development of balance and co-ordination is implicit in this activity (Adams et al. 1975).

Special considerations for the teacher
(i) Although riding is a suitable form of activity for children with most types of disability, there are some for which it is not so. Children with hip joint disorders should not ride if this is likely to aggravate their condition, and children with quadriplegia or advanced muscular dystrophy are generally not advised to ride because of their inability to balance and their poor arm control.

(ii) For riders with a disability of one arm, an adaptive rein bar can be fashioned to fit between the reins at a suitable distance from the horse's mouth. The rider holds the bar in his unaffected hand and uses movements of the wrist to simulate the effect of having two hands on the reins.

(iii) For children with only partial control over the trunk muscles, various high-backed saddles are available.

Rowing

This activity incorporates both competitive rowing or sculling and the non-competitive recreational activity commonly observed on municipal boating lakes.

For rowing in competition an oarsman must have the 'full use of both hands, at least one leg and some mobility in the upper part of the body' (Croucher 1974). No such restrictions are placed upon the coxswain however: his only qualifications are an ability to swim and a not too heavy body-weight (preferably under 10 stone).

Non-competitive rowing on the other hand is open to anyone, although as with all other water sports each participant should at least be able to swim.

Special considerations for the teacher
(i) Apart from the physical requirements for children wishing to row in competition, in boats built for speed the ability to maintain one's balance on a very narrow surface should not be underestimated.

(ii) Experience of ordinary row-boats, which normally have wide hulls and

are therefore very stable, might make a useful initiation into the art of oarsmanship for children interested in taking up canoeing or competitive rowing.

(iii) All boats should have sufficient buoyancy to support the crew in the event of a capsize. If this is not built-in, it can be improved by the use of buoyancy bags secured to the inside of the boat.

Sailing

Dinghy sailing, either single-handed or in two-man craft, is practised by paraplegics, amputees, cerebral palsied and many other disabled as well. It is a sport which is currently growing in popularity both among able-bodied and handicapped people and provides an excellent opportunity for integrated recreation. As with all other water sports, participation should not be encouraged unless the would-be sailor is also a competent swimmer – even though life-jackets are worn.

In all small sailing craft those unable to walk have to devise a means of transferring from their wheelchair to the dinghy, as the chair has to be left on the side. In larger craft, canal barges, river boats and such like, it is sometimes possible for the chair to be taken on board as well. In fact a number of boats are now available for hire which have been specially converted to facilitate this process. In one particular case, this has made it possible to take as many as ten people in wheelchairs at one time, and a number of ambulant disabled as well.

Special considerations for the teacher

(i) Many handicapped sailors, in particular the paralysed, prefer to sit on the floor of the boat rather than on the seat (which tends to be rather narrow). Alternatively, it is sometimes possible to fill in the space between the seats (e.g., with sponge matting) so that the difference between the level of the seat and that of the floor is not so great.

(ii) Many cerebral palsied children and some paraplegics have a tendency to go into spasm when suddenly immersed in cold water. To prevent the obviously dangerous consequences of such an eventuality, it is advisable for such children to wear wet-suits.

(iii) Some high-level paraplegics, quadriplegics and other severely handicapped children may find that they have insufficient postural control to prevent frequent falls when sailing. *Under no circumstances* should they be provided with any form of harness, as this would trap them underwater in the event of a capsize. Such children are probably better advised to seek alternative forms of recreation.

Skiing

Skiing is obviously only possible for those children whose handicap does not prevent them from standing, walking and maintaining a position of balance

while moving. Not surprisingly, it is a sport which has a considerable following amongst amputees. Apart from the disadvantage of having only one leg, the lower-limb amputee has certain advantages over other handicapped skiers, namely

(i) he has a much keener 'sense' of balance, and

(ii) he almost certainly has had experience of using sticks.

This does not mean however that skiing should be restricted to amputees. There are a large number of children in special schools whose handicap is sufficiently minimal to enable them to ski quite successfully.

Although skiing is not possible for children who use wheelchairs, one activity which is similar in its effect is specially designed so that its participants are either sitting or lying down: this is the sport of tobogganing. However, even though such toboggans can be fitted with safety straps, there is unavoidably quite a sizeable risk-factor with this sort of activity and extreme caution should be exercised.

Special considerations for the teacher

(i) Although children with below-knee or arm amputations can ski quite successfully in the conventional fashion by wearing their prostheses, this is not so successful for above-knee amputees. For these a Three-Track Ski system has been devised which enables them to wear one ski on their sound leg, to leave behind their artificial limb, and to use elbow crutches with short skis attached (Fig. 26).

(ii) With able-bodied children wishing to take up skiing, it is sometimes recommended that they precede their introduction to snow skiing with a few sessions of instruction on an artificial slope. The teacher in the special school has to weigh against this convenience the possibility of injury incurred by handicapped children falling on this rather firm surface.

(iii) Even though down-hill tobogganing is unavoidably hazardous, the element of risk involved in tobogganing on gentle slopes or tobogganing on level ground using a tow should not be excessive, even for paraplegics.

Water Skiing

Like snow skiing, skiing on water demands an ability to stand and to maintain one's balance while in motion. Not surprisingly therefore, it is once again the amputee population and the blind who have shown a particular penchant for this activity.

For the child in the wheelchair, the aquatic version of tobogganing is called aquaplaning and incorporates a board or aquaplane being attached by a rope to a power boat and towed across the water. As in tobogganing, the child can sit or lie down and in this case he can kneel as well.

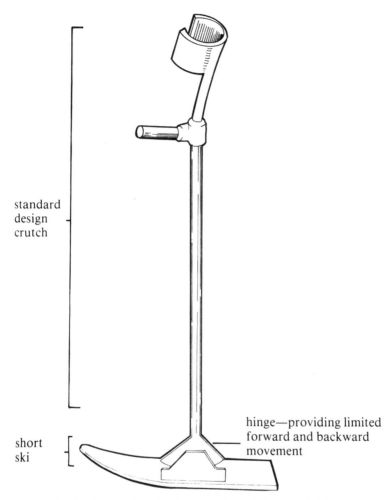

standard
design
crutch

hinge—providing limited
forward and backward
movement

short
ski

Figure 26 Standard outrigger ski guide (adapted from Adams et al. 1975)

Special considerations for the teacher

(i) Because of the sudden acceleration, water skiing in particular should only be undertaken by children with strong arms and legs.

(ii) As the possibility of capsize is presumably quite high in both of these activities, they should only be performed by children who are very confident in the water, reasonably strong swimmers and well able to tread water for several minutes.

(iii) Whether water skiing or aquaplaning, any capsize at speed is likely to cause the participant to hit the water with some considerable force. These activities are not suitable therefore for children who have brittle bones or are otherwise fragile or delicate.

Summary

The activities outlined above can all provide a most useful complement to the gymnastic, games and swimming components of the conventional physical education programme. In addition, they can be of particular value as an alternative to the contribution made by the major competitive sports, providing the same sort of physical challenge, with similar benefits to motor fitness, whilst at the same time not requiring the same intense involvement in competition.

The teacher should remember, however, that the majority of these outdoor pursuits require trained leadership and proper equipment. Only when these conditions have been met should such activities be incorporated into the school physical education programme.

REFERENCES

Adams, R. C., Daniel, A. N. & Rullman, L. (1975) *Games, sports and exercises for the physically handicapped.* Lea & Febiger: Philadelphia.
Croucher, N. (1974) *Outdoor pursuits for disabled people.* Disabled Living Foundation: London.
Guttmann, Sir L. (1976) *Textbook of sport for the disabled.* HM & M Publishers: Aylesbury.
Riding for the Disabled Association (1971) *Annual Journal.* Riding for the Disabled Association: Kenilworth.
Roberts, K. (1976) *Integrated water sports holidays.* A paper presented at the National Aids for the Disabled Conference 'Naidex '76' held in Brighton, England.
Shivers, J. S. & Fait, H. F. (1975) *Therapeutic and adapted recreational services.* Lea & Febiger: Philadelphia.

10

Only the beginning

It is usual in the last chapter of a textbook to draw conclusions, to 'sew up all the loose edges' and at least to attempt to leave no questions unanswered. In this case however, it is perhaps more appropriate to consider this not as the end, but the beginning. In the preceding chapters various problems have been discussed relating to the introduction of a programme of physical education for physically handicapped children, not in such a way as to be encyclopaedic in their coverage, but rather in an attempt to familiarise the reader with the tools of his trade. In this way, hopefully, he might be able to go forward from this book and apply what he has read to each new situation as it arises.

The first chapter outlined the basic philosophy behind the teaching of physical education, highlighting factors which influence not only the physical development of children but their psychological and sociological development as well. It went on to relate this concept to the needs of physically handicapped children.

To give the discussion some relevance, Chapter 2 put beside this philosophical construct a description of the sort of school in which such children are taught, the type of facilities which exist and the activities provided in them. But just as no two schools are identical, so physical education is not a static concept. It is a dynamic and ever-changing phenomenon, assimilating and accommodating to the demands of time, taking on a slightly different form in each different situation. Consequently, the teacher should develop his own notions of the sort of physical education which is appropriate to his school, based upon an evaluation of the needs of the children within that school.

Chapters 3 and 4 were offered in an attempt to give the reader some insight into the aetiology, character and prognosis of the more common handicaps, and to point out some of the less obvious behavioural disorders often accompanying these handicaps. But these too were structured in such a way as to make similar analysis possible for any other condition which might be encountered in an individual case.

Having thus provided the reader with an adequate background, Chapters 5 through 9 gave an indication of those activities which might usefully be taught to physically handicapped children. But here again, although various teaching progressions were described and attention was drawn to certain special features, it was left to the reader to decide which child with which handicap is

suitable for which activity. Admittedly, guidelines have been offered, but the point cannot be stressed too strongly that children are much more than agglomerations of bone, nerve and muscle.

Individuals are not just input-decision-output machines, satisfied by the extent to which their neuro-muscular equipment fits the requirements of a particular activity. (Munrow 1972).

Children are different; not only because of their physical condition, but because they think differently, because they have different likes and dislikes, because they have good moods and bad moods, strong points and weak points and so on. For example, it is not sufficient for the teacher to maintain that as archery is good for paraplegics, it is therefore an appropriate activity for all paraplegics. Although there might be some advantage in teaching the basics of archery to all paraplegics, sooner or later the time has to come when children decide that they do, or do not, want to pursue it any further. As Oliver (1972) puts it:

Because of the intimate relationship of the functioning of all aspects of growth an individual cannot be divided into two parts; therefore, we do not believe that one type of experience trains the body and that another type of experience educates the mind . . . We believe that each individual reacts to each experience in his own unique way and this may leave him slightly changed. This change we call education.

The activities which have been mentioned in these chapters are but examples of the sort of activity which *might* be appropriate, and they are supported by considerations for the teacher which *might* be appropriate. It is for the reader to decide which are and which are not. Such decisions can only be reached when assessment and evaluation are made in terms of a child as an individual and not as the personification of a physical handicap.

But despite the fact that most of the opinions expressed in this book have been left open-ended, it is at least hoped that its contents will enable the reader to feel better equipped to introduce such a programme of physical education to the special school by giving him a better idea of the range of activities which can be enjoyed by even the most severely physically handicapped child. It could even be argued that the significance of a programme of physical education is even greater to the handicapped child than it is to the able-bodied child.

The following quotation from a paper written by Sir Ludwig Guttmann is rather lengthy, but it gives a summary account of the principles upon which all physical education with the physically handicapped is based, and thus conveys the principle message behind this book as well.

Sport is of much greater significance for the severely disabled than for the able-bodied person. Serious physical handicap interferes to a greater or

lesser degree with bodily function and co-ordination and leads to abnormal patterns of movement. These often induce psychological tensions that make social contact with the outside world difficult or even impossible. If the (handicapped) person is continually stared at, he may develop an inferiority complex characterised by anxiety with loss of self-confidence and personal dignity; the result is self-pity, self-centred isolationism, and anti-social attitudes. Taking an active part in sporting activities restores his psychological equilibrium and enables him to face up to life in spite of his physical disability . . . From the physical point of view, sport is of immense therapeutic value. It is the most natural form of remedial exercise and can be used successfully as a complement to the conventional methods of physiotherapy . . . The great advantage of sport over formal remedial exercise lies in its recreational value, which is a motivating force in the enjoyment of life. Recreation thus becomes an important factor in achieving the psychological equilibrium so necessary to the disabled person in coming to terms with his physical defect. The final, and possibly noblest aim of sport for the disabled person is to help him (establish) contact with the world around him. By restoring activity to mind and body – by instilling self-respect, self-discipline, a competitive spirit, and comradeship – sport develops mental attitudes that are essential for successful social (re)integration and, in particular, for useful employment (Guttmann 1967).

After school – what next?

No matter how comprehensive the physical education in school, it can only have any lasting effect upon the health and mental attitudes of the children involved if there is provision for similar activity once they have left school. Unfortunately this is not always the case, and quite often at this stage it appears that the efforts of the teacher have all been in vain.

Any school, 'special' or not, exists to provide children with an education, and much of this education, for handicapped children in particular, is concerned with preparation for independence and adulthood. So what possible value can there be in providing children with a balanced programme of physical education throughout their childhood if, at sixteen years of age, they leave school either to find that there is no opportunity to continue with these activities, or that they have no idea how to locate them?

Although the teacher in the special school only has a close relationship with his pupils until they are sixteen, there is still a lot that he can do to influence their post-school welfare. And the physical education teacher in particular is probably in as good a position as anyone to do something about 'bridging the gap' between childhood dependence and adult independence.

At a local level this is probably best achieved in three different ways:

(i) by providing opportunities for older children to visit and use local sports facilities whilst they are still at school. In this way, the children are made aware

of what is available outside of school, and the staff in the centres used are reminded of their obligation to provide a service for *all* members of the public and not just a select few;

(ii) by inviting representatives of local sports organisations to come into the school, both to lend of their expertise by giving coaching sessions, either on a one-off basis or as a regular part of the programme, and to talk to the children about how best they might set about continuing with such activity once they have left school;

(iii) by encouraging one of the local sports centres to set aside its facilities for one period a week (on a fee-paying basis if necessary) so that interested adult disabled – and those about to leave school – might have an opportunity to form their own Sports Club for the Disabled (Price 1973).

Although more is said below about the relative merits of segregated sports and integrated participation, the sort of provision outlined under (iii) has many advantages. Not only does it provide an opportunity for adult disabled to try their hand at recreational activities in a sheltered and sympathetic environment, and give to the more reticent of them a reason to venture beyond their homes, but it also provides for the more out-going disabled person a resource centre, a place to go for information and advice, for example on how he might set about joining an able-bodied sports club.

On a broader front, the teacher is likely to be best served if he affiliates his school to the appropriate national governing body of sport (in the British case, the British Sports Association for the Disabled).

Apart from the National Games which the B.S.A.D. organises for both children and adults in a wide range of activities, and which themselves are a useful vehicle by which to provide children with contacts, the Association itself is nationally recognised as a co-ordinating and advisory body on all matters relating to sport for the disabled. Its permanent staff are always willing to come into schools to talk to children and through its regional officers the teacher should be able to find information on all sorts of matters, ranging from the dates of regional, national and international competitions, through details of coaching courses and training meets, to the addresses of all the local sports organisations which might be of help to his pupils on leaving school.

In addition to the B.S.A.D., there are also certain other organisations with responsibility for particular handicaps, e.g., the British Deaf Sports Association, the British Association for Sport and Recreational Activities for the Blind, and the British Paraplegic Sports Society, each of which might be able to provide the teacher with further information. (For a list of such organisations, see Appendix 4.)

Segregation v. integration

Although this is a popular subject for debate, it is very much a red herring in this context as it implies that one of the two alternatives might possibly be right

for all people and all situations. Restating what has been emphasised throughout this book, i.e., that what is appropriate for one person is not necessarily so for another, it can be appreciated that under different circumstances *both* situations might be desirable.

Not only are personality differences likely to be a determining factor in such decisions, but also the nature of the activity in which people are interested is likely to be significant. One handicapped person might be sufficiently confident to pitch into a fully integrated situation straight away, even at the risk of 'sticking out like a sore thumb'. Another might prefer to stay permanently in the supportive atmosphere of a segregated society, and yet another might be happier attempting a gradual transition from segregation to integration. As for the activity, obviously there is a far greater likelihood of a disabled angler integrating with other anglers than there is of a wheelchair basketball player mixing with ambulant basketball players.

At the present time, as we have seen, most children with a physical handicap are educated in segregated special schools. As a result, the physical education offered to these children has to be adapted to suit the needs of this predominantly unskilled population. It is not surprising, therefore, that some of the activities taught are somewhat rudimentary, and certainly not likely to be found in similar form in ordinary schools. But even in this situation, as the children grow and begin to show the benefits of this adapted programme of physical education, it becomes increasingly possible to introduce them to recreational activities in which they can participate on equal terms with their able-bodied peers.

It is only when they have left school that this question of segregation or integration crops up in more complex situations. For not only is the activity which is pursued likely to be segregated, but also the situation in which that activity is played may be segregated as well. In mathematical terms, therefore, there are four possibilities:

    (i) an integrated activity in an integrated situation;

    (ii) an integrated activity in a predominantly segregated situation;

    (iii) a segregated activity in an integrated situation;

    (iv) a segregated activity in a segregated situation.

And of the four it must surely be the last alternative which is the least desirable.

Let me give an example. Any activity in which participation is possible by able-bodied and physically handicapped on more or less equal terms, such as angling or archery, is likely to be pursued in a situation in which the physically handicapped are in the minority. This is a natural form of integration. But activities which are played only by the handicapped, such as wheelchair basketball, are commonly played in special centres (hospital gymnasia or such like) where the able-bodied form the minority. This is the least desirable situation as it can create an introspective, isolationist attitude to society.

In theory there is no reason why even totally segregated activities cannot be

played in ordinary sports centres alongside ordinary people. At least in this situation the social intercourse is likely to be integrated. It is in this respect, unfortunately, that community recreation provision in Britain is lacking. Although almost without exception sports and leisure centre managers are sympathetic to this cause, only rarely do they have suitably knowledgeable personnel on their staff to implement the requirements of handicapped people. Perhaps there is a lesson to be learned from the United States, where the therapeutic recreation profession has already established itself in a community setting (Shivers et al. 1975 and O'Morrow 1976).

But in Britain too there are signs of change. Given appropriate leadership from the physical education profession, recreation management, and those at the helm of such organisations as the British Sports Association for the Disabled, the situation could improve both significantly and rapidly.

Conclusions

Whatever the nature of the provisions made for the physically handicapped, the instrument of such change has to be the handicapped themselves. There can be little point either in sports organisers laying on courses to introduce the disabled to their sphere of activity, or in architects and planners taking account of the need for ramped entrances, wide corridors, the installation of lifts, etc., if the disabled themselves are not going to come forward and make use of such provisions.

Obviously for the handicapped person who is already in his adult years, the awareness of what is available and, more important, what is possible is going to come gradually. But the handicapped teenager, having been given a comprehensive physical education in school, should be there 'knocking at the door', knowing that he is able, and simply asking for acknowledgement of his right to join in.

If, even in a small way, this book is helpful in preparing the handicapped child to take his place in society, it will have been worthwhile.

REFERENCES

Cratty, B. J. (1975) *Remedial motor activity for children*. Lea & Febiger: Philadelphia.
Guttmann, Sir L. (1967) The Stoke Mandeville Games. In Richardson, R. G. (Ed.) *Abbottempo*. Vol. 5, Book 3, pp. 2–7. Abbott Universal Ltd.: Netherlands.
Munrow, A. D. (1972) *Physical education: A discussion of principles*. Bell: London.
Oliver, J. N. (1972) Physical activity and the psychological development of the handicapped. In Kane, J. E. (Ed.) *Psychological aspects of physical education and sport*. Routledge & Kegan Paul: London.
O'Morrow, G. S. (1976) *Therapeutic recreation: a helping profession*. Reston: Virginia.

Price, R. J. (1973) How a sports club for the disabled came to Lincoln. In *Sport and recreation.* Vol. 15, No. 1, pp. 42–43.

Shivers, J. S. & Fait, H. F. (1975) *Therapeutic and adapted recreational services.* Lea & Febiger: Philadelphia.

Glossary

ABDUCTION   Movement of a body part away from the axis of the body.

ABILITY   Power to perform mental or physical acts with the present level of training and development.

ABIOTROPHY   Phenomenon of an abnormal gene remaining undetected at birth and exerting its effect progressively during post-natal life.

ACHILLES TENDON   Tendon which attaches the muscles of the calf to the heel.

ACTIVITY   Any learning situation involving change or motion; in physical education this is one of the organised games, sports or elements in which students demonstrate skill and initiative, and which is selected and conducted for specific outcomes.

ADAPTED PHYSICAL EDUCATION   Any programme of developmental activities, games, sports and rhythms suited to the interests, needs, capacities and limitations of individuals with disabilities.

ADDUCTION   Movement of a body part towards the axis of the body.

AEROBIC   Requiring the presence of oxygen.

AETIOLOGY   Science or study of the causes of disease and mode of operation.

AFFERENCE   Transmission of impulses from the periphery to the nerve centres; opposite of efference.

AGNOSIA   Inability to process information even though sensory mechanisms are intact.

AGONIST   Muscle which, in moving a part, is resisted by a muscle that relaxes sufficiently to permit the movement; (see 'antagonist').

AMBULATION   Process of walking or other movement on the feet.

AMPUTATION   Surgical removal of an extremity or other projecting body part.

ANAEMIA   Deficiency in the number of red blood corpuscles and/or the amount of haemoglobin in the blood stream; symptoms include pallor, general weakness and giddiness.

ANAESTHESIA   Absence of sense of touch; lack of feeling in a body part.

ANOMALY   Mental, physical or sensory disorder, derangement, deviation or deformity.

ANOXAEMIA   Lack of sufficient oxygen in the blood; (sometimes used synonymously with anoxia).

ANOXIA   Inadequate oxygen supply in body tissues or fluids with consequent disturbance in body function.

ANTAGONIST   Muscle which acts in opposition to the pull of another muscle; (see 'agonist').

ANTERIOR   Located in the front; opposite of posterior; (sometimes used synonymously with ventral).

APHASIA   i) Receptive aphasia – inability to understand speech;
ii) Executive aphasia – inability to use speech even though speech organs are intact.

APRAXIA   Inability to execute planned movements despite conservation of sensation, mobility and coordination.

ARTHROGRYPOSIS   Congenital condition in which several joints are fixed at birth as a result of incomplete development of skeletal muscle.

ASPHYXIA   Loss of consciousness due to oxygen deprivation.

ASTHMA   Allergic condition characterised by wheezing and difficulty in exhalation.

ASTIGMATISM   Eye condition leading to faulty vision, caused by irregularity in the curvature of the cornea or lens.

ATAXIA   Condition of motor incoordination, characterised by lack of balance and/or directional control; occasional manifestation of cerebral palsy due to lesion of the cerebellum.

ATHETOSIS   Slow, involuntary, vermicular movements of the limbs, trunk, etc; occasional manifestation of cerebral palsy due to lesion of the basal ganglia.

ATROPHY   Wasting of tissues (usually muscle) as a result of inactivity or disuse.

AUTONOMIC NERVOUS SYSTEM   Efferent system of peripheral nerves responsible for innervation and regulation of smooth muscle and glands.

AUTOSOME   Genetic character *not* sex-linked.

BALANCE   Ability to maintain or regain posture or position; typically either static or dynamic.

BASAL GANGLIA   Part of the brain; large collection of motor neurons deep in the cerebral cortex.

BIOPSY   Removal and examination of tissue from the living body for diagnostic purposes.

BLIND   Total or serious loss of sight; visual acuity of 20/200 or less.

CALIPER   Orthotic aid designed to restrict movement and/or lend support, e.g. leg brace.

CAMPING   Form of organised recreation involving living out-of-doors in a more or less close relationship with the natural environment.

CARDIAC   Pertaining to the heart.

CARDIOVASCULAR   Pertaining to the heart and blood vessels.

CAUDAL   Towards the tail or inferior end; opposite of rostral.

CAUDOCEPHALIC   Progression from the tail to the head.

CENTRAL NERVOUS SYSTEM   Part of the nervous system comprising the brain and spinal cord.

CEPHALIC   Pertaining to the head (more specifically to the brain).

CEREBELLUM   Part of the brain located beneath the cerebrum; concerned with strength, range and smoothness of muscle contraction, and with maintenance of balance or equilibrium.

CEREBRAL PALSY   Paralysis due to lesion of the cerebrum or other motor areas of the brain.

CEREBROSPINAL   Pertaining to the brain and spinal cord.

CEREBRUM   Two hemispheres forming the superior and larger part of the brain.

CERVICAL   Pertaining to the upper region of the spine; uppermost seven vertebrae; neck region.

CHRONIC   Continuing for a long time or recurring frequently.

COAGULATION   Clotting of blood; natural defence against excessive bleeding.

COCCYGEAL   Pertaining to the coccyx or to the spinal nerve issuing from the coccyx.

COCCYX   Rudimentary tail; bottom-most vertebra in the spinal column.

CO-CONTRACTION   Synchronous tension of agonist and antagonist muscles.

COGNITION   Process of knowing, remembering, imagining, conceiving, judging or reasoning.

COMPETITION   Friendly struggle or rivalry; typically, highly organised and played according to a predetermined set of rules.

CONGENITAL   Condition or characteristic present at birth because of hereditary or environmental factors.

CONTRACTURE   State of prolonged contraction of a muscle; failure of a muscle to return to normal length after contraction; muscular rigidity.

CONTRALATERAL   Situated or having an effect on the opposite side; opposite of ipsilateral.

CORTEX   Outer layer of a organ; typically cerebral or cerebellar.

CRANIUM   Portion of the skull forming the enclosure for the brain, i.e. excluding the lower jaw.

CURRICULUM   Progressive series of courses and/or experiences at a particular educational level and/or in a specific field of learning for a definite, predetermined purpose.

CYSTIC FIBROSIS   Disease of children involving the endocrine glands, resulting in pancreatic insufficiency and chronic pulmonary disease.

DEAFNESS   Total or serious hearing loss; typically, hearing loss in excess of 75 decibels.

DELICATE   Impaired physical condition; typically, not as serious as is implied by the term 'handicapped'.

DIPLEGIA   Paralysis affecting like parts on both sides of the body; occasional manifestation of cerebral palsy due to a bilateral lesion of the pyramidal tracts.

DISABILITY   Loss or reduction of functional ability and activity that is consequent upon impairment.

DISINHIBITION   Inability to refrain from producing an immediate, impulsive and often inadequate response.

DISLOCATION   Complete tearing of some part of a joint capsule, with displacement of the head of the bone from its normal position; (synonymous with luxation).

DISTAL   Away from the source; farther from the point of origin; opposite of proximal.

DISTRACTIBILITY   Condition where concentration of attention is disturbed by irrelevant stimuli; inability to refrain from attending to such stimuli.

DORSAL   Towards the back or rear surface of a body or organ; opposite of ventral; (sometimes used synonymously with posterior).

DORSIFLEXION   Flexion towards the back; typically, bending the foot upwards by flexing the ankle.

DRILL   Repetition of an activity to increase facility or skill, or to fix associations in the memory.

DYNAMIC   Energetic; active; not static.

DYSFUNCTION   Defective, deficient or abnormal performance of an organ, movement or activity.

DYSKINESIA   Loss of sense of movement; loss of motor function in a body part which is not paralysed.

DYSPLASIA   Abnormality of development; impairment of growth processes.

DYSTONIA   Abnormal tonus of voluntary muscle.

ECTODERM   Cell layer forming the dorsal portion of the embryonic disc; derivatives include the outer skin and the nervous system.

ECTOPIA VESICA   Congenital condition in which the bladder is abnormally situated.

EFFERENCE   Transmission of impulses from the central nervous system to the periphery, to organs and to superficial tissues; opposite of afference.

EGOCENTRICITY   Self-centredness; tendency to interpret everything solely in terms of one's self without regard for the interests of others.

EISENMENGER'S SYNDROME   Congenital heart defect.

ELECTROMYOGRAM   Record or tracing of the electric response in a contracting muscle.

EMBRYOLOGY   Branch of biology dealing with eggs and their development into adult organisms.

ENDODERM   Cell layer forming the ventral portion of the embryonic disc; derivatives include the digestive and respiratory tracts.

ENDOTHELIUM   Membrane lining various vessels and cavities of the body.

ENDURANCE   Ability to persist in specific acts of strength, skill or speed without exhaustion or undue fatigue.

EPILEPSY   Chronic nervous disease characterised in the pronounced form (grand mal) by general motor convulsions and loss of consciousness; and in the milder form (petit mal) by momentary dizziness or loss of consciousness.

EPITHELIUM   Cell layer forming the cuticle upon the skin, the inner surface of the bowels, and the lining of ducts and hollow organs.

EQUILIBRIUM   State in which the resultant of all forces acting on or in the object is zero; an evenly balanced state.

EQUINUS   See 'pes equinus'.

EXECUTIVE   Pertaining to the output of a body or system.

EXERCISE   Systematic activity for the purpose of training or developing the body or mind; regular series of movements designed to strengthen or develop some body part, system or faculty.

EXHALATION   Process involved in expelling air from the lungs; breathing out; opposite of inhalation.

EXTENSION   Movement of a body segement by which the adjacent parts are brought into straighter alignment; movement in a joint resulting in the movement of the two adjacent parts away from each other; opposite of flexion.

FENESTRATION   Pertaining to the tympanum or ear drum.

FETAL   Pertaining to the unborn child or fetus.

FIBRIN   Substance formed in the blood as an aid to clotting.

FITNESS   Degree to which a person is able to function; including physical, mental, social and emotional fitness.

FLACCID   Absence of muscle tonus; typically due to a spinal lesion.

FLEXIBILITY   Ability to move, bend or rotate the body parts easily and normally in all their joints and articulations without undue muscular or structural restrictions.

FLEXION   Movement in a joint by which the two adjacent parts approach each other; opposite of extension.

FORAMEN   Small, natural opening in a bone; (pl. foramina).

FORCED RESPONSIVENESS   Inability to refrain from responding to a stimulus even though it may be irrelevant or unimportant to the situation at hand.

FRONTAL   Pertaining to or located in the front; typically the foremost part of the cerebrum.

GENETIC   Pertaining to or originating in the genes, by which all hereditary factors are conveyed from one generation to another.

GRAND MAL   See 'epilepsy'.

HAEMARTHROSIS   Bleeding into a joint cavity; often caused by injury or, in the haemophiliac, by spontaneous bleeding.

HAEMOPHILIA   Hereditary disease characterised by a tendency to uncontrollable haemorrhage.

HAEMORRHAGE   Any escape of blood from the vessels which naturally contain it; internal or external bleeding.

HAEMOSTASIS   Normal state of affairs in the blood; condition wherein all the usual constituents of blood are present in all the usual amounts.

HANDICAP   Defect in physique, intellect or other behaviour; disadvantage that is consequent upon impairment or disability.

HEMIANOPIA   Loss of half the usual field of vision; affected persons may see either everything to the left or to the right, or just that which is directly in front, or, thirdly, only those objects which are far out on both sides; depending in each case on the location of the brain damage.

HEMIPLEGIA   Paralysis affecting only one side of the body, such as the right arm and right leg; occasional manifestation of cerebral palsy due to unilateral pyramidal tract involvement.

HEREDITY   Transmission of characters and traits through factors in the genes from one generation to the next.

HYDROCEPHALUS Condition in which there is an abnormal accumultion of cerebrospinal fluid within the skull; commonly associated with spina bifida.

HYDROTHERAPY Treatment of muscles, bones or tendons by the application of water and/or controlled movement in water.

HYPERTONUS Chronic high muscular tension.

HYPERTROPHY Increase in the size of body parts (tissues or organs) as a result of activity or some factor other than normal growth.

HYPOTHERMIA Chronic loss of body heat; commonly due to overexposure to cold temperatures.

HYPOTONIA Chronic low muscular tension.

IMPAIRMENT Disturbance of or interference with the normal structure and functioning of the body, including the mental function.

INANITION Emptiness, especially from lack of nourishment.

INCONTINENCE Inability to control the evacuation of bladder and/or bowel.

INFARCTION Change in an organ due to the sudden blockage of an artery.

INFERIOR Towards the feet; below the midpoint; opposite of superior.

INHIBITION Blocking, restraint or arrest of a function; especially a nerve or mental function.

INTEGRATION Bringing together or unification of different persons, acts, processes or functions.

IPSILATERAL Situated or having an effect on the same side; opposite of contralateral.

ISCHAEMIA Deficient blood supply to a body part.

KERNICTERUS Severe disease of the newborn characterised by anaemia and jaundice; caused by haemolysis or breakdown of the red blood cells.

KINAESTHESIS Sensation or awareness of position and movement of parts of the body; perceived through nerve endings in muscles, tendons and joints.

KYPHOSIS Exaggeration of the normal anterior-posterior curvature of the spine (convex); most common in the thoracic or dorsal region.

LABYRINTHINE Pertaining to the labyrinth or vestibular organ of the inner ear; associated with the sense of balance.

LESION Wound or injury; typically of nerve.

LOCOMOTION Movement from one place to another, such as in walking, running, hopping, etc; usually applied to self-propulsion.

LORDOSIS Exaggeration of the anterior-posterior curvature of the spine (concave); most common in the lumbar region.

LUMBAR Pertaining to the small of the back; those five vertebrae between the twelfth thoracic vertebra and the sacrum.

LUMEN Space or cavity; (pl. lumina).

LUXATION See 'dislocation'.

MALADJUSTMENT   Mode of response to one's environment that is detrimental to the individual, to society or to both.

MEDIAL   Plane passing in an anterior-posterior direction through the body which divides the body into equal left and right parts.

MEDULLA   Most caudal part of the brain stem; (alternatively 'medulla oblongata').

MENINGES   Membranes covering the brain and spinal cord; pia mater, arachnoid and dura mater.

MENINGITIS   Inflammation of the meninges.

MENINGOCELE   Least common and least serious form of spina bifida cystica in which only the meninges (and not the nerve cord itself) are involved.

MENINGOMYELOCELE   More common and generally more severe form of spina bifida cystica in which (in addition to the meninges) part of the nerve cord proper is also involved; alternatively 'myelomeningocele').

MENINGOMYELOCYSTOCELE   Most common and most serious form of spina bifida cystica in which the nerve cord is not only involved but also severely damaged; (alternatively 'myelomeningocystocele').

MENTAL DEFICIENCY   Inability to think logically in a manner appropriate to one's age.

MESENCHYME   Inner wall of the embryo.

MESODERM   Diffuse collection of cells between the ectoderm and endoderm in the embryonic disc; derivatives include the skeleton, muscles, connective tissue, the heart and blood vessels.

MONOPLEGIA   Paralysis of one extremity or limb; occasional manifestation of cerebral palsy.

MOTIVATION   Process of applying incentives, arousing and sustaining interest for the purpose of causing a pupil to perform in a desired way.

MOTOR   Pertaining to a muscle, nerve or centre that effects or produces movement.

MUSCLE SPINDLE   Sensory receptor in skeletal muscle which is stimulated by tension changes in the muscle.

MUSCULAR DYSTROPHY   Condition in which wasting takes place in certain muscles, with or without previous increase in the bulk of these muscles, and apparently without any affection of the nervous system; genetically-determined, degenerative, primary myopathy.

MYELODYSPLASIA   Arrestation in the development of the neural tube; characterised by incomplete formation and closure of the vertebral arches.

MYOCARDIAL   Pertaining to the musculature of the heart.

MYOPATHY   Disease of muscle.

MYOPIA   Near-sightedness; a refractory defect which causes the focal image to form in front of the retina.

MYOTOME   Mode of identification of spinal cord segments and those muscles which are innervated via such segments.

NECROSIS   Death of a tissue or organ; typically bone or muscle.

NEONATE   New-born child.

NEUROMERE   Segment of spinal cord which corresponds to one vertebra.

NEUROPATHY   Nervous disease.

NOTOCORD   Embryonic neural tube from which develop the spinal cord and the brain.

OCCIPITAL   Pertaining to the occiput, the lower part of the back of the head.

ORTHOPAEDIC   Pertaining to that branch of medicine concerned with the prevention and correction of deformities, especially in children.

ORTHOTIC   Pertaining to an artificial aid such as a caliper; *not* a replacement for a missing body part (see 'prosthesis').

PALSY   Paralysis.

PANCREATIC   Pertaining to the pancreas; a long secreting gland situated in the back of the abdomen.

PARALYSIS   Loss of muscular power due to interference with the nervous system.

PARANATAL   During childbirth.

PARAPLEGIA   Paralysis of both legs; usually accompanied by incontinence.

PARESIS   Incomplete or partial paralysis.

PARIETAL   Pertaining to the sides of the head, especially the parietal bones of the skull and the parietal lobes of the cerebrum.

PAROXYSMAL   Pertaining to a fit of disease.

PATHOLOGY   Branch of medicine which investigates diseases, disorders and abnormal conditions of the body.

PELVIS   Basin-shaped ring of bones (ilium, ischium and pubis) situated at the base of the trunk; supports the spinal column and provides the sockets for the hip joints.

PERCEPTION   Integration of sensations and the attachment of meaning to such sensations; process of recognition or identification of an object affecting a sense organ.

PERINATAL   Before, during and immediately after childbirth.

PERIPHERY   Outermost part of a body or organ; outer surface or boundary.

PERSEVERATION   Apparent inability or unwillingness to transfer attention from one object or activity to another.

PES   Foot.

PES CAVUS   Exaggeration of the plantar arch of the foot.

PES EQUINUS   Foot deformity in which a person walks only on the toes or forefoot.

PES PLANUS   Flat foot; undue flatness of the sole and arch.

PETIT MAL   See 'epilepsy'.

PHAGOCYTOSIS   Destruction of injurious cells or particles by phagocytes or white blood cells.

PHYSICAL EDUCATION   Phase of education which is concerned with the adjustment and development of an individual or group in or through total-body activities, usually of a playful type; adjustment and development accruing from organised instruction or direction in such total-body activities.

PHYSIOTHERAPY   Treatment of disease and injury by physical means, such as heat, cold, water, massage and exercise.

PLACENTA   Vascular structure developed early during pregnancy, and attached to the inner wall of the uterus, through which the fetus is supplied with nourishment and oxygen and through which it also gets rid of its waste products; afterbirth.

PLANTAR   Pertaining to the bottom or sole of the foot.

PLANTAR FLEXION   Extension of the ankle joint; pointing the toes.

PLAY   Pleasurable activity carried on for its own sake, without reference to ulterior purpose or future satisfactions.

POLYMYOSITIS   Inflammatory disease of muscle.

PONS   Nerve fibres which bridge across the brain stem to the cerebellum on either side; part of the hindbrain.

POSTERIOR   Located in the back; opposite of anterior; (sometimes used synonymously with dorsal).

POSTNATAL   After birth.

POSTURE   Position or attitude of the body as a whole or of parts of the body with respect to one another.

PRENATAL   Before birth.

PROGNOSIS   Prediction as to the probable result of a disease or injury.

PRONATION   Medial rotation of the hand or foot; opposite of supination.

PRONE   Lying or leaning face down; opposite of supine.

PROPHYLACTIC   Preventive; measure taken to prevent or ward off disease or deformity.

PROPRIOCEPTION   Sense of position in space; appreciation of movement and position of the body and parts of the body based on information from other than visual, auditory or superficial cutaneous sources.

PROSTHESIS   Artificial body part, usually an arm or leg.

PROXIMAL   Nearest the source; opposite of distal.

PSEUDOHYPERTROPHY   Giving the appearance of hypertrophy, typically of muscle.

PSYCHOSOMATIC   Pertaining to a mental-physical relationship; physical disorder originating in or influenced by the mental and/or emotional state.

PULMONARY   Pertaining to the lungs.

PYRAMIDAL   Pertaining to the pyramid, a region of the ventral medulla, through which runs the corticospinal or pyramidal tract, a column of motor efferent nerves.

QUADRIPLEGIA   Paralysis of all four limbs; occasional manifestation of cerebral palsy wherein the legs are more severely affected in the spastic case and the arms more involved in the athetoid case.

QUESTIONNAIRE   List of planned, written questions related to a particular topic submitted to a number of persons for reply; commonly used in the measurement of attitudes, opinions, provision of services, etc.

RECEPTOR   Specialised sensory organ in which the sensory nerve fibres terminate peripherally and which is stimulated by some specific type of environmental disturbance, typically heat, cold, light, sound or touch.

RECREATION   Individual or group experience motivated primarily by the enjoyment and satisfaction derived therefrom; commonly artistic or sporting.

REFLEX   Constant, inherited, involuntary motor response resulting from stimulation of sensory receptors.

RENAL   Pertaining to the kidney(s).

RESPIRATORY   Pertaining to the exchange of gases between the body and the atmosphere.

RIGIDITY   Stiffness; immobility; occasional manifestation of cerebral palsy.

ROLLATOR   Frame on wheels used as a walking aid.

ROSTRAL   Towards the head or superior end; opposite of caudal.

ROTATION   Angular movement of a bone or body segment about its own axis.

SACRAL   Pertaining to the sacrum, that part of the spinal column between the fifth lumbar vertebra and the coccyx.

SAGITTAL   Plane passing in an anterior-posterior direction through the body; any plane parallel to the medial plane.

SARCOLEMMA   Cell membrane of striated muscle fibre.

SCLEROMERE   Vertebral equivalent of the neuromere; (see 'neuromere').

SCOLIOSIS   Abnormal rotary-lateral curvature of the spine; commonly 'C' type consisting of a long convexity to one side, or 'S' type consisting of reverse curvatures to the right or left in the upper back and in the opposite direction in the lower back.

SEGREGATION   Separation of the handicapped from their able-bodied peers for education and/or participation in certain activities.

SENSATION   Receipt of an impulse by one of the sense receptors.

SHUNT   Valve system introduced surgically to drain excess cerebrospinal fluid from the brain into the bloodstream, usually in the region of the heart.

SMOOTH MUSCLE   Involuntary muscle occurring in the walls of hollow viscera and controlled by the autonomic nervous system.

SOMATOTOPIC   Represented in the human form, i.e., head, neck, chest, arms, abdomen, legs, feet; arranged in that same order.

SPASM   Involuntary, excessive muscular contraction.

SPASTICITY   Condition showing a tendency to spasm; typically either 'tonic' (prolonged, firm contraction) or 'clonic' (quick, alternate contractions and relaxations).

SPECIAL EDUCATION   Education of children who deviate so far from the norm (physically, mentally or emotionally) that the standard curriculum is not suited to their needs.

SPHINCTER   Circular muscle which surrounds the opening of an organ; commonly used with regard to the bladder and rectum.

SPINA BIFIDA   Birth defect characterised by incomplete formation and closure of the vertebral arches; typically a rupture occurs in which the meninges, cerebrospinal fluid and sometimes part of the nerve cord protrude out of the spinal canal and appear beneath the skin; varying degrees of severity are manifest in more (s.b. cystica) or less (s.b. occulta) complete paralysis below the site of the lesion.

STRENGTH   Capacity for resistance or for overcoming resistance.

STRIATED MUSCLE   Voluntary, skeletal muscle whose contraction produces movements of parts of the body; controlled by the central nervous system.

SUBCUTANEOUS   Immediately beneath the skin.

SUBLUXATION   Partial dislocation (or luxation) of articulating bones.

SULCUS   Groove.

SUPERIOR   Towards the head; above the midpoint; opposite of inferior.

SUPINATION   Lateral rotation of the hand or foot; opposite of pronation.

SUPINE   Lying on the back with face upwards; opposite of prone.

SYNDROME   Group of typical symptoms or conditions that characterise a deficiency or disease.

TACHYCARDIA   Abnormally rapid heart beat; opposite of bradycardia.

TACTILE   Pertaining to the sense of touch.

TALIPES   Deformity of the foot and ankle in which the foot is twisted out of position; club-foot.

TALIPES VALGUS   Club-foot condition in which the individual walks on the inner border of the foot, the sole being turned outwards.

TALIPES VARUS   Club-foot condition in which the individual walks on the outer border of the foot, the sole being turned inwards.

TENDON   Tough cord or band of connective tissue that unites a muscle to a bone.

TETRAPLEGIA   Synonymous with quadriplegia.

THALIDOMIDE   Drug administered to pregnant women during the late 1950s; unexpected side-effects of which included children born severely handicapped with limbs malformed or absent.

THORACIC   Pertaining to the chest region; those twelve vertebrae between the seventh cervical and the first lumbar vertebra.

TONUS   State of continued slight contraction of a muscle (as if) in readiness for work.

TOXAEMIA   Form of blood-poisoning due either to the absorption of bacterial products formed at some local site of infection or to defective action of some excretory organ such as the kidney.

TOXIC   Pertaining to a bacterial poison or toxin.

TRAUMA   Wound or injury; (pl. traumata).

TREMOR   Continuous muscular spasm of limited range; occasional manifestation of cerebral palsy due to a lesion of the cerebellum and/or the basal ganglia.

TRIPLEGIA   Paralysis of three extremities; typically both legs and one arm; occasional manifestation of cerebral palsy.

TROPHODERM   Layer of epithelial cells which surrounds the embryo maintaining contact with the maternal blood supply.

VALGUS   Outward turning; (see 'talipes').

VARUS   Inward turning; (see 'talipes').

VASCULAR   Pertaining to the blood vessels.

VENTRAL   Towards the front or front surface of a body or organ; opposite of dorsal; (sometimes used synonymously with anterior).

VENTRICLE   Chamber or cavity.

VERTEBRA   Bone of the spinal column of which there are seven cervical, twelve thoracic, five lumbar, five (fused) sacral, and one coccygeal.

VERTIGO   Dizziness; inability to maintain one's balance, usually due to dysfunction of the semi-circular canals, the cerebellum and/or the cerebrum.

VISCERAL   Pertaining to the viscera or internal organs.

RECOMMENDED READING

Drever, J. (1952) *A dictionary of psychology*. Penguin: Harmondsworth.

Gardner, E. (1968) *Fundamentals of neurology*. W. B. Saunders: Philadelphia.

Gunn, S. L. (1975) *Asic terminology for therapeutic recreation and other action therapies*. Stipes: Champaign, Illinois.

Hunter, M. D. (1966) *A dictionary for physical educators*. University Microfilms Inc.: Ann Arbor, Michigan.

Thompson, W. A. R. (1971) *Black's medical dictionary*. 29th edition. A. & C. Black: London.

Wood, P. H. N. (1975) *Classification of impairments and handicaps*. World Health Organization: Geneva.

Appendix one

Types of case admitted to special schools for physically handicapped and delicate children—as defined by the Department of Education and Science (1974)

A.
1. Debility, malnutrition and anaemia
2. Respiratory conditions (non-tuberculous)
3. TB contact
4. Primary pulmonary tuberculosis
5. Active respiratory tuberculosis
6. Quiescent respiratory tuberculosis
7. Coeliac disease
8. Rheumatism, chorea and rheumatic heart disease
9. Diabetes
10. External eye disease
11. Non-contagious skin disease
12. Contagious skin disease
13. TB and other diseases of bones and joints
14. Other forms of non-respiratory TB
15. Congenital deformities
16. Amputations
17. Poliomyelitis
18. Cerebral palsy, other forms of paralysis
19. Muscular dystrophy and atrophy
20. Spina bifida
21. Fragilitas ossium
22. Haemophilia
23. Congenital heart defect

B. Certain of these schools also accept children with the following handicaps
24. Epilepsy
25. Maladjustment
26. Educational subnormality

Appendix two   The questionnaire

A. *THE CHILDREN*

(i) What is the school's total population?

1–50	51–100	101–150	More

(ii) Which of the following most closely represents the age-range of your pupils?

2–16 yrs	2–10 yrs	10–16 yrs

(iii) How many children fit the following categories?

HANDICAP	NUMBERS						
	0	1–5	6–10	11–15	16–20	21–25	if more how many?
Spina bifida							
Cerebral palsy							
Muscular dystrophy							
Delicate							
*							
Wheelchair							
Sticks etc.							
Ambulant (unaided)							

*Please indicate any other numerically significant conditions.

B. *THE FACILITIES*

(i) a) Do you have access to the following items?

FACILITY/APPARATUS	NO	YES—IN SCHOOL	YES—ELSEWHERE
Assembly Hall/Gym			
Purpose-built Gym			
Sports Hall			
Climbing Apparatus			
Swimming Pool			
Physiotherapy Dept.			
Grass Areas			
Hard Court/Playground Areas			
Adventure Playground			
Changing Rooms			
Showers			

b) If YES—ELSEWHERE, are the facilities within reasonable walking distance?

YES	NO

(ii) a) How many facilities or items of equipment have been specially adapted/designed/made?

NONE	A FEW	A LOT

b) If YES, please outline below:

C. *TIME ALLOCATION*

(i) What is the average time allocated to each child for the following activities?

ACTIVITY / TIME	NONE	NO. OF MINUTES IN ANY ONE DAY	NO. OF DAYS PER WEEK
'P.E.'			
Games			
Swimming			
Individual Activity Sessions			

(ii) How much extra-curricular time is devoted to organised physical recreation?

NONE	0-5 HOURS PER WEEK	6-10 HOURS PER WEEK	MORE

(iii) How often does competition feature in your activities?

NEVER	OCCASIONALLY	USUALLY	ALWAYS

D. *STAFF—PUPIL INVOLVEMENT*

(i) How often are children grouped according to the following criteria?

CRITERION / FREQUENCY	NEVER	OCCASIONALLY	USUALLY	ALWAYS
Age				
Sex				
Type of Handicap				
Ability—i.e. Mixed Handicap				
Mobility—i.e. Wheelchair/Ambulant				

(ii) What is the average number of pupils for each activity?

ACTIVITY	NUMBER				
	None	1–5	6–10	11–15	If more how many?
'P.E.'					
Games					
Swimming					

(iii) Which members of staff are responsible for/involved in the following sessions? If more than one, please indicate accordingly.

ACTIVITY	STAFF				
	P.E. SPECIALIST	CLASSROOM TEACHER	PHYSIO-THERAPIST	REMEDIAL GYMNAST	OTHER
'P.E.'					
Games					
Swimming					

E.   ACTIVITIES

To what extent are your pupils engaged in the following activities?

ACTIVITY / INVOLVEMENT	NEVER	OCCASIONAL	REGULAR
Archery			
Athletics			
Badminton			
Basketball			
Bowling			
Canoeing			
Climbing			
Cricket			
Cross Country			

ACTIVITY \ INVOLVEMENT	NEVER	OCCASIONAL	REGULAR
Cycling			
Dance (Modern Educational)			
Dance (Folk etc.)			
Fencing			
Golf			
Gymnastics (Educational)			
Gymnastics (Traditional)			
Handball			
Hockey			
Judo			
Keep Fit			
Lacrosse			
Netball			
Orienteering			
Riding			
Rounders			
Rowing			
Sailing			
Shooting			
Shinty			
Slalom			
Skating (Ice)			
Skating (Roller)			
Skiing			
Soccer			
Swimming			

ACTIVITY	INVOLVEMENT	NEVER	OCCASIONAL	REGULAR
Table Tennis				
Tennis				
Trampolining				
Volleyball				
Weight Training				
*				
*				

*Please indicate any other activities.

Signed . . . .

School . . . .

Appendix three

A selection of films on sport, recreation and/or education for the physically handicapped

Access to angling   16mm   Colour/Sound   40mins
Produced by the National Anglers' Council and the Disabled Living Foundation, this film looks at the various problems facing disabled people who wish to take up any of the three major disciplines: coarse, game and sea fishing. Its main themes are to alert appropriate authorities to these problems, to encourage able-bodied anglers to give of their expertise and to promote increased participation by the disabled themselves.
The film is available from Town and Country Productions, 21 Cheyne Row, LONDON SW3 5HP.

I want to be   16mm   Colour/Sound   35mins
Produced by the Invalid Children's Aid Association, this film examines the many problems which face handicapped children and their families. The contribution of the ICAA is outlined and reference is made to a number of individual case studies, including one of an asthmatic boy whose main hobby is now parachuting.
The film is available from Town and Country Productions, 21 Cheyne Row, LONDON SW3 5HP.

It's ability that counts   16mm   Colour/Sound   25mins
Produced by the British Sports Association for the Disabled and Cinexsa Films, this film describes the work of the BSAD and demonstrates the tremendous value of sport to the disabled 'as a means to a fuller and happier life within the community'. Activities shown include swimming, athletics, slalom, wheelchair basketball, fencing and table tennis.
The film is available from BSAD, Stoke Mandeville Sports Stadium, Harvey Road, AYLESBURY, Bucks. HP21 8PP.

Not just a spectator   16mm   Colour/Sound   35mins
Produced by the Disabled Living Foundation, this film bears witness to the tremendous increase in opportunities for disabled people to enjoy a wide range of indoor and outdoor activities. Through reference to 'the many and sometimes unlikely activities that give pleasure to a great number of people with different disabilities' it demonstrates that, whatever one's interest, 'whether it be climbing, basketball, angling, wheelchair dancing or even birdwatching, there are both facilities and leadership'.
The film is available from Town and Country Productions, 21 Cheyne Row, LONDON SW3 5HP.

Riding towards freedom   16mm   Colour/Sound   35mins
Produced by the Riding for the Disabled Association, this film describes the structure
and work of the RDA, showing how largely through the efforts of volunteers the joys
and thrills of horse riding have been brought to countless thousands of physically and
mentally handicapped children.
The film is available from Town and Country Productions, 21 Cheyne Row, LON-
DON SW3 5HP.

Riding for the disabled   16mm   Colour/Sound   35mins
Produced by the Riding for the Disabled Association, this film describes how volun-
teers, physiotherapists and members of the medical profession co-operate to set up a
new centre for handicapped riders.
The film is available from Town and Country Productions, 21 Cheyne Row, LON-
DON SW3 5HP.

So we're different but . . .   16mm   Colour/Sound   31mins
Produced by the Central Office of Information for the Department of Education and
Science, this film examines 'the role of the special school in educating the physically
handicapped to achieve and accept the fine balance which must exist between
dependence and independence' and includes contributions from both professionals and
pupils. There are also some good shots of swimming, riding, tenpin bowling and wheelchair handball.
The film is available from Central Film Library, Bromyard Avenue, LONDON W3
7BJ.

Water free   16mm   Colour/Sound   35mins
Produced by the Association of Swimming Therapy, this film details the way in which
a specialist voluntary organisation and a local authority collaborated to demonstrate
how, by simple though scientifically proven methods, people of all ages with different
disabilities are able to enjoy a remarkably high degree of mobility – through swimming. More specifically, it shows the tremendous potential of the Halliwick Method of
swimming instruction for the teacher of handicapped children.
The film is available from Town and Country Productions, 21 Cheyne Row, LON-
DON SW3 5HP.

Appendix four

Names and addresses of organisations which promote sport and/or the welfare of the disabled

A. Professional associations
Association for Special Education
19 Hamilton Road, WALLASEY, Cheshire L45 9JE.

National Council for Special Education
17 Pembridge Square, LONDON WC2.

National Council for Schools' Sports
Hon. Sec. Mr E. Burden, 190 Nether Street, West Finchley, LONDON N3 1PE.

Physical Education Association of Great Britain & Northern Ireland
Ling House, 10 Nottingham Place, LONDON W1M 4AX.

B. National co-ordinating organisations
British Sports Association for the Disabled
Stoke Mandeville Sports Stadium, Harvey Road, AYLESBURY, Bucks. HP21 8PP.

Central Council for Physical Recreation
70 Brompton Road, Knightsbridge, LONDON SW3 1EX.

Scottish Sports Association for the Disabled
22 Charlotte Square, EDINBURGH EH2 4DF.

Scottish Sports Council
4 Queensferry Street, EDINBURGH EH2 4PB. (c/o Miss N. Smith)

Sports Council
70 Brompton Road, Knightsbridge, LONDON SW3 1EX. (c/o Miss E. Dendy)

Sports Council for Northern Ireland
49 Malone Road, BELFAST BT9 6RZ. (c/o Miss A. Moorhead)

Sports Council for Wales
National Sports Centre for Wales, Sophia Gardens, CARDIFF CF1 9SW. (c/o Miss R. Morgan)

Welsh Sports Association for the Disabled
c/o Mr M. Davey, Crescent Road, CAERPHILLY, Mid-Glamorgan.

C. Sports organisations specifically for disabled people

Advisory Panel on Water Sports for the Disabled
c/o Miss E. Dendy, Sports Council, 70 Brompton Road, Knightsbridge, LONDON SW3 1EX.

Association of Swimming Therapy
c/o Mr J. McMillan, 24 Arnos Road, LONDON N11.

British Amputees Athletic Club
c/o Mr L. Softley, 25 Sandringham Road, NORTHAMPTON.

British Association of Sports and Recreational Activities for the Blind
c/o Mr S. Palmer, 5 Curzon Road, THORNTON HEATH, Surrey.

British Deaf Sports Council
c/o Mr J. Hudson, 140 Green Lane, Cookridge, LEEDS LS16 7JQ.

British Paraplegics Sports Society
Stoke Mandeville Sports Stadium, Harvey Road, AYLESBURY, Bucks. HP21 8PP.

British Ski Club for the Disabled
14 Easton Road, HIGH WYCOMBE, Bucks.

Calvert Trust (Outdoor Pursuits for the Disabled)
Old Windebrowe, KESWICK, Cumbria CA12 4NT.

Disabled Campers Club
c/o Mr F. Strong, 28 Coote Road, BEXLEYHEATH, Kent.

Handicapped Adventure Playgrounds Association
3 Oakley Gardens, LONDON SW3.

National Association of Swimming Clubs for the Handicapped
c/o Mr D. Braham, 4 Hillside Gardens, NORTHWOOD, Middlesex.

National Association of Visually Handicapped Bowlers
c/o Mr P. Mepsted, 2 Rose Lane, ELMSWELL, Suffolk.

National Wheelchair Dance Association
c/o Mr A. Edwards, 8 Starvecrow Close, Shipbourne Road, TONBRIDGE, Kent TN11 9NW.

Riding for the Disabled Association
c/o Miss C. Haynes, Avenue 'R', National Agricultural Centre, KENILWORTH, Warks.

D. National governing bodies of sport
Where names are given, these are the N.G.B.s officers with responsibility for the disabled. In all other cases, the addresses are those of the headquarters.

Angling
National Anglers' Council
c/o Mr L. Warren, Flat D, St George's Lodge, Muswell Hill, Hornsey, LONDON N10 3TE.

Archery
Grand National Archery Society
c/o 20 Broomfield Road, CHELMSFORD, Essex.

Appendices

Athletics
Amateur Athletics Association
c/o Sports Council, 70 Brompton Road, Knightsbridge, LONDON SW3 1EX.

English Schools Athletics Association
c/o 26 Coniscliffe Road, STANLEY, Tyne & Wear DH9 7RF.

Badminton
Badminton Association of England
c/o Mr C. Landrey, 44–45 Palace Road, BROMLEY, Kent BR1 3JU.

Basketball
English Basketball Association
c/o Mr M. Welch, Calomax House, Lupton Avenue, LEEDS LS9 7DD.

Bowling
English Bowling Association
c/o Mr E. Crosbie, 150 Wellington Road, ENFIELD, Middlesex EN1 2RH.

British Tenpin Bowling Association, 19 Canterbury Avenue, ILFORD, Essex.

Canoeing
British Canoe Union
c/o Sports Council, 70 Brompton Road, Knightsbridge, LONDON SW3 1EX.

Caving
National Caving Association
c/o Mr F. Baguley, 15 Elm Grove, Gadlys, ABERDARE, Mid-Glamorgan CF44 8DN.

Cricket
The Cricket Council
Lords Cricket Ground, LONDON NW8 8QN.

Cycling
British Cycling Federation
c/o Sports Council, 70 Brompton Road, Knightsbridge, LONDON SW3 1EX.

Cyclists' Touring Club
c/o Cotterell House, 69 Meadrow, GODALMING, Surrey.

Fencing
Amateur Fencing Association
c/o Mr L. Veale, 14 Kingsley Park Grove, SHEFFIELD S11 9HL.

Handball
British Handball Association
c/o Mr J. Timmins, 38 Lea Road, HODDESTON, Herts.

Hockey
The Hockey Association
c/o Mr L. Bone, 17 the Drive, BUCKHURST HILL, Essex.

Orienteering
British Orienteering Federation
c/o Mr M. Collett, 3 Oakbank House, Skelsmergh, KENDAL, Cumbria.

Rambling
The Ramblers Association
1–4 Crawford Mews, York Street, LONDON W1H 1PT.

Rounders
National Rounders Association
1 Chantrey Close, BEESTON, Nottinghamshire.

Rowing
Amateur Rowing Association
c/o Dr E. O'Brien, 20 Weltje Road, LONDON W6 9DJ.

Sailing
Royal Yachting Association
c/o Mr R. Bond, Training Manager, Victoria Way, WOKING, Surrey.

Skiing
National Ski Federation of Great Britain
118 Eaton Square, LONDON SW1.

Soccer
The Football Association
16 Lancaster Gate, LONDON W2 3LW.

Swimming
Amateur Swimming Association
c/o Mrs S. Dobie, Harold Fern House, Derby Square, LOUGHBOROUGH, Leicestershire.

Royal Life Saving Society
Desborough House, 14 Devonshire Street, LONDON W1N 2AT.

Table Tennis
English Table Tennis Association
c/o Mr S. Dane, 21 The Ridgeway, Southgate, LONDON N14.

Volleyball
English Volleyball Association
c/o Mr T. Jones, 45 Fairford Avenue, BEXLEYHEATH, Kent.

Water Skiing
British Water Ski Federation
c/o Sports Council, 70 Brompton Road, Knightsbridge, LONDON SW3 1EX.

E. Voluntary associations of/for disabled people
Association for Spina Bifida and Hydrocephalus
Devonshire House, 30 Devonshire Street, LONDON W1V 2EB.

British Association of the Hard of Hearing
26 Osborne Road, HORNCHURCH, Essex RM11 1HA.

British Deaf Association
38 Victoria Place, CARLISLE, Cumbria CA1 1EX.

British Epilepsy Association
3–6 Alfred Place, LONDON WC1.

Appendices

British Polio Fellowship
Bell Close, West End Road, RUISLIP, Middlesex.

Chest and Heart Association
Tavistock House North, Tavistock Square, LONDON WC1 9JE.

Disabled Living Foundation
346 Kensington High Street, LONDON W14.

Haemophilia Society
P.O. Box 9, 16 Trinity Street, LONDON SE1 1DE.

Multiple Sclerosis Society
4 Tachbrook Street, LONDON SW1V 1SJ.

Muscular Dystrophy Group of Great Britain
26 Borough High Street, LONDON SE1 9QG.

National Fund for Research into Crippling Diseases
Vincent House, 1 Springfield Road, HORSHAM, Sussex.

National Society for Mentally Handicapped Children
Pembridge Hall, 17 Pembridge Square, LONDON W2 4EP.

Physically Handicapped and Able Bodied (Youth Clubs)
42 Devonshire Street, LONDON W1N 1LN.

Royal Association for Disability and Rehabilitation
25 Mortimer Street, LONDON W1N 8AB.

Royal National Institute for the Blind
224–228 Great Portland Street, LONDON W1N 6AA.

Royal National Institute for the Deaf
105 Gower Street, LONDON WC1E 6AH.

Spastics Society
12 Park Crescent, LONDON W1N 4EQ.

Spinal Injuries Association
24 Nutford Place, LONDON W1H 6AN.

Index

To Shelagh and Ben

Acknowledgements

The debt of gratitude I owe to the staff and children of Saint Francis School, Lincoln, in particular to the Headmaster, David Williams, is immeasurable. Much of what is written in this text is based on my experiences at the school as teacher in charge of physical education. Without such experiences, good and bad, it could never have been written. Thanks are again due to David Williams for allowing me to use photographs taken at Saint Francis. These were taken with considerable skill and patience by Graham Jones to whom I also express my thanks.

I am similarly indebted to Peter Morris, Senior Lecturer at the Carnegie School of Physical Education, Leeds, who was my tutor during my presentation of the thesis which was the starting point of this book. Also to John Whiting, now of the Free University of Amsterdam, who provided the initial encouragement and *savoir faire* to get the book under way; and to the many teachers and therapists in schools throughout England and Wales who found the time to complete and return my questionnaires.

Thanks also to Shelagh, my wife, not least for learning to type so that my first draft might be made legible; and to my publishers for being so patient and considerate in leading me for the first time through the rigours of publication.

attention is paid to the nature and extent of movement difficulties or limitations which are manifest in them. From this it is hoped that the reader will be better able to recognise the movement capabilities of children with different types of handicap, and so to determine those activities which can be taught to all the children, and those which are suitable only for particular groups within the whole.

iii) *Chapter 4* considers the less obvious defects which are associated with these conditions, such as specific behavioural and learning problems, including perceptual difficulties, distractability, disinhibition and short attention span. These factors, whilst they are not so readily diagnosed as the major physical disabilities, play a large part in hampering a child's progress in the learning of new skills. Consequently a proper understanding of their nature is an essential prerequisite to any consideration of lesson plans or teaching method.

iv) *The remaining chapters* educe certain observations from the earlier part of the book, to suggest ways in which a physical education programme might be developed in a school for physically handicapped children. Special attention is paid (in consecutive chapters) to movement education, major games, swimming and outdoor pursuits.

At the end of the book there is a glossary to help explain some of the special terms whose use in certain places could not be avoided, and a series of appendices which, hopefully, will serve as kindling to the spark which this book attempts to create.

realise that their problems are not only more acute than those of their able-bodied peers but also more varied and far-reaching in their effect. In a nutshell, they are just as different from one another as any other children.

For children who are physically handicapped, by nature or by accident forced to come to terms with a life of immobility or uncoordination, the benefits which can accrue from a programme of physical education are immense. But they can only be realised if the programme is well balanced, well executed and tailored to suit the needs of the individual. In this situation perhaps more than any other, the teacher needs to know his subject *and* his subjects.

This then is what this book *is* about. The author, having in the past introduced such a programme of physical education to a special school for physically handicapped children – as comprehensive in its scope as one would find in a comprehensive school – sets out to consider some of the problems which were either encountered on the way or which he was fortunate enough to have avoided. More tentatively, the book seeks to offer guidance to others working with physically handicapped children by highlighting common pitfalls and by drawing attention to areas likely to be of particular value.

Depending upon the background and experience of the reader, certain parts of the text will need more (or less) careful reading than others. It has not been possible to avoid this because of the diversity of professions now offering their services to this sector of education. Basically, it can be subdivided into four distinct parts:

i) *Chapters 1 and 2* set the scene, providing the philosophical and historical framework upon which the rest is built. The values of physical education to the physiological, psychological and social development of the child are indicated and an attempt is made to describe a 'typical' special school. Particular reference is made to the results of a questionnaire which was sent out to schools for physically handicapped children in England and Wales (see Appendix Two) and which sought information on each of the following areas:

    a) The number of children in each of these schools and the proportional representation of the major handicapping conditions;

    b) the nature and extent of the facilities which were available for use by these schools;

    c) the proportional allocation of time to different aspects of the physical education syllabus;

    d) the ways in which children were grouped for participation in these physical activities;

    e) the staff:pupil ratios which were considered suitable for these activities;

    f) the nature of the activities themselves.

ii) *Chapter 3* looks at each of the major handicapping conditions. These are examined from the point of view of aetiology and prognosis, and particular

Preface

I can think of no better way to begin this preamble than with a statement of what this book is not. It is *not* an attempt to provide the reader with a ready-made programme of physical education which can be slotted wholesale into the curriculum of a special school. Such programmes as do exist may be useful as an aid to diagnosis and a guide to remediation, but they provide neither the flexibility, the variety nor the challenge that one associates with a conventional programme of physical education.

It was with such admittedly negative thoughts in mind that the book's title 'Physical education and the physically handicapped child' was chosen. To have called the book 'Physical education for physically handicapped children' – my original intention – could have implied that this sort of physical education was somehow different from that which is provided for able-bodied children. And, despite the fact that I have been told by one rather eminent physical educationist that this *is* the case, this was not the impression that I wished to create.

In its present form the title bears witness to a firm conviction that physical education is physical education, no matter where, by whom or to whom it is taught. Any differences that may be apparent are manifestations either of the way the subject is taught (reflecting qualities and ambitions in the teacher) or of qualities inherent in the children under instruction. But it is not my intention to suggest that the teaching of physical education should be standardised or that all aspects of the subject should be taught in the same way. On the contrary, I wish only to underline a belief in physical education as a subject area with an enormous contribution to make not just to the physical but to the overall development of children and, because of this totality of effect, as a subject area which in its teaching and its content must reflect an awareness that *all children are different*.

Even in our so-called normal schools each child brings to the physical education lesson characteristics that are unique, abilities (and disabilities) that are peculiar to the individual, and a good teacher adjusts his input accordingly. In the special school too, this 'one-to-one' relationship is vitally important. The children have been brought together for their education because of certain exceptional qualities which they all have in common and which render them unsuitable for education 'under the normal regime of ordinary schools'. But one does not have to spend long with such children to

Contents

First published 1980 by Lepus Books
an imprint of Henry Kimpton (Publishers) Ltd
7 Leighton Place, Leighton Road, London NW5 2QL

British Library Cataloguing in Publication Data

Price, Robert J.
  Physical education and the physically handicapped child.
  1. Physical education for handicapped children
  I. Title
  371.9'1   GV445
        0089877
ISBN 0 86019 035 8

Typesetting by Malvern Typesetting Services
Printed in Great Britain at the
University Press, Cambridge

107542

371. 9044 796
PRI

PHYSICAL EDUCATION

AND THE

PHYSICALLY HANDICAPPED

CHILD

ROBERT J. PRICE

MA, BEd, DPE

LEPUS BOOKS

LONDON

PHYSICAL EDUCATION
AND THE
PHYSICALLY HANDICAPPED
CHILD